The Meaning of Evil

James Sias

The Meaning of Evil

James Sias
Dickinson College
Carlisle, Pennsylvania, USA

ISBN 978-1-349-95401-8   ISBN 978-1-137-56822-9 (eBook)
DOI 10.1057/978-1-137-56822-9

© The Editor(s) (if applicable) and The Author(s) 2016
Softcover reprint of the hardcover 1st edition 2016
This work is subject to copyright. All rights are solely and exclusively licensed by the Publisher, whether the whole or part of the material is concerned, specifically the rights of translation, reprinting, reuse of illustrations, recitation, broadcasting, reproduction on microfilms or in any other physical way, and transmission or information storage and retrieval, electronic adaptation, computer software, or by similar or dissimilar methodology now known or hereafter developed.
The use of general descriptive names, registered names, trademarks, service marks, etc. in this publication does not imply, even in the absence of a specific statement, that such names are exempt from the relevant protective laws and regulations and therefore free for general use.
The publisher, the authors and the editors are safe to assume that the advice and information in this book are believed to be true and accurate at the date of publication. Neither the publisher nor the authors or the editors give a warranty, express or implied, with respect to the material contained herein or for any errors or omissions that may have been made.

Printed on acid-free paper

This Palgrave Macmillan imprint is published by Springer Nature
The registered company is Nature America Inc., US

*For Molly—
who almost certainly is not evil*

Acknowledgments

I have been thinking about the ideas contained in this book for many years, but I only began thinking about how they might come together like this in the Spring of 2014. And that was only because one of my colleagues, Chauncey Maher, told me, "You should write a book about that." So I did. The first person to thank, then, is Chauncey. I really doubt this book would have been written if he hadn't insisted that he was being serious when he told me to write it. Thanks also to Susan Feldman and Jeff Engelhardt for help and support throughout the entire process.

During the Fall 2014 semester, while researching for the book, I taught an undergraduate seminar on the topic of evil. For better or worse, many of our discussions involved me thinking out loud for several minutes at a time, trying to work through some of my own thoughts. So I want to thank those students for their patience and understanding, and for letting me bounce ideas off of them. They are Zachary Brode, Harper Clark, Sarah Curt, Ashley Doyle, Katelyn Eby, Brittany Horgan, Catherine Munger, Duong Nguyen, Sam Portelance, Mia Scanlon, Meghan Shippe, Jake Silvaggio, Elizabeth Smith, and Rachel Stern. I also want to thank Adam Berman, Kirsten Dedrickson, and Paul Gaver for being helpful sounding boards along the way.

Research for Part I of the book was especially difficult. It is one thing to investigate various philosophical theories of evil. It is quite another thing, I have found, to familiarize oneself very closely with evil in the real world. During those months especially, the encouragement of friends and family was invaluable. Most of all, I want to thank Molly for putting up with me for these past few years. This book is dedicated to her.

Contents

1 An Introduction to Evil — 1

Part I The Psychology of Evil: Some Case Studies — 21

2 Serial Murder, Psychopathy, and Objectification — 23

3 Genocide, Ideology, and Dehumanization — 53

4 Money, Greed, and Commodification — 85

Part II The Philosophy of Evil: Puzzles, Problems, and Theories — 115

5 Three Puzzles about Evil — 117

6 Theories of Evil Personhood — 157

7 A New Theory of Evil — 187

Index — 227

CHAPTER 1

An Introduction to Evil

During the 2008 United States presidential election, Saddleback Church hosted an event that gave voters a unique look into the minds of John McCain and Barack Obama. Basically, the format was this: each candidate would be interviewed by pastor Rick Warren, while the other candidate was waiting somewhere off-stage, unaware of his opponent's responses to Warren's questions; and importantly, both candidates were asked the same questions. Combining the virtues of an ordinary presidential debate with those of an episode of "The Newlywed Game," the event allowed viewers to compare and contrast each candidate's thoughts on a wide range of issues, but without having to suffer through the discomfort of watching two adult humans trying to talk over each other.

At one point during the interviews, Warren asked each candidate the following: "Does evil exist? And if it does, do we ignore it, negotiate with it, contain it, or defeat it?" McCain answered, "Defeat it"—presumably, an admission that evil *does* exist—and then promised prospective voters that he would bring Osama bin Laden to justice. Obama answered, "Evil does exist," followed by a somewhat more careful and nuanced acknowledgment of the different forms that evil might take: from the genocide in Darfur to parents who viciously abuse their children.

Now, for some contrast, consider a recent experience of my own. I was teaching a course on issues in moral psychology, and we were about to begin a unit on psychopathy. Over the next few weeks, I wanted the class to wrestle with questions like: Do psychopaths "know right from wrong"? Are psychopaths morally responsible for their actions? Are psychopathic serial killers evil? So to get the discussion started, I had students write down their answers to a few more general questions: Can a person be genuinely morally evil? If no, why not? And if yes, what would it take for someone to count as genuinely morally evil?

Of the 13 students in the class, 11 answered that there is *no such thing* as a genuinely evil person. (I address their responses to the "Why not?" question in a later chapter.) And of the two students who allowed that there *can* be a genuinely evil person, one insisted that the conditions a person must satisfy in order to count as evil are so extreme that probably no one in the real world has ever actually been morally evil.

Looking back, that was the day that I began working on this book. I can certainly understand my students' reluctance to admit that genuine moral evil exists, but I believed then, and still now, that they are mistaken. Some people really are evil. And while it may sound as if I have a couple of allies in John McCain and Barack Obama, I actually suspect that the two presidential candidates (McCain especially) were talking about something importantly *different* from what will be my focus in the following chapters. Let me explain.

Four Uses of "Evil"

In practice, we use the term "evil" in all sorts of ways. McCain used it to refer to such serious *wrongdoers* as Osama bin Laden, while Obama used it to refer both to serious wrongdoers (abusive parents) and to the serious *wrongs* themselves (genocide in Darfur). But in an immeasurably less serious context, my wife and I might joke that the "dessert guy" at a nice restaurant is evil—a modern-day "serpent in the garden," slithering through the dining room with his cart of treats, tempting people into making decisions that they may regret later.

Children are introduced to the nature and language of evil at a very early age, in such villainous characters as Cinderella's "*wicked* stepmother" and the "*evil* Queen Maleficent." In fact, a quick search on Imdb.com reveals no fewer than 200 movies, television shows, and video games containing the word "evil" in their titles. As you can probably guess, most are in the horror genre, and feature such charming characters as flesh-eating zombies, bloodthirsty vampires, demons, ghosts, werewolves, and other monstrous and supernatural threats to humanity.

The term itself has Germanic origins, and comes to us from the Old English "yfel," meaning *over* or *beyond*. Throughout its history, the word "evil" and its etymological ancestors were used generally to refer to things considered *bad*, *wicked*, *cruel*, *ill*, or *defective*. In modern parlance, though,

I think we can recognize four distinct ways in which the term is commonly used, only one of which will be the subject of this book.

Political "Evil"

Perhaps the most common way in which the term "evil" gets used these days is also the most problematic, in my view. This is when it is used as part of a more general phenomenon of resorting to extreme moral or evaluative language in order to express our attitudes toward things. Comedian Louis C.K. once joked that we have gotten especially careless with our use of such evaluative terms as "hilarious," "genius," and "amazing." In a stand-up comedy special—appropriately titled *Hilarious*—he said,

> We go right for the top shelf with our words now. We don't think about how we talk. "Dude, it was amazing! It was *amazing*!" Really, you were amazed? You were *amazed* by a basket of chicken wings? Really? Amazing? What are you going to do with the rest of your life now? What if something really happens to you? [...] What are you going to call *that*? You used 'amazing' on a basket of chicken wings.

Whatever the reason, it does seem to be popular now for people to resort to unnecessarily extreme terms for what are apparently just rhetorical and expressive purposes. Desserts are not merely tasty; they are "literally the best thing I've ever tasted." The night the power went out was not merely inconvenient; it was "the worst night of my life."

We do this with moral language as well and perhaps most often in heated political contexts. As political divisiveness in America continues to heighten, so does the tendency to label one's opponents using the most extremely negative of moral terms. If two or more people disagree over some political matter, and the matter itself—as these things often do—happens to strike at some very deeply held values, then it is only a matter of time before one party to the disagreement assures the rest of us that its opponents are a lot like the Nazis. And in these contexts, labels like "despicable," "monstrous," and "evil" become common rhetorical currency.

At the time of writing this, a Google search of the phrase "Adolf Hitler was evil" reveals fewer than a million hits. By contrast, a search of the phrase "George Bush is evil" brings up more than 15 million hits. In fact, opposition to Bush got so irrationally fierce here in the United States, comparisons of Bush to Hitler so ubiquitous, that the term "Bushitler" actually became a thing. And of course, divisiveness in American politics is no less acute today than it was a decade ago, so we should expect to find—and in fact, do find—the same thing happening with respect to Bush's successor. Googling "Barack Obama is evil" will give you a list of over 10 million related links, and he is still in office!

For better or worse, though, one does not have to be the president of the United States in order to be considered evil by one's political opponents. To many who are pro-life, abortion and its defenders are evil; but to many others who are pro-choice, opposition to abortion is evil. To many who oppose homosexual marriage, gay pride parades are celebrations of evil; but to many defenders of gay rights, it could only be evil to try to prevent two loving adults from marrying. And which is the more evil economic system, capitalism or socialism? Care to guess what many capitalists and socialists will say?

Rather than going on and on with more examples of this politically oriented use of the term "evil," I will simply make two critical remarks before moving on to discuss another common use of the term. First, whatever such extreme language *has* in terms of its ability to enable the expression of one's attitudes, it *lacks* in terms of its ability to enable rational and responsible public discourse. Quite the contrary, in fact, terms like "evil" often have the effect of *shutting down* such discourse—after all, if someone is not just wrong or misguided, but *evil*, then we have no more reason to seriously consider his beliefs and values than we have for those of any other madman or inhuman monster. Just as it would be a waste of time—and perhaps even a moral misstep in itself—to try to "see things from Hitler's point of view," it could only be similarly useless (and maybe immoral) to even entertain the ideas of those on the other side of the abortion debate, or debates about gay rights, or whatever. Whether or not people who resort to such extreme language intend to imply such a thing about the targets of terms like "evil," it is an implication of the language nonetheless.

My second point can be framed as a kind of philosophical dilemma. As the term "evil" is commonly used in these heated moral and political contexts, its meaning is either purely *expressive*—in the sense that speakers use it only to *express* their disdain or disapproval of moral and political opponents—or else it is (at least partly) *descriptive*—in the sense that speakers use it to *report or describe* some moral fact of the matter. Now, this book takes for granted that there are objective moral facts of the matter, and sets out to discern what those facts are—specifically those to do with the nature and reality of evil. Since this is the case, if there are contexts in which the term "evil" is used for purely expressive purposes—as often seems the case with respect to moral and political disputes—then those uses of the term are of no interest to us here. (Used in this way, "evil" functions more like a *pejorative* or *slur* than the name of an actual moral property.)

On the other hand, if people actually do mean to be reporting or describing some moral fact of the matter when they apply the term "evil" to George Bush or Barack Obama, opponents or defenders of abortion, capitalists or socialists, and so forth, they are almost certainly misusing the term in the vast majority of these cases. There just are not any plausible theories of evil according to which someone counts as evil simply for opposing or defending abortion, or gay marriage, or free markets, or for doing any of the things that Bush and Obama have done. (If you disagree, stick around until at least Chap. 6, where I discuss some of the more prominent theories of evil.)

So, as the term "evil" is popularly used in heated moral and political contexts, its meaning is either expressive—in which case it has nothing whatsoever to do with the aims of this book—or else it is descriptive—in which case it is being misused far more often than not, and so we would do well to simply ignore these uses of the term. Either way, my focus from this point forward will be on a much more careful and restricted use of "evil."

Religious "Evil"

For some, the term "evil" really only applies to figures or entities of a distinctly religious or supernatural nature. Used in this way, the category of evil might include such characters as the Devil and demons, ghosts, zombies, vampires, and perhaps even a few Disney villains, but it would apparently not include any actual human beings. Is there any reason to think that evil might be an *essentially* religious or supernatural concept?

Philosophers sometimes distinguish between *pure* and *impure* evil.[1] To understand the difference, think of the distinction between means and ends. I want to get into better shape—that is my end. So I begin exercising and dieting—these are both means to that end. Now, nobody doubts that human beings cause each other to suffer all the time, and in all sorts of ways. But whenever we do so, it always seems to be done as a means to some further end. We might cause others to suffer for the sake of revenge, for instance, or for financial gain, or even just for pleasure. In fact, the end might even be something in itself positive—for example, if I were to steal from the wealthy (thereby causing them some suffering) in order to benefit the poor. Either way, the mark of impure evil is supposed to be that suffering (or the *causing of* suffering) is a means to some further, different end. Obviously, human beings are capable of impure evil.

Pure evil, on the other hand, is when suffering is both the means *and the end*—that is, when suffering is caused not for things like revenge, financial gain, or even pleasure, but rather only *for its own sake*. When you think about what this would involve, it is actually very difficult to even comprehend the frame of mind someone would have to occupy in order to engage in pure evil. Remarking on this idea of causing suffering for its own sake, Phillip Cole writes,

> [T]his verges on the incomprehensible, to such an extent that many thinkers have argued that mere human beings are incapable of it. Human agents can only be evil in the impure sense, while pure evil, it if exists at all, belongs to the supernatural.[2]

And from here, some might argue that *pure* evil is the only *real* evil. After all, if every instance of suffering caused by humans, whatever the end, is to count as an instance of (impure) evil, then apparently, most (if not all) human moral wrongdoing is evil, in this impure sense—from serial murder and genocide to cutting in line at Starbucks or stealing a co-worker's lunch. But surely, the very usefulness of the concept of evil depends on our being able to distinguish its instances from those of other moral concepts, like *morally wrong* and *morally bad*. And just as surely, stealing a co-worker's lunch may be morally wrong, but it is not evil. So if we want to affirm that there *is* a useful concept of evil, it seems we are left saying that it must apply only to cases of pure evil—which, if Cole is right, is something of which only a supernatural being could be capable. If this is right, then maybe evil is an essentially religious or supernatural concept.

For my own part, while I do not want to deny that there may be a perfectly legitimate use of the term "evil" according to which it applies only to religious or supernatural beings or entities, I also think that there is a perfectly legitimate and straightforwardly *secular* concept of evil, according to which certain persons and certain behaviors are evil, and these can be distinguished from those that are morally wrong or morally bad. The key here is that I think we should reject the distinction between pure and impure evil outright, since it is either useless or misleading. For one thing, notice that the category of impure evil, as it has been used to this point, will even include actions that are perfectly morally innocent—such as a dentist causing a patient to suffer while performing a root canal. But suppose we have a way of separating the morally wrong impure evils from those that are not. Even still, the remaining category of wrongs is apparently going to include an immensely wide variety of instances of suffering—from the frustration of having one's lunch stolen by a co-worker to the horror of being tortured and raped by a sadistic murderer—all for the sake of a similarly wide variety of ends. As far as the category of impure evil is concerned, neither *the nature of the suffering* nor *the end for which suffering is caused* really matters—all that matters is that the suffering and the end are *different*. But of course these things matter! And importantly, they matter to our thoughts about evil. In fact, as we will see in Chap. 6, according to one prominent theory of evil, evil is a matter of causing suffering for the end of pleasure.

At the end of the day, the pure–impure distinction just does not seem to mesh very well with the way we ordinarily think about evil. Surely the systematic extermination of several million innocent Jews was as *real* an evil as there ever has been, despite having been carried out by fellow humans; and surely it does not belong in the same category as such other "impure" evils as cutting in line at Starbucks or stealing a co-worker's lunch. So again, I suggest that we reject the pure–impure distinction outright. Maybe a capacity to cause suffering for its own sake is indeed the distinguishing mark of religious or supernatural figures of evil. Or maybe it is something else, like a conscious opposition to, or perversion of, goodness—as when Milton's Satan says, "Evil be thou my good." I am happy to leave the religious use of terms like "evil" or "wicked" to scholars of religion and theology.

In this book, I develop a secular theory of the concept of evil. By calling it secular, I mean a few different things. First, the theory will make no essential reference to anything religious or supernatural, as it would, for instance, if it were to define evil in terms of something like opposition to the interests or purposes of God. Second, it is a theory to which all people, of all religious or non-religious beliefs, can in principle agree. Third, the theory I defend suggests that evil is in fact "human, all too human," to adapt a line from Nietzsche. In other words, according to the theory taken up in Chap. 7 (as well as the theories critiqued in Chap. 6), evil is hardly something of which only religious or supernatural beings are capable. Indeed, if I am right, all of us are likely to *engage* in evil at some point in our lives, even if only a few of us will ever *be* evil.

Metaphysical "Evil"

Until relatively recently, philosophers typically used the term "evil" to refer to the opposite of whatever is referred to by "good." Consequently, for the better part of the history of philosophy, "evil" was used primarily to refer to *badness of any kind*—or, sometimes, to *the absence (privation) of goodness of any kind*. So defined, the category of evil includes not only serious moral wrongdoing like genocide and serial murder, but also things like natural disasters, diseases, and birth defects. (Recall from above that "evil" and its etymological ancestors have been used to refer not only to things that are *wicked* and *cruel*, but also to things that are *bad, ill,* or *defective*.)

This conception of *evil as badness* lies at the heart of the so-called "problem of evil" in the philosophy of religion. In simplest terms, the problem of evil is the problem of reconciling the existence of things like moral wrongdoing, diseases, natural disasters, and birth defects, on the one hand, with the supposed existence of a God who is omnipotent, omniscient, and morally perfect, on the other. If God is *omnipotent*, then presumably, he has the power to prevent these things. If he is *omniscient*, then presumably, he knows when these things will occur and also how to prevent them. And if God knows when and how to prevent them, and has the power to do so, but does not, then he is not *morally perfect*. So if God is supposed to have all three of these properties—omnipotence, omniscience, and moral perfection—then why do these terrible things exist?

Now, given this characterization, it should be obvious that the real significance of evil—as far as the problem of evil is concerned—lies not so much in *what it is like*, or *how bad it is*, or even in *how much of it there is*. Rather, the significance of evil lies primarily in *the fact that it exists at all*, in a world in which we might expect otherwise. Strictly speaking, the problem of evil would still be a problem if there were no genocide, no murder, no cancer, no earthquakes, none of this. Indeed, it is a problem as long as there exists badness or suffering of any kind—or at least, any kind that is not apparently justified by some greater good. A single toothache might be enough to challenge the existence of a loving and perfectly good God with unlimited power and knowledge. After all, unless there is some greater good that could only be realized as a result of that toothache, shouldn't such a God prevent even *that* suffering?

Since the significance of evil so understood lies ultimately in its mere existence, I call this "evil" in the *metaphysical* sense. (For those who do not know, metaphysics, roughly speaking, is the philosophical study of what exists.)

There are some who think—and I am inclined to agree with this—that it is unfortunate that this worthwhile philosophical problem has come to be known as "the problem of *evil*." After all, we often associate the term "evil" with the most morally despicable of actions, persons, and instances of suffering. But as I have just explained, these are not the only things we would expect an omnipotent, omniscient, and morally perfect God to prevent. Naturally, we would expect him to prevent *all* gratuitous suffering, not just the worst of it. So for this reason, some prefer to refer to this not as the problem of evil, but rather as the problem of *suffering*.

I do find this to be an incredibly fascinating topic. But it is a topic that I will avoid in this book, for two reasons. The first is simply that so much good stuff has already been written on this problem. I just do not think that another book on the problem of evil is what anyone needs at this point.[3]

The second reason is similar to my reason for rejecting the distinction between pure and impure evil. As I explained earlier, as long as the category of impure evil can include everything from genocide and serial murder to stealing a co-worker's lunch, then it is effectively useless as a guide to the nature moral evil—whatever is required for one of us to count as genuinely morally evil, surely more is required than helping ourselves to a sandwich that is not our own. Likewise, when "evil" is used in this metaphysical sense, to refer to *badness of any kind*, it effectively ignores distinctions that are central to our ordinary concept of evil. In fact, this metaphysical use of the term "evil" ranges over an even broader and more diverse set of phenomena, since it includes all instances of suffering, and not just those caused by moral agents for the sake of some end. There may be *some* sense of "evil" in which even a toothache counts as evil, but it is not the sense that interests me here.

In recent years, philosophers have begun distinguishing between *wide* and *narrow* conceptions of evil. The wide conception of evil is the one that lies at the heart of the so-called problem of evil, since "evil" here refers widely to *all* instances of badness or suffering. But in the last century—and especially since the Holocaust—philosophers began to recognize a narrower conception of evil. Basically, the thought then, and now, is that we fail to fully appreciate the moral uniqueness of the Holocaust if we place it in the same category alongside things like natural disasters and birth defects. Indeed, even alongside other instances of serious moral wrongdoing—like murder and other forms of mass murder—the Holocaust stands out as *something other*, morally speaking. Perhaps most famous for her work on Nazi totalitarianism and the Holocaust, Hannah Arendt used the term "*radical* evil"—which she borrowed and adapted from Kant—to refer to this separate, and narrower, moral category.

Since my aim in this book is just to elucidate this narrow conception of evil, additional terms like "radical" will be unnecessary for my purposes. So, unless otherwise noted, I shall henceforth use "evil" to refer *only* to this separate moral category, that is, to whatever it is that makes the Holocaust and perhaps some other actions, events, and persons, so morally unique.

Moral "Evil"

What I want to uncover in this book is the meaning of "evil" as it is used in a more explicitly *moral* sense. In the sense that I have in mind—as opposed to the sense of "evil" at work in the problem of evil—the category of evil includes only certain persons and actions, and excludes all nonmoral causes of suffering, such as diseases and natural disasters. Evil in this moral sense is not just a problem for theists; it is a problem for all of us.

Many of us have a sense—even if only a loose one—that some actions are not just *morally wrong*, or even *extremely* morally wrong; rather, they are evil. To say that the Holocaust was "morally wrong" would be to engage in pretty serious understatement, and perhaps even to misuse the moral term entirely. Likewise, we have a sense that some people are not just *bad* or *immoral*; they are evil. If Sam cheats on his wife on multiple occasions, gambles away his children's college funds, and spends his career engaging in shady business practices, he may indeed count as a bad person, fully deserving of blame, resentment, scorn, and the like. But, for as bad as he is, Sam is no Hitler. With these sorts of examples in mind, Daniel Haybron writes, "Prefix your adjectives [like 'wrong' and 'bad'] with as many 'verys' as you like; you still fall short. Only 'evil', it seems, will do."[4]

What went on at Auschwitz is perhaps comparable to similar events, like Rwanda and Cambodia, but it defies comparison to most other wrongs. And despite the tendency of some today to liken just about anyone with whom they deeply disagree to Adolf Hitler, in reality, his is an evil that defies likeness. The real question for us, though, will be whether or not it also defies *understanding*. Can any *sense* be made of such evil?

For that matter, what would it even mean to say that we understand, or can make sense of, sadistic serial murderers like Ted Bundy and Edmund Kemper? Bundy engaged in necrophilia; he kept the severed heads of several victims in his apartment as keepsakes; and his final victim was a 12-year-old girl whose body he left to rot under a hog shed. One of Kemper's last victims was his own mother. He decapitated her and raped her severed head, before cutting out her vocal cords and shoving them down the garbage disposal. These actions are different from the genocides mentioned above in many important ways, but they are alike in defying comparison to most other wrongs.

Simply put: there is *wrongdoing*, and then there is *evil*. There are *bad* people, people whose characters warrant disapproval, and then there are *evil* people. Like I said, I think many of us *sense* the difference between these moral categories, even if we do not have a clear idea of what *makes* the difference. Can any sense be made of what distinguishes evil from the merely wrong or bad? What *is* moral evil, and what is its significance? These are questions that I want to answer in this book.

Evildoers, Evil People, and Evil Actions

Suppose Bob tells a lie. Does that make him a *liar*? Before you answer yes, what if I told you that everyone who knows Bob considers him a very honest person? What if it is genuinely "out-of-character" for Bob to lie to someone? Is he nonetheless a liar, just for telling the one lie?

In one sense, it seems like the answer has to be *yes*. After all, what else could the word "liar" mean except *someone who lies or has lied*? And even if Bob has only lied *once*, that is all it takes to count as *someone who lies or has lied*. (For comparison: how many people would Bob have to kill in order for him to count as a *killer*?) What if Bob lied *to you*? Wouldn't that be all it takes for you to think of him as a liar?

But in another sense, it also seems a bit hasty and unfair to call Bob a liar on the basis of just one lie. Surely there is an important difference between Bob, someone widely regarded as honest, and Bill, someone known for being extremely dishonest. Suppose Bill tells lies as often as Bob doesn't. If *both* of these men deserve the label "liar," then *everybody* does, and the word "liar" is effectively rendered practically useless. After all, *everyone* is *someone who lies or has lied*.

Crucially, though, when Bill lies, he is not acting "out-of-character," like Bob. Rather, when Bill lies, he is acting "in-character." He is the sort of person who lies. So perhaps a more useful meaning of the term "liar" would be something like *the sort of person who lies*, or *someone for whom it is characteristic to lie*. This is useful because it allows us to distinguish between people like Bob and people like Bill. When "liar" is used in this more specific way, the difference between them is clear: Bill is a liar, but Bob is not. And the difference is not only clear, but important as well: Bob can be trusted, for instance, but Bill cannot.

Sometimes we apply moral and other evaluative labels to people solely because of their *actions*, and sometimes we do so for a deeper reason, one to do with their *characters*. And oftentimes, when these labels are used solely on the basis of actions, this renders them practically useless, as we have just seen with "liar," as applied to Bob and Bill.

Now, what about the label "evil"? You may just have to take my word for it for now, but I think the lesson here is actually very similar to the one we just learned with respect to "liar." Sometimes, as we have seen with Bob, lies are told by people who are not liars. In fact, I think this happens quite often. And in just the same way, I think it is possible for evil actions to be committed by people who are not evil. In fact, I think decent folks like you and me regularly commit evil acts, and oftentimes with disturbing ease—a conclusion supported not only by history, but also by about a half-century's worth of research in social psychology. (We will explore some of this research together in later chapters.)

As long as it is possible for decent people to occasionally do evil things, though, we will have to take some care with our language here as well. Let us use the term "evildoer" to refer to *anyone who performs or has performed an evil action*. Later in the book, I will have an answer to the question, "What makes an action evil?" So for now, again, you will just have to take my word for it that probably most adult humans are evildoers at some point in their lives. But this is like saying that both Bob and Bill have told lies. In contrast, I shall use the term "evil person" to refer to someone who is *the sort of person who performs evil actions*, or *someone for whom it is characteristic to perform evil actions*. So defined, you earn the label "evildoer" by *acting* a certain way, and you earn the label "evil person" by *being* a certain way.

With this distinction between evildoers and evil persons in place, we can make the following two claims, both of which I think are true. First, not all evildoers are evil people. This is just to say that not all people who perform evil actions are *the sorts of people* who would do such a thing. In other words, it is possible to perform an evil action out-of-character. Second, not all evil persons are evildoers. Strictly speaking, it is at least possible for someone to be *the sort of person* who would do evil, and yet—perhaps for lack of opportunity—to never actually perform an evil act. Similarly, it seems possible for someone to be the sort of person who would tell lies, and yet, for whatever reason, to never actually lie.

This distinction between evildoers and evil persons is useful for at least two other reasons. First, the distinction will be important in later chapters—especially Chaps. 6 and 7—as it will help us to understand and evaluate different theories of evil. Second, it allows me to further clarify the central questions that I seek to answer in this book. At the heart of the book is a question very similar to the one I asked my students: *What makes someone an evil person?* As should now be clear, the answer cannot be as simple as saying, "*Performing evil actions* is what makes someone an evil person." For one thing, we still do not know what an *evil action* is. And for another, this answer would just collapse the distinction between evildoers and evil persons.

What is it that separates an evil person, then, from a mere evildoer? What has to be true of a person's character in order for him to be the sort of person who performs evil acts? These are different ways of asking what is the central question of the book.

For the record, there is some controversy in the philosophical literature on evil about which is the more fundamental concept—*evil action* or *evil person*? Some, like Luke Russell, believe that evil action is the more basic concept, the implication being that we cannot understand what an evil person is until we first understand what an evil action is.[5] So he goes to great lengths explaining what he thinks an evil action is, before then defining evil character or personhood in terms of a disposition to perform actions of that type. Others, like Haybron, "suggest that we reverse the usual order of explication and understand the evil action in terms of its relation to the evil character: e.g., perhaps, an action is evil if it manifests the sensibilities characteristic of an evil person."[6]

For my own part, I think it best not to take a side on the matter. Instead, I shall proceed on the assumption that the concept of *evil* is equally fundamental to both evil action and evil person. Throughout the book, I focus primarily—though certainly not exclusively—on the concept of evil personhood, not because I consider it more basic or fundamental, but only because I happen to consider it a more interesting route to an understanding of the general concept of evil.

Previewing Evil: An Outline of the Book

This book aims to be scientific in its method, and philosophical in its means. When I say that it is "scientific in its method," I mean that it follows a familiar pattern common to scientific investigation: gathering data, evaluating existing hypotheses in light of the data, and formulating new hypotheses, if and when necessary. In this case, though, the "data" consists in a fact-based examination of several real-life cases of apparent human evil, and the "hypotheses" will be various philosophical theories of evil. When I say that the book is "philosophical in its means," I mean that it is, at its heart, an exercise in conceptual analysis—in this case, an analysis of the concept of *evil*.

Let me say a bit more about the general method that will guide me throughout the chapters to follow. When philosophers are grappling with a particular concept—like the concept of *knowledge*—they often begin by surveying a number of cases in which people ordinarily use words like "know," "knows," and "knowledge," before then asking, "What, if anything, do all or most of these cases have in common?" Basically, the presumption is that most people not only *have* a concept of knowledge, but they *share* a concept of knowledge, more or less; and even if most people are unaware of the exact nature of this concept, we can at least begin to get a sense of its contours by analyzing the various ways in which they use the relevant terms. For instance, even if I manage to correctly guess how many fingers you are holding up behind your back, most people will nonetheless say that I do not *know* how many fingers you are holding up. This suggests that, even if these people have never actually taken a moment to contemplate the nature or essence of knowledge, they nonetheless share a concept according to which beliefs based solely on guesses cannot count as knowledge, even if those beliefs happen to be true.

Now, to be clear, I am not suggesting that we can uncover the nature of all of our concepts simply by sitting back and reflecting on the ways in which people ordinarily use the relevant terms. In many cases, much more will be needed; for instance, we needed scientists to tell us that the stuff everyone calls "water" is composed of two hydrogen atoms and an oxygen atom. Rather, all I am saying is that ordinary language use can often be especially revelatory when it comes to the nature of our concepts, and this is particularly important when the concept itself is something that apparently cannot be settled by hard science—for example, concepts like *knowledge, justice*, and *beauty*. I also assume that the full nature of a concept can actually be unknown to a person who not only possesses it, but even uses it competently. We were competent users of the concept *water* long before we knew its chemical composition; and people who never once read a book, or took a course, on epistemology might nonetheless spend a lifetime using the concept *knowledge* perfectly competently.

All of this applies equally well to the concept of evil—even in the narrower, specifically moral sense discussed above. I believe that people have, share, and even competently use such a concept, even if its exact nature is unclear. For those of us who are interested in analyzing this concept, I think a useful place to start would be by examining the various ways in which people ordinarily put this concept to use. In other words, if we are trying to get a sense of what makes a person evil, then we ought to begin by asking: What sort of person, or people, do we ordinarily consider evil?

As I mentioned earlier, there is an unfortunate tendency among some to resort to extreme moral language when discussing those they perceive as political enemies—such as George Bush and Barack Obama. For this reason, it can be difficult to get a clear sense of how people *really* deploy the concept of evil when they are being sincere and clear-headed. (Do you *really* think that Bush or Obama belongs in the same category as genocidal dictators and sadistic serial murderers? Or are you just being hyperbolic for the sake of expressing your extremely contemptuous attitudes?)

Thankfully, we may not have to rely on merely observing people's casual uses of the term "evil." For a couple of recent studies, and drawing from a couple of "true crime" books written for popular audiences, Peter Brian Barry "compile[d] a list of 49 different individuals as plausible examples of evil people."[7] He then constructed a survey to be taken online in which respondents were given the names of two individuals from the list and asked, "Who is a better example of an evil person?" (Respondents could choose either name, or, if unsure, a third button labeled "I can't decide.") The result—after nearly 2,000 votes were cast—was a list of individuals ranked from best to worst examples of an evil person, according to respondents' intuitions. Among the 20 highest-ranked people are (a) Ted Bundy, Jeffrey Dahmer, John Wayne Gacy, Donald "Pee Wee" Gaskins, Richard Ramirez; and (b) Adolf Hitler (unsurprisingly, he was ranked highest by a significant margin), Adolf Eichmann, Heinrich Himmler, Josef Mengele, and a number of other genocidal dictator-type individuals, including Pol Pot, Joseph Stalin, Benito Mussolini, and Mao Zedong.[8]

I find these results both unsurprising and striking at the same time. They are unsurprising in that I likely would have guessed that many of these names would have appeared somewhere on the list, perhaps with the exception of Gaskins, who is a lesser-known serial killer compared to the others. But the results are striking in that the most highly ranked candidates for evil can apparently be divided into two recognizable types, as indicated by the two lists into which I divided them above. What sorts of people do we ordinarily consider evil? Apparently: (a) psychopathic serial murderers and (b) leaders of totalitarian and genocidal regimes. (Correspondingly, we can probably guess that serial murder and genocide would rank highest among the types of *action* most likely to be deemed evil.)

What I find perhaps most curious about Barry's list of candidates for evil—and, in his defense, this is apparently just a consequence of constructing his own list from lists made by others—is the conspicuous absence of a third type of person commonly regarded as evil, namely, someone who seeks financial profit from the misuse or destruction of others. Here I have in mind everyone from Wall Street "confidence men" and corrupt CEOs (like Bernie Madoff and "Chainsaw" Al Dunlap) to drug lords (like Pablo Escobar) to human traffickers. After all, at the risk of resorting to cliché, it cannot be for nothing that people so commonly regard a love of money as "the root of all evil." Now, probably, people like Madoff and Escobar would not have ranked nearly as high as your "average" serial killer or genocidal dictator—and, perhaps, deservedly so. But the fact that we so commonly associate such extreme and criminal pursuits of financial gain with evil suggests that they have nonetheless earned their place in a discussion of the nature of evil personhood.

So, for the purpose of gathering the data required to properly evaluate philosophical theories of evil, and then to construct one of my own, Part I of the book examines the psychological mechanisms involved in these purported instances of evil: psychopathic serial murderers (Chap. 2), perpetrators of genocide (Chap. 3), and various money-related evils (Chap. 4). The basic idea is essentially the same as what I described earlier with respect to the concept of knowledge. Just as epistemologists often take for granted that we are *onto something* when we call some things knowledge and others not—that is, that we are using the concept of knowledge mostly competently, in a way that reveals something about its nature—I similarly assume that people are *onto something* when they call certain types of people, but not others, "evil." So, just as a close examination of cases of purported knowledge can reveal something important about our concept of knowledge, a close examination of cases of purported evil might likewise reveal something important about our concept of evil.

Other theorists shy away from such close examinations of real-life cases of evil. Here, for instance, is how Russell explains his reluctance to do so:

> While it is true that often we cannot fully understand why a specific evil action occurred without locating that action in its detailed context, it is also true that theories of evil action can be skewed and incomplete if they focus too closely on only one kind of example of extreme wrongdoing.[9]

Russell's point here is well taken. And in fact, we can see an example of what he is talking about in Philip Zimbardo's recent contribution to the literature on evil, *The Lucifer Effect: Understanding How Good People Turn Evil*. While Zimbardo does occasionally mention in passing other evils, such as the genocides in Germany and Rwanda, the vast majority of his book focuses exclusively on two cases in particular—his now-famous

Stanford Prison Experiment and the abuse of prisoners at the Abu Ghraib Prison in Iraq—and the comparisons that he attempts to draw between them. Indeed, Zimbardo himself admits, "The driving force behind this book was the need to better understand the how and why of the physical and psychological abuses perpetrated on prisoners by American Military Police at the Abu Ghraib Prison in Iraq."[10] But one result of this excessively narrow focus on only two (relatively similar) cases is that Zimbardo ends up saying things about the nature of evil that simply do not apply to other paradigm instances, such as that people only "turn evil" when they are under the influence of especially powerful situations or settings (e.g., the artificial prison environment that he created in the lower level of Stanford's psychology department and the very real prison environment of Abu Ghraib). This might be true of the many Nazi henchmen who willingly participated in genocide, but it does not obviously apply to any of the Nazi leaders mentioned earlier, and it almost certainly does not apply to psychopathic serial murderers. (For a more thorough critique of Zimbardo's views on this and other points, stick around for Chap. 5.)

So again, Russell's point is well taken, and apparently, well founded. But there is another concern that runs in the opposite direction: if we do not look *closely enough* at particular cases of apparent evil, we risk missing out on important features, certain very subtle similarities between them, which might give us some valuable insight into the nature of the phenomenon. If you settle for surface appearances, you end up defining "water" as *a clear, colorless, potable fluid*. It is not until, and unless, you look closer that you discover that it is H₂O. Likewise, if you settle for cursory glances at a few of the surface appearances of cases of purported evil, you may end up defining it in terms that do not really "carve the moral reality at its joints," to adapt an expression often used in metaphysics. The way to resolve or avoid both of these concerns, I think, is to look very closely at a sufficient number of relatively diverse real-life cases. That is the aim of Part I of the book.

In Part II, with all of the psychological data gathered in Part I in mind, we turn our attention to the philosophy of evil. This begins in Chap. 5 with a discussion of three philosophical puzzles. The first puzzle is this: Isn't evil fundamentally *incomprehensible*? In other words, don't we just call people evil whenever we cannot understand them or their behavior? And if so, why think that a philosophical *theory* of evil is even possible, if the point of such a theory is to make some sense of the relevant concept? (A related worry will be: If we attempt to *understand* evil people, do we not thereby risk *justifying* or *exonerating* them?) The second puzzle is this: Do the people we encounter in Part I of the book really deserve to be called evil, if their behavior is ultimately rooted in things like brain malfunction, personality disorder, or abuse suffered as a child? And the third puzzle arises out of research in social psychology conducted over the course of the past half-century (here Zimbardo will re-enter the discussion). What this research seems to show is that people do the things they do primarily because of the influence of features of their situations, and not because of any traits of character or personality, as is commonly assumed. But if this is right, it has a number of troubling implications. For one, it implies that you or I might just as well have done the same things as some of the people discussed in Part I, if only we had faced the same situations. And for another, it apparently undermines the common assumption that some people do what they do *because they are evil*.

Then in Chap. 6, with those puzzles out of the way, I examine some of the more prominent philosophical theories of evil personhood. These theories can be divided into roughly four types: *extremity* theories, *action-based* theories, *desire-based* theories, and *affect-based* theories. For each type, I will explain its distinguishing features, provide an example or two of theories of that type, and explain why these theories do *not* do a good enough job of capturing our concept of moral evil.

Finally, in Chap. 7, I offer my own theory of evil. Since my view is very much inspired by some of the work of Hannah Arendt, mentioned above, I begin the chapter with a discussion of three of Arendt's more noteworthy claims about the nature of evil. This will lead me to the conclusion that evil is a matter of what I call *moral disregard*. After defining the notion of moral disregard, by locating it among other more familiar ethical concepts, I defend a view according to which a person is evil as long as he or she *has* a kind of moral disregard for others, and an action is evil as long as it *shows* a kind of moral disregard for others. I also explain how the theory can apply to other things, such as evil institutions, evil policies, and evil events. Then, after defending the theory against a number of potential objections, I close the book with some speculative remarks about two issues that arise in earlier chapters: if evil is indeed a matter of moral disregard, then (1) what, if anything, can we *do* about it? and (2) what does this imply with respect to *moral sainthood*, if, as many assume, the evil person is supposed to be a kind of perverse mirror image of the moral saint? In response to this second question, I will suggest that the common assumption that the opposite of evil is *goodness* is mistaken. The opposite of evil is not goodness, but something else.

Notes

1. See, e.g., Cole (2006: 3–4) and Feinberg (2003: 142ff).
2. Cole (2006: 3).
3. For treatments of the problem of evil geared toward popular audiences, I recommend Lewis (1957) and Craig and Sinnott-Armstrong (2004) (especially pp. 83–98, 112–127). For more philosophically rigorous treatments of the problem, I recommend Mackie (1955), Hick (1966), Plantinga (1974), Rowe (1996), Adams (1999).
4. Haybron (2002: 260).
5. Russell (2014: 31–34).
6. Haybron (2002: 280).
7. Barry (2013: 28).
8. Barry (2013: 30–31).
9. Russell (2014: 7).
10. Zimbardo (2007: 18).

References

Adams, Marilyn McCord. 1999. *Horrendous Evils and the Goodness of God*. Ithaca: Cornell University Press.
Barry, Peter B 2013. *Evil and Moral Psychology*. New York: Routledge.
Cole, Phillip. 2006. *The Myth of Evil: Demonizing the Enemy*. Westport: Praeger.
Craig, William Lane, and Walter Sinnott-Armstrong. 2004. *God? A Debate between a Christian and an Atheist*. New York: Oxford University Press.
Feinberg, Joel. 2003. Evil. In *Problems at the Roots of Law: Essays in Legal and Political Theory*, 125–92. Oxford: Oxford University Press.
Haybron, Daniel. 2002. Moral Monsters and Saints. *The Monist* 85(2): 260–284.
Hick, John. 1966. *Evil and the God of Love*. New York: Harper and Row.
Lewis, C.S. 1957. *The Problem of Pain*. London: Fontana Books.
Mackie, John L. 1955. Evil and Omnipotence. *Mind* 64: 200–212.
Plantinga, Alvin. 1974. *God, Freedom, and Evil*. New York: Harper and Row.
Rowe, William. 1996. The Evidential Argument from Evil: A Second Look. In *The Evidential Argument from Evil*, ed. Daniel Howard-Snyder, 262–285. Bloomington: Indiana University Press.
Russell, Luke. 2014. *Evil: A Philosophical Investigation*. Oxford: Oxford University Press.
Zimbardo, Philip. 2007. *The Lucifer Effect: Understanding How Good People Turn Evil*. New York: Random House.

PART I

The Psychology of Evil: Some Case Studies

CHAPTER 2

Serial Murder, Psychopathy, and Objectification

A recent television program entitled *Most Evil* documents the lives and criminal behaviors of a number of notorious murderers; at the end of each segment, the murderers are then rated on a "scale of evil" developed by Michael Stone, forensic psychiatrist and professor of clinical psychiatry at Columbia. At the lower end of the scale are those who kill from such "ordinary" motives as jealousy and rage. At the higher end of the scale are psychopathic serial murderers, who often rape and torture their victims before killing them. Here again, as we saw in the previous chapter, psychopathic serial murderers tend to rank highly among those most commonly regarded as morally evil. The purpose of this chapter is to take some steps toward understanding why this is the case. What is it, specifically, about serial murder—as opposed to other violent acts, and even other forms of murder—that ignites our thoughts about evil? And what, if anything, does psychopathy have to do with it? For that matter, what really *is* psychopathy?

Throughout Part I of the book, we will look relatively closely at the psychological mechanisms underlying real-life cases of purportedly evil people. As I explained in the previous chapter, one of my aims in doing this is to avoid potentially missing out on important features of these cases, which might lend valuable insights to our later philosophical investigation of the nature of moral evil. This will be especially important in this chapter, for a few reasons. For one, as I explain below, there are a number of misconceptions surrounding the nature and implications of psychopathy, such as what causes psychopathy, whether psychopaths understand what goes on in others' minds, and whether psychopaths "lack a conscience." But even more directly relevant to the topic of the book, while it is very common for people to assume that psychopathic serial killers are driven primarily by sadistic desires (usually sexual in nature), I think a closer examination of the lives, actions, and statements of real-life psychopathic serial killers will reveal that there is something even more basic that motivates them. Of course, many of them *are* sexual sadists. But this is not what makes them evil—or so I shall argue.

So the chapter begins with a brief biographical sketch of the life and crimes of perhaps the most notorious serial killer ever, Ted Bundy. Bundy will not be the only psychopathic serial murderer discussed in this chapter, but he will serve as a kind of "main character," if you will. Since many readers will already be familiar with his crimes, however, I shall do my best to focus on elements of the Bundy story that are less widely known. Then I will turn my focus to the questions raised above. What is it about serial murder in particular that so consistently stirs our thoughts about evil? What is psychopathy, and what explains its apparent connection to serial murder? Is it fair or accurate to describe psychopaths as lacking a conscience? If so, does that mean that psychopathic serial murderers do not really know that what they are doing is morally wrong? And if they do not, does that mean that they are not morally responsible for their actions? And if they are not morally responsible for their actions, how could they be any more *evil* than, say, a rabid dog?

As you can see, we have a lot of interesting ground to cover. And as you can probably imagine, some of it is going to be very disturbing and difficult to read. So please be forewarned. Now, with that warning issued, let me introduce you to Ted.

TED BUNDY

Ted Bundy was not the most prolific of serial killers. Indeed, he is not even the most prolific of *American* serial killers, a dishonor that currently belongs to "Green River Killer" Gary Ridgeway. Nor were his crimes any more gruesome than those of other lesser-known murderers, like Albert Fish or Richard Trenton Chase. Bundy has no signature nickname, like "the Night Stalker," "the Zodiac," or "Son of Sam"; he did not leave "calling cards" at the scenes of his crimes; and he did not encourage his own popularity by sending cryptic letters to the press. Yet, despite all of this, he is widely regarded as one of the most fascinating and notorious serial killers in history.

Bundy was arrested on February 15, 1978, in Pensacola, Florida, on suspicion of vehicle theft (his now infamous Volkswagen Beetle had been reported as stolen), and later charged with the murder of two members of the Chi Omega sorority at Florida State University. (A month earlier, Bundy had broken into the sorority house during the night and attacked four young women as they slept, murdering two and leaving the other two seriously injured.) He stood trial for the murders the following summer—his trial was the first to be nationally televised—and on July 24, 1979, the jury returned a guilty verdict. Several months later, Bundy stood trial for another of his Florida murders—a 12-year-old girl named Kimberly Leach. He walked Leach right off of her school grounds in broad daylight, raped and killed her, and then left her body under an abandoned hog shed. For all three murders, Bundy received death sentences; and nine years later, on January 24, 1989, he was executed by electrocution.

While on death row, Bundy reluctantly agreed to a series of interviews with journalists Stephen Michaud and Hugh Aynesworth. The circumstances surrounding these interviews are fascinating in their own right. Almost immediately after the trials, Bundy had wanted to tell his story, in the form of a book; however, at the time, and despite overwhelming evidence of his guilt and a total lack of any kind of alibi for any of the murders, he nonetheless maintained that he was completely innocent. So he was initially uncooperative when he felt that Michaud and Aynesworth were looking for something like a confession. However, when they "repackaged" the proposal by making it appear to Bundy as if they were simply seeking his invaluable insight into the kind of person who could do the sorts of things he had been accused of doing, his demeanor changed entirely. He grabbed the tape recorder, cradled it in his lap, and opened up—unwittingly giving us (often behind the guise of third-person) what is now regarded as "probably the most complete self-portrait ever painted by a serial killer."[1]

Surprisingly little is known about Bundy's childhood. Unlike most serial killers, it does not appear to be the case that Bundy himself was ever a direct victim of abuse. But he did spend a lot of time around—and later claimed to have greatly admired—his maternal grandfather, Samuel Cowell, who was apparently very violent (especially toward his wife and the family dog) and possibly mentally ill. Bundy had no relationship at all with his biological father, unless, as some rumors have it, he was conceived as a result of Cowell raping his daughter, Bundy's mother, Louise. Bundy's relationship with Louise was strange, to say the very least. For a while, Bundy was forced to pretend that he and Louise were siblings, and not mother and son. Bundy never expressed any resentment toward his mother, but did confess that their relationship was hampered to some degree by Louise's inability to discuss anything even remotely personal with him.

Two details in particular about Bundy's psychological development stand out as potentially relevant to the criminal that he would eventually become. The first is a profound sense of personal inadequacy that manifested itself in a number of ways. For one, he was extremely materialistic, harboring "an arrogant disdain for anything he regarded as common."[2] Bundy was mortified, for instance, by the modest possessions, such as clothing and vehicles, which his mother and stepfather's salaries could afford. But perhaps nothing fueled his sense of inadequacy stronger than the news of his own illegitimacy. After discovering his birth certificate and seeing "Unknown" in the space for his father's name, friends and relatives report that Bundy seethed with bitterness and hostility. Bundy himself tells a somewhat different story, though, describing the event as "an opportunity to make a decision about who I was."[3]

The other early warning sign was a kind of social ineptitude that came to a peak when he entered high school. Up to that point, Bundy never really struggled to get along with and relate to others. But around this time, while friends and classmates advanced further in their social development, he stayed put. And as a result, other people became alien to him. "I didn't know what made things tick," Bundy himself explained. "I didn't know what made people want to be friends. I didn't know what made people attractive to one another. I didn't know what underlay social interactions."[4] Stories of his friends' sexual escapades were equally fascinating and utterly perplexing to Bundy. He excelled in formalized environments like the classroom, where the rules were always very clear, but he struggled in environments where the "rules" were more of the "unspoken," conventional variety—that is, rules that required a kind of sensitivity to others' intentions, desires, and expectations, which Bundy seemed to lack.

Bundy began his criminal career as a petty thief, but unlike many thieves, he never stole money, and he never stole items with the intention to sell them later. Rather, "[h]e stole a television, a stereo, home furnishings, cookware, clothing, and artwork—things that he wanted to own. Possessions."[5] This was, after all, a way for him to satisfy his materialistic impulses, and to thereby assuage to some degree his deep sense of inadequacy. It was also around this time that Bundy developed a taste for violent pornography, and his habit of prowling around his college campus and town looking for things to steal soon turned into a habit of prowling around and peeping into women's bedrooms.

Eventually, Bundy's urges escalated to such a point that, on the night of January 4, 1974, he entered the bedroom of a sleeping young woman through the window of her basement apartment, beat her unconscious with a metal rod, and violently thrust a speculum into her vagina, causing serious internal injuries. She survived, despite spending several months in a coma, but remembered nothing of the event. Less than a month later, Bundy struck again—once again entering the bedroom of a young woman named Lynda Healy through her window in the middle of the night and savagely beating her unconscious. However, this time, after dressing Healy in clean clothes and making her bed, Bundy took her body with him when he left. A year later, Healy's skull was found in a wooded area on Taylor Mountain, in Washington, alongside the remains of at least five other women.

There is some debate about whether the Healy case was actually Bundy's first murder. But what is well known is that, with Healy, Bundy began a career of serial murder that would span four years, several states—from Washington to Florida—and result in the gruesome deaths of nearly three dozen young women, the last of which was 12-year-old Kimberly Leach. He often baited his victims by pretending to be injured and in need of help. According to some reports, he once abducted two women on the same day, took them both to the same location, and forced each to watch as he raped the other. He sometimes dressed his victims' lifeless bodies in outfits that pleased him, and applied makeup to their faces. On several occasions, he visited his victims' remains so that he could "relive what he had done to them."[6] And he would occasionally keep their severed heads with him in his apartment as souvenirs.

Even in those moments during his prison interviews at which Bundy came closest to confessing, he was reluctant to shoulder much, if any, of the blame. A persistent theme throughout these interviews was the effect that he believed pornography had on him. Reflecting (again, in the third person) on this issue in particular, Bundy once said,

> Maybe he focused on pornography as a vicarious way of experiencing what his peers were experiencing in reality. Then he got sucked into the more sinister doctrines that are implicit in pornography—the use, the abuse, the possession of women as objects.[7]

Another tactic that Bundy employed for deflecting blame was to posit what he called "an entity," or "malignant being," inside him that would take over during his homicidal rampages:

He [Bundy] called it a "hybrid situation," a pathology in which the "entity" was both in and *of* the killer, not some alien presence or second self, but a purely destructive power that grew from within.[...]

[...] Only by means of his astounding capacity to compartmentalize had Bundy been able to keep the hunchback from raging through the mask and destroying him. When at last it did, *Ted* became the hunchback. No longer its protector, he and the entity fused.

I [Michaud] felt I was encountering a wholly novel form of derangement. Rather than being overwhelmed, defeated by his illness, Ted appeared to be inhabited by it. The two, man and hunchback, interacted. Above all, I saw elements of will, *conscious* will, taking part in the creation of this entity, as if Ted had *wanted* to become a killer.[8]

But as you can see, those who observed Bundy closely did not get the impression that he was possessed and overtaken by some murderous entity. Rather, *he was the entity*.

As I mentioned in the previous chapter, serial killers are among the people most commonly regarded as evil, and Ted Bundy is the serial killer *par excellence*. But what is it about serial murder that so often stirs people's intuitions about evil?

SERIAL MURDER

At one point, the Federal Bureau of Investigation (FBI) defined "serial murder" as the killing of three or more people, in three or more separate locations, with a kind of emotional cooling-off period between incidents. But there are a number of problems with this definition. For one, it seems a misnomer to describe the time between murders as a "cooling-off period." Just as important as whatever "cooling-off" a serial killer might do between attacks is the gradual "heating-up," or intensifying, of his homicidal urges. For another thing, it is completely irrelevant that the incidents take place at separate locations. Many serial killers—such as Jeffrey Dahmer, John Wayne Gacy, and Fred and Rosemary West—lure their victims back to a single, familiar location to be tortured and killed. Finally, while "serial" obviously implies a series, why must it be a series of *three* or more? In light of these and other worries, the FBI revised its definition in 2008 to this: "The unlawful killing of two or more victims by the same offender(s), in separate events."[9]

As far as the FBI and other law enforcement agencies are concerned, the main purpose of defining "serial murder" in the first place is to have a formal means by which to distinguish instances of serial murder from other types of multiple murders. For instance, depending on how we are to delineate between "events," this definition sets serial murder apart from both *mass murder*—which typically involves the killing of many people in a single event, and at the same location (e.g., school shootings)—and *spree killing*—which is identical to mass murder, but spread across multiple locations (e.g., the Port Arthur massacre).

What the FBI definition still misses, however, is the peculiar psychological nature of most instances of serial murder. Mass murderers and spree killers are typically of the "ticking time bomb" variety, resorting to murder only after reaching a kind of psychological tipping point. It is relatively common, for instance, for people to engage in mass or spree killings after significant and unfortunate life events, such as getting a divorce or losing a job. Serial murderers, however, are typically of a more predatory type. The National Institute of Justice's (NIJ's) definition of "serial murder" agrees with the FBI's in its reference to two or more victims, killed in separate events. But the NIJ adds that the perpetrator's behavior and crime scenes often reflect sadistic, sexual overtones. While this is certainly not an essential feature of serial murder—so-called Angel of Death serial killers, usually nurses, doctors, or other medical personnel, often murder out of a warped sense of mercy—it is arguably common enough to be characteristic, and surely deserves mention alongside any attempted definition of the crime.

The reference to sexual sadism is important, but also potentially misleading. Although it is certainly true that most serial murderers are sexual sadists, what is more important for our purposes is to understand what it is about inflicting harm, often of a sexual nature, that they find so stimulating. Harold Schechter, a crime writer who specializes in serial murder, explains it thus:

> [T]he vast majority of serial killers were subjected to extreme forms of psychological abuse as children. They were made to feel utterly helpless and humiliated. As a result, they grew up with a malevolent need to inflict the same condition on others. The only way to overcome their deep-rooted feelings of impotence is by asserting total control over another human being. […] In its most extreme form, the serial killer's need for control involves

turning another human being into a completely passive object, a kind of doll that belongs entirely to him.[10]

It is a common assumption that serial killers are driven simply by a predatory and sexually sadistic impulse. No wonder, then—as we will see in Chap. 6—that it is so common for people to associate *evil* either with a desire to inflict significant harm upon another, or with a tendency to take pleasure in the harming of others. However, while I certainly do not deny that serial killers are often sadistic and that this gives their crimes a particularly disturbing feel, there is a serious risk here of settling too quickly for how things appear on the surface, rather than digging below the surface for understanding. For what truly motivates most serial killers is not a sexual desire for another's pain, but rather something deeper than that: a desire for total control, total dominance, total possession of another human being. Somewhat surprisingly (especially if one has settled for a simple diagnosis of sexual sadism), Bundy himself

> insisted that violence was never an end in itself, that the sex was almost perfunctory, and that to the extent it was possible the victims were spared pain. Not that the "entity" was moved by any humanitarian impulses; it was just that *gratification lay not in the assault, but in possession—the key to understanding Ted*.[11]

It is perhaps worth noting, for instance, that Bundy often began his attacks by knocking the victim unconscious. So it was apparently not a desire for her conscious pain or suffering that he was attempting to satisfy.

Even aside from their motive, however, serial killers can often be distinguished by a set of traits or features that, while certainly not essential, are nonetheless common enough to make up a kind of stereotype. For instance, most serial killers are white males between the ages of 20-40. Most have an above-average IQ (but are rarely geniuses, as is commonly assumed). Most perform poorly in school and rarely stay at one job for very long, and as a result, often end up poorly skilled as adults. Perhaps most significantly, most serial killers come from seriously troubled and dysfunctional families or households, often with a long history of psychiatric problems, drug and alcohol abuse, and other criminal behavior. It is common for serial killers to have some combination of either (a) an absent or abusive father, (b) a domineering mother, or (c) both. With predictable regularity, this combination later gives rise to a corresponding (a) difficulty with male authority figures, (b) intense hostility toward women, or (c) both. Nearly all serial killers were victims of some sort of abuse as children, often sexual.

Someone who fits the stereotype perfectly—perhaps even better than Bundy—is Edmund Kemper. Unlike Bundy, Kemper struggled in school, despite being exceptionally bright. Also unlike Bundy, Kemper had a very close relationship with his father, but the relationship was lost when his parents divorced while he was still a young boy, an event that left Kemper confused and devastated. From that point on, he was forced to live with his mother, Clarnell, a mentally unstable woman who abused alcohol and constantly belittled and humiliated him. Predictably, Kemper developed an intense hatred of women, a hatred that drove him to rape and murder several young women, earning him the nickname "The Co-ed Killer," and which climaxed in his brutal attack on Clarnell herself. Kemper bludgeoned her with a claw hammer, decapitated her, raped her severed head, and finally, in a symbolic act meant to "shut her up once and for all," cut out her vocal chords and forced them down the garbage disposal.

Here too, however, it would be too simplistic, to the point of being downright mistaken, to describe Kemper as a sexual sadist. First and foremost, he wanted total possession of, and total control over, another human being. Indeed, here is how Kemper *himself* described his own state of mind at the time: "It was more or less making a doll out of a human being and carrying out my fantasies with a doll, a living human doll."[12]

There are a handful of novels that have achieved a kind of ill fame as favorites among serial killers. One such novel is *The Collector*, by John Fowles. In the book, a young man named Frederick Clegg, who captures and collects butterfly specimens as a hobby, becomes obsessed with a young woman named Miranda Grey. Eventually, the obsession boils over to such a point that he kidnaps her and keeps her captive in his basement, initially in the hope that she might one day fall in love with him. The first part of the book follows the story from Frederick's perspective; the second part consists of entries in a diary that Miranda kept during her captivity. In one such entry, finally realizing how he has transferred his desire to possess and control butterflies onto her, she writes,

> I am one in a row of specimens. It's when I try to flutter out of line that he hates me. I'm meant to be dead, pinned, always the same, always beautiful. He knows that part of my beauty is being alive, but it's the dead me he wants. He wants me living-but-dead. I felt it terribly strong today. That my

being alive and changing and having a separate mind and having moods and all that was becoming a nuisance.[13]

And indeed, earlier in the book, Frederick admitted himself, "What she never understood was that with me it was having. Having her was enough. Nothing needed doing. I just wanted to have her, and safe at last."[14] One naturally wonders if serial murderers might identify so strongly with Clegg because they, too, seek not a gratification of sadistic sexual desires, but ultimately, the sensation of so utterly dominating another person that this other person is reduced to being a mere thing, a specimen, an object, over which they have total ownership and total control.

What has so far gone unmentioned is the curious coincidence of serial murder and *psychopathy*. Very few psychopaths are serial killers. If somewhere around 0.75 % of adults are psychopaths,[15] and according to recent census statistics, there are around 245 million people in the United States over the age of 18, then the total number of psychopaths in the United States is something close to 2 million. But the total number of active serial killers in the United States at any given time is only estimated to be between 25 and 50. So again, very few psychopaths engage in serial murder. However, of the 25–50 people currently engaged in serial murder in this country, you can bet that nearly all of them are psychopaths. So now that we have some idea of the characteristic motive of a serial murderer—that is, total domination or possession of another human being—it is important for us to dig a little deeper into the sort of character or personality that most commonly underlies this motive. And in order to do that, we will need to come to grips with the nature of psychopathy.

Psychopathy

During the nineteenth century, psychiatrists referred to patients who appeared to lack a conscience, or exhibited a notable disregard for the rights of others, as "moral imbeciles," or as "morally insane." It was not until sometime around 1900 that they began using the term "psychopath" fairly regularly—a term meaning, quite literally, *mentally* (*psyche*) *ill* (*pathos*).[16] By the middle of the twentieth century, however, mental health professionals came to prefer the term "sociopath," in part as a way to emphasize the profoundly *social* impact of this particular disorder. Nowadays, both terms are equally popular, and sometimes—though mistakenly, as I will explain below—used interchangeably.

The *Diagnostic and Statistical Manual of Mental Disorders* (DSM), now in its fifth edition, still makes no mention of psychopathy (or sociopathy, for that matter). Instead, these disorders are assumed to fall under the more general category of Antisocial Personality Disorder (ASPD). The main problem with this, as Blair et al. argue, is that

> there are many routes to antisocial behavior. The advantage of the concept of psychopathy is that it identifies a population who share a common etiology, a dysfunction in specific forms of emotional processing. In contrast, the DSM-IV [and now, the DSM-V] diagnoses identify the broad category of individuals who engage in antisocial behavior. As such, they identify a highly heterogeneous population who do not share a common etiology.[17]

In fact, only about 20–25 % of individuals with ASPD are psychopaths. So what, specifically, is psychopathy?

While we are now beginning to get a much clearer sense of the particular neurobiological underpinnings of the disorder, psychopathy is still commonly defined as a *syndrome*—that is, a cluster of more or less integrated psychological and behavioral symptoms or traits. The now-definitive list of traits is known as the Psychopathy Checklist-Revised (PCL-R). Developed by psychologist Robert Hare in the 1970s, and then revised throughout the 1980s and early 1990s, the PCL-R was initially inspired by a similar list published earlier in Hervey Cleckley's groundbreaking study of psychopathy *The Mask of Sanity* (1941).[18] The two lists diverge on some interesting points—for instance, only Cleckley's list mentions an absence of delusions and anxiety, and only Hare's list mentions childhood delinquency—but it is where the two lists converge that we get a clear picture of the psychopathic personality. Among the traits mentioned on both lists are glibness and superficial charm; proneness to manipulation and deception; egocentricity and overconfidence; impulsivity and failure to engage in long-term planning; a deficient sense of responsibility, often manifested by a lack of emotions like guilt and shame; general emotional shallowness; and a lack of empathy for others.

The lists themselves dispel a number of common misconceptions. For instance, psychopaths are commonly thought to be terrible at mind reading, that is, "reading" the mental states of others (e.g., beliefs, attitudes, intentions, and emotions) from such cues as their facial expressions, vocal tones, and body language. Now, to be sure, there is something to this. (Recall Bundy's self-professed bafflement at how people formed friendships, attractions, etc.) But the simple fact of the matter is that one cannot engage in manipulative and deceptive behavior, intentionally and successfully, without having some knowledge of the beliefs and expectations of others, some awareness of their changing states of mind, and so forth, together with an ability to adapt one's own behavior to the real-time feedback received from others. Manipulation and deception are cognitively very sophisticated, and would be almost impossible for psychopaths if they really were as "blind" to the minds of others as some assume.

This particular misconception, I think, is rooted in a misunderstanding of the nature of empathy. If empathy is conceived as (partly) a matter of "getting into the minds of others," or "seeing things from their perspective," and psychopaths are supposed to *lack* empathy, then of course you would expect them to struggle with mind reading. But again, this appears not to be the case. In reality, it is not so much that psychopaths are unempathetic in the sense of being *unaware* of others' mental states, but rather that they are unempathetic in the sense of being *unaffected* by others' mental states—or at least, they are not affected by them in the same ways as the rest of us. I will have more to say about this later.[19]

Of course, both lists also mention a proneness to antisocial behavior of some form or another, but as Blair et al. explain, what is unique about psychopaths is not *that* they engage in antisocial behavior, but *how*. Often unmentioned in discussions of ASPD and psychopathy is a distinction between *reactive* and *instrumental* forms of aggression. Aggression is reactive when it is displayed in response to some perceived offense or threat, and apparently without regard for any specific desire or goal. Aggression is instrumental when it is used as a means to accomplish some goal, for example, to acquire a victim's possessions or to increase one's status within a group hierarchy. Individuals with ASPD typically engage in antisocial behavior in a mostly reactive manner. Psychopaths, however, "present with highly elevated levels of both instrumental and reactive aggression."[20] In other words, for the psychopath, violence and other forms of aggression—much like superficial charm and outright lies—are ultimately tools in his toolkit, devices to be used for purposes of manipulating others in order to get what he wants.

As I mentioned earlier, we are now beginning to get a clear sense of the peculiar neurobiological underpinnings of psychopathy.[21] Basically, the real heart of psychopathy is an emotional impairment, and contrary to what is often assumed, this impairment has genetic, and not social, origins. Specifically, it begins with a reduced responsiveness of the neurons in the amygdala, one of the most crucial regions of the brain involved in emotional processing. The resulting amygdala dysfunction manifests itself in a variety of ways. For instance, in healthy individuals, the connection between the amygdala and the sensory cortex allows for perceived emotional stimuli (e.g., emotion words, emotional expressions in others, etc.) to "stand out," or to capture our attention. This is very important for purposes of socialization: we cannot learn how to properly *respond* to emotional cues without first being primed to *attend* to those cues. But in psychopaths, and directly as a result of genetically prior dysfunction in the amygdala, this amygdala–sensory cortex connection is impaired. In this way, and others, a malformed amygdala inhibits the psychopath's capacity for emotional learning.

For a while now, there has been a kind of "chicken or the egg" debate among researchers of psychopathy: what comes first in the development of a psychopath—poor socialization or emotional impairment? Are they emotionally impaired as a result of how poorly they socialize? Or do they socialize so poorly because they are emotionally impaired? We now appear to have an answer: emotional impairment, rooted in amygdala dysfunction, comes first.[22]

Importantly, though, this genetically rooted emotional impairment will not *necessarily* lead to the full suite of behavioral traits associated with psychopathy. In healthy individuals, the amygdala's sensitivity to emotional cues in others, especially during the course of socialization, works as a kind of built-in inhibitor, or governor, significantly limiting how inclined we are to engage in antisocial behavior of *any* kind, but especially of the *instrumental* variety. (Even if some form of instrumental aggression *could* be used to accomplish one of our goals, the very prospect of potentially witnessing expressions of pain and emotional suffering in would-be victims inhibits the properly socialized individual from doing so.) But, in the psychopath—and again, due primarily to dysfunction in the amygdala—this natural inhibitor never really takes root. So the claim is not that the associated emotional impairment will definitely lead to displays of reactive and instrumental aggression; rather, the claim is only that, for psychopaths, such behavior is not inhibited in the way that it is for the rest of us.

What about the "nurture" side of the familiar "nature versus nurture" debate? If someone with the psychopath's characteristic emotional impairment is raised in a stable, supportive, and socio-economically advantaged household, the range of behavioral options available to him will likely be much wider than it is for someone raised in an unstable, unsupportive, and disadvantaged environment; and as a result, the former will be less likely to engage in antisocial behavior instrumentally. Even if they both lack the behavioral "inhibitor" described above, the incentives will still be different: the prospect of stealing $50 will be much more attractive to someone who is socio-economically disadvantaged than it will be for someone who is already very wealthy, even if the wealthy person is also a psychopath.

[E]motional dysfunction increases the probability that the individual will learn antisocial motor programs for the achievement of goals. Whether they do or not will depend on the individual's social environment and learning history; i.e., a wealthy child might have more prosocial ways to gain rewards available to them.[23]

So, while experts agree that psychopaths cannot be *created* by such social factors as abuse, neglect, and socio-economic disadvantage, these factors do contribute a great deal to the likelihood that a psychopathic individual will, later in life, engage in the sorts of behaviors that we commonly associate with psychopaths—reactive and instrumental forms of aggression.

What we find in the developmental stories of psychopathic serial murderers, then, is a deeply unfortunate "perfect storm" sort of scenario. First, these people typically come into the world with brains that are already impaired in ways that are crucial to proper socialization. So they lack inhibitors that ordinarily function partly to prevent antisocial behavior. Then, these already psychopathically primed individuals are often subjected to some of the worst forms of verbal and physical (often sexual) abuse, which, a number of studies show, only has further detrimental effects on the brain.[24] This abuse frequently takes place in environments of severe socio-economic disadvantage. As a result of all of this, as we have already seen, they develop as one of their "goals" a desire to totally dominate, totally possess, other human beings—something they are especially likely to pursue by means of instrumental forms of aggression like capture, torture, rape, and ultimately murder. Whereas the immediate effects of such aggressive behavior—displays of physical and emotional distress in victims—would typically command a healthy person's attention in a markedly *inhibitive* way, they do not have the same effect on the psychopathic sadist. If anything, such distress cues only serve as signs that their goals are being achieved.

DO PSYCHOPATHS LACK A CONSCIENCE? ARE THEY MORALLY RESPONSIBLE?

A common trope in descriptions of psychopaths is that they are people who "lack a conscience." Interestingly, this is a point often made in connection to the matter of whether or not psychopathic serial murderers are evil. However, the connection here might be supposed to run in either of two opposite directions. On the one hand, one might think that such people are evil *because* they lack a conscience—that is, that their lack of a conscience is what makes them evil. On the other hand, one might think that they *cannot* be evil if they lack a conscience. After all, if they lack a conscience, then presumably, they do not really understand the moral significance of their actions. And if they do not understand the moral significance of their actions, then they are no more evil than a rabid dog.

Part of the problem here is that there are at least two ways in which a "lack of conscience" claim can be understood, paralleling the two ways of understanding *empathy* noted above. Just as empathy might be conceived either as an *awareness of* or as a *concern for* the mental states of others, conscience might similarly be conceived either as an awareness of or as a concern for the moral significance of things. In other words, on a more or less *epistemic* conception, conscience is essentially a faculty of moral intuition or perception—it is the means by which we "see" moral reality. But according to a more *psychological* or *motivational* conception, conscience is not simply a faculty of perception, but a capacity to be appropriately moved or motivated by moral reality.

What would it mean to say that psychopaths lack a conscience, according to the epistemic conception? Essentially, it would be to say that they suffer from a kind of blindness. Here, for instance, is how Cleckley describes the psychopath's awareness of such things as beauty, ugliness, goodness, evil, love, horror, and humor:

> It is as though he were color-blind, despite his sharp intelligence, to this aspect of human existence. It cannot be explained to him because there is nothing in his orbit of awareness that can bridge the gap with comparison. He can repeat the words and say glibly that he understands, and there is no way for him to realize that he does not understand.[25]

Building on Cleckley's analogy (and adapting Hare's use of the same basic analogy[26]), imagine someone born completely color-blind, able to see the world only in black, white, and shades of gray. But suppose also that this person has a kind of handheld device, like a laser pointer with a screen, that, when pointed at an object, will tell him the object's color. So when he points the laser at a stop sign, the screen reads "RED," and when he points it at a particular patch of a painting, it reads something like "OCHER," and so on. Finally, imagine that our color-blind man has lived for many years with this color-detecting device, and has an exceptional memory for the colors of things. In fact, while he always has the device in his pocket, these days, he rarely has a need for it, since he has already memorized the colors of most objects in his ordinary day-to-day experience.

Now, on the one hand, if you were to have a conversation with this man that somehow involved a discussion of the colors of things, he might very likely fool you into thinking that he can see colors just like you, since the combination of his memory and use of the device will enable him to "say all of the right things." He, too, will say that the stop sign is red, and so forth. On the other hand, my guess is that most will nonetheless agree that his knowledge of colors—indeed, if it is even right to say that he "knows" the colors of things—is *deficient* in some way. After all, if someone were to replace a familiar item in his house with another item of a different color, but similar tone, he would likely never notice.

Some think that the psychopath's understanding of morality is essentially the same as the color-blind man's understanding of color. On the one hand, psychopaths typically pay close enough attention to the ways in which those around them use terms like "right," "wrong," "good," "bad," "just," and "unjust," so that they can very reliably reproduce these claims in ways that would convince you and me that they are fully aware of the moral significance of things. In other words, when it comes to matters of morality, psychopaths often "say all of the right things." He, too, will say that murder is wrong, and so forth. But on closer examination, when they are posed with questions or dilemmas that require the kind of proficiency with these concepts that most ordinary people possess, psychopaths often do and say things that betray a deeper lack of awareness or understanding, as would be the case, for instance, if and when the color-blind man failed to notice that we switched his red coffee mug with one that is ocher. What evidence is there for this deeper lack of understanding?

Before I describe the evidence, consider another analogy: if I am looking at two birds, a sparrow and a hawk, I will probably be able to tell you which is the sparrow and which is the hawk; but if I am looking at two sparrows, I probably will not be able to tell you which is the *lark* sparrow and which is the *fox* sparrow. This is because, while I do know what a sparrow is (enough, at least, to tell one apart from a hawk), I do not know what a lark sparrow is, except that it is a type of sparrow. This sort of case illustrates an intuitive rule for knowledge by acquaintance: knowing *what something is* typically requires that the knower be able to distinguish it from other things that it is *not*. Here is another example: imagine someone sincerely asserting, "I know what a basketball is," but then, when asked to grab the basketball from a bin containing various sports balls, grabbing a football instead. Would we not regard this as some evidence that he or she does not *really* know what a basketball is?

In a now famous study, Blair examined whether or not psychopathic criminals could distinguish between two importantly different kinds of wrongdoing, namely, moral and conventional.[27] Moral wrongdoing tends to be more serious, less permissible, and less contingent upon authority than conventional wrongdoing. Think of the difference between, say, students eating food in class and students making racist remarks to their classmates. In general, overt racism is more serious and less permissible than eating food in a place where it is ordinarily discouraged or forbidden. And even if the teacher were to announce, "In my class, it's perfectly acceptable to eat food and make racist remarks," most would agree that it is still wrong to make racist remarks, even if it is no longer wrong to eat food in that class. This is because the wrongness of eating food in class, but not the wrongness of racism, is contingent upon authority.

Even as early as age three, most psychologically normal individuals display a sensitivity to these differences between moral and conventional wrongdoing.[28] But according to Blair's study, psychopaths apparently fail to recognize any such difference, rating instances of moral and conventional wrongdoing as similar along such dimensions as seriousness, permissibility, and authority-contingence. What are we to make of this? Well, if a person's failure to distinguish between lark and fox sparrows is evidence that he does not *really* know what a lark sparrow is, and if a person's failure to tell a basketball apart from other balls is evidence that he does not *really* know what a basketball is, then presumably, the psychopath's apparent failure to see a difference between moral and conventional wrongdoing ought similarly to be regarded as evidence that he does not *really* know what moral wrongness is.

On the basis of Blair's research, some have argued that psychopathic offenders are not morally responsible for their actions, since they apparently do not really know that what they are doing is morally wrong. Specifically in the context of psychopathic serial murderers, Manuel Vargas argues that they are not morally responsible, for two reasons.[29] First, he claims that psychopaths suffer from what he calls "blindness to harm." As I have already argued, though, this cannot be right. Psychopaths are not *blind* to others' states; rather, they just are not *affected* by those states in the ways that the rest of us are typically affected. (Think about it: if psychopathic serial murderers were really *blind* to the harm that they cause, then it could only be an amazing and unfortunate coincidence that they just happen to be drawn to precisely the sorts of actions that cause intense harm to their victims.) And second, and explicitly on the basis of Blair's study, Vargas claims that psychopathic serial killers are *unaware* of the fact that their behavior is seriously morally wrong. And for that reason, at least, they should not be blamed for the things that they do.

Interestingly, though, Vargas also argues that, even though they are not morally responsible, psychopathic serial killers are nonetheless morally evil. Why? Because according to Vargas, a person is evil as long as he "desire[s] to see other people harmed for no reason beyond the desire itself."[30] So, as long as this is an apt description of the psychopathic serial murderer, he is an evil person, even if he is no more *blameworthy* than a rabid dog. This is a very controversial view, for a couple of reasons. For one, many will have the intuition that if a person is no more blameworthy than a rabid dog, then he also cannot be any more *evil* than a rabid dog. Second, many think that calling a person evil is *itself* an act of blaming, or holding responsible. If this is right, then Vargas's view is incoherent. (I will return to these issues later.)

Recently, however, Blair's findings have come under some attack. One of the more surprising results of Blair's original study was that psychopaths seemed to regard moral and conventional wrongdoing both as *morally wrong*—that is, rather than treating all wrongs as merely conventional, as Blair predicted they would, they instead treated all wrongs as if they had the same seriousness, impermissibility, and authority-independence of moral wrongs. Blair speculated that this was actually a strategic move on their part: the inmates were trying to manipulate the researchers into thinking that they had been properly reformed, and attempting to do so by acting as if they now took all wrongdoing very seriously. This kind of behavior is sometimes referred to as "impression management." But this raises the following possibility: maybe psychopaths really *can* distinguish between moral and conventional wrongness, but in their attempt to manage others' impressions, they gave responses that misleadingly suggest that they cannot.

In order to put this possibility to the test, Aharoni et al. introduced what is called a "forced-choice method" into Blair's moral–conventional task. Rather than presenting subjects with descriptions of wrong acts, and for each one, giving them the opportunity to rate it as either moral or conventional—thereby making it possible for them to rate all wrong acts as one or the other—the forced-choice method involves telling the subjects ahead of time that "exactly half of the listed acts were prerated by members of society to be morally wrong, and instruct[ing] them to determine which half met that criterion."³¹ And lo and behold, when forced to choose between rating acts as either morally or conventionally wrong in this way, psychopathic criminals perform no worse than non-psychopathic criminals, and not significantly worse than a comparison sample of college undergraduates. Aharoni et al. state unequivocally, and in direct opposition to Blair, that there is no correlation between psychopathy and poor performance on the moral–conventional task, once the incentive for impression management is removed. On the basis of studies like this one, more and more researchers are concluding, contrary to what has long been assumed, that "psychopaths *know* right from wrong but don't *care*," as another study puts it.³²

Even if psychopaths really do understand (to some degree, at least) the difference between moral and conventional wrongdoing, there may yet be another reason for doubting that psychopathic offenders like Ted Bundy really do "know right from wrong": namely, the very fact that they apparently "don't care." According to a philosophical thesis known as *motivational internalism*, it is a necessary condition for *genuinely having* a moral belief that the believer be *motivated* to some degree to behave accordingly. So, for instance, if I claim to believe that I have a duty to help the needy, but never once exhibit even the slightest motivation to help anyone in need, even when given relatively low-risk and cost-efficient opportunities to do so, motivational internalists will say that I must not *really* believe that I have such a duty. In other words, at least with respect to moral matters, motivational internalism implies that it is impossible for one to believe something *without also caring* (to some degree) about the thing believed.

If this is true, then the suggestion that "psychopaths know right from wrong but don't care" is actually incoherent. If they truly do not care, the motivational internalist will say, then they do not genuinely believe; and according to a long-standing and nearly universally accepted epistemological doctrine, one cannot *know that p* unless one first *believes that p*. So regardless of how psychopaths perform on the moral–conventional task, and regardless of whatever they might claim to know about morality, their apparent lack of motivation to behave in accordance with the things they profess to believe is reason to think that they do not really believe them. And if they do not really believe these things, then it cannot be the case that they know them either.³³

The most significant problem with this argument, however, is just that motivational internalism is a very controversial thesis. Presumably, motivation is something that comes in degrees. If I am currently motivated both to continue writing and also to stop writing and go for a jog, then whatever I spend the next few moments of my life doing will be determined by which of these is the *stronger* motivation. Surely, though, the internalist claim cannot be that believing some moral proposition *p* requires that one's motivation to behave according to *p* always be strong enough to override competing motivations. For then, apparently, no wrongdoer has ever genuinely believed, at the time of wrongdoing, that the relevant action is or was morally wrong. (And consequently, if belief is required for knowledge, and knowledge is required for being morally responsible, as Vargas and others assume, no one has ever been morally responsible for his or her wrongdoing.) But then, how are we to specify the degree of motivation necessary in order for a moral belief to count as being genuinely or sincerely held by the believer? And how are we to know that psychopathic serial killers are not *often* motivated *to that degree* to refrain from serial murder?

Philosophers sometimes distinguish between *strong* and *weak* versions of motivational internalism. According to the stronger thesis, one must be *overridingly* motivated to act in accordance with moral proposition *p* in order for *p* to count as genuinely or sincerely *believed*. Most philosophers reject this thesis. Weak motivational internalism, on the other hand, simply claims that a person must be motivated *to some degree* to act in accordance with *p* in order for *p* to count as genuinely or sincerely believed. And as far as I can tell, weak motivational internalism is perfectly compatible with the claim that psychopathic serial murderers *know*, on some level, that their own actions are morally wrong, since it is perfectly compatible with their wrongful behavior that they were nonetheless motivated *to some degree* to refrain.

Neither Blair's study (nor any other such study of which I am aware) nor the argument from motivational internalism gives us strong enough reason to doubt that psychopathic serial murderers are well aware of the fact that what they are doing is seriously morally wrong.[34] If there is any sense in which psychopaths "lack a conscience," it is not in the epistemic sense of being unaware of the moral significance of things. We must not confuse *defiance* of morality with *ignorance* of morality. So, at this point, I see no reason to doubt that they are fully morally responsible for their actions.[35] Furthermore, while psychopathic serial killers clearly are not *sufficiently motivated* to refrain from behavior they know is morally heinous, as far as attributions of moral responsibility are concerned, what many think matters more than motivation is whether or not they are sufficiently *in control* of themselves while engaging in such behavior. And while it may be tempting to assume that these people are psychotic, bloodthirsty animals who are no more able to control themselves than rabid dogs, this, too, would be a mistake. Consider, for instance, the following chilling accounts from Kemper and Bundy.

Two of Kemper's earliest victims were a pair of hitchhiking college students that he picked up in the Berkeley, California, area in May 1972. Kemper drove to a secluded area and fatally stabbed both young women, before then taking their bodies back to his home to mutilate and rape the corpses.[36] According to Kemper,[37] not long before his arrest the next year, he was once again driving the Berkeley area, specifically trying to trigger his own sadistic impulses, in order to see whether or not he could control them. In a remarkable coincidence, he once again found a pair of young women hitchhiking, picked them up, and agreed to take them to their desired destination, Mills College. On the way, the two women asked to be taken a particular route, because they mistakenly believed it was the way to the college. But Kemper knew that they were mistaken, and insisted on taking a different route, which, as you can imagine, frightened the two women. But more significantly, had Kemper taken the route that the women requested, they would have driven past the same secluded area where he had killed the two other women a year before. And according to Kemper himself, had they done so, he very likely would have given in to his urges and killed them as well. Describing his refusal to go the way they asked, Kemper said in an interview, "I'm trying to save their lives!" As it happened, Kemper did deliver the two women safely to their dormitory, where they ran from the car, never looking back. He added, "I don't think they know, to this day, how close that came."

At one point in his interviews with Michaud and Aynesworth, Bundy describes how he saw his victims—not as women, but rather more as *symbols* of women. "They wouldn't be stereotypes necessarily," he explains, "But they would be reasonable facsimiles to women as a class. A class not of women, per se, but a class that has almost been created through the mythology of women and how they are used as objects."[38] Later, when describing parts of his modus operandi, he explains in fascinating detail how, when luring a victim through conversation, he took pains to manage the interaction ever so carefully so that she would not "emerge as a person and thereby lose her symbolic value."[39]

"What was going on in his mind on the way to his place?" [Michaud asked, playing Bundy's game of referring to the killer in the third-person]

"Conversation," Ted said. "*To remove himself from the personal aspects of the encounter*, the interchange. Chattering and flattering and entertaining, as if seen through a motion picture screen. He would be engaging in the pattern just for the purpose of making the whole encounter seem legitimate [...] and to keep her at ease. He didn't want this girl to get second thoughts about going with him to his place. And also, he was afraid if he started thinking about what he was going to do he'd either become more nervous or lose his concentration or in some way betray himself."[40]

It is one thing to use superficial charm as a tool or instrument for manipulating others. As we have seen, this is characteristic of all psychopaths. It is another thing entirely to recognize that the use of such charm and superficiality is necessary in order to keep potential victims from appearing too much like *real people*, thereby jeopardizing one's own willingness to kill them, and then to engage in superficially charming conversation *for this reason*. Bundy later describes a time when he, like Kemper, decided to test himself to see if he could keep from killing even when he had an easy opportunity to do so. He had a young woman over for a one-night stand, thought several times throughout the night about killing her, but ended up returning her safely, the next morning, to the area where she lived.[41]

If these accounts are to be believed—they are, after all, coming from psychopaths—they imply that both Bundy and Kemper actually had a remarkable capacity for exerting higher-order control over their own violent and sadistic impulses, and could use this capacity either to spare potential victims or to ensure their demise. If this is right, then we can apparently ascribe to psychopathic serial murderers two of the most common features on which attributions of moral responsibility are supposed to depend, namely, knowledge and control. They are aware of the greater seriousness, lesser permissibility, and lesser authority-contingence of morally wrong acts like rape, torture, and murder. And as the accounts from Bundy and Kemper make clear (and there are many other such accounts, from many other killers), psychopathic serial murderers are hardly the psychotic, out-of-control monsters that many often assume. Quite the contrary, they are able to act as both actor and director, knowingly and intentionally manipulating not only other people, but also even the circumstances surrounding the manipulation.

In light of all of this, it is apparently a mistake for Vargas and others to suggest that psychopathic serial murderers are not at all morally responsible for their actions. In fact, barring further evidence or arguments, I think we should conclude at this point that Bundy, Kemper, and others are every bit as morally responsible as the rest of us. Whether or not they are *evil*, however—and if so, *why*—remains to be seen.

Concluding Thoughts

Psychopathic serial murderers are almost always mentioned in discussions of moral evil as paradigm instances of what an *evil person* is. But why? What is it about the serial sex murderer that sets him so distinctly apart from other murderers with multiple victims? For example, in 2014, a police officer in Utah named Joshua Boren shot and killed his wife, their two children, and his mother-in-law. Then, after arranging the bodies of his wife and kids on a bed, he lay down beside them and took his own life. An investigation later revealed that Boren struggled with drug and pornography addictions, as well as pent-up anger stemming from abuse that he suffered as a child. This all contributed to the collapse of his eight-year marriage, and on January 16, 2014, hours after his wife threatened to take their children away from him, he snapped.[42]

Obviously, Boren's actions are terrible, tragic, and seriously morally wrong. Were he still alive, most would agree that he is fully deserving of blame, condemnation, and very harsh punishment. But my guess is that most people would nonetheless refrain from calling him evil, despite the heinousness of his crimes, and the fact that he has a greater victim count than even many serial killers. So what is the relevant difference between someone like Boren, on the one hand, and psychopathic serial murderers like Bundy and Kemper, on the other, such that the label "evil" is so much more befitting of the latter?

In Chap. 6, I critically examine several philosophical theories of evil. As we shall see, some will say that people like Bundy and Kemper are evil in virtue of the specific types of action they perform, or are disposed to perform. Others will say that it has something to do with certain persistent desires of theirs. And still others will argue that Bundy, Kemper, and other psychopathic serial murderers are evil in virtue of the sadistic pleasure they took in causing so much suffering, which, it is fair to assume, was not the case with Boren.

For my own part, I agree that Bundy, Kemper, and others like them are evil, but not for any of these reasons. Rather, I think the reason has something to do with what was described earlier as the basic motivation of most, if not all, psychopathic serial killers: the desire to totally dominate, to completely possess, another human being. So, in the interest of foreshadowing my discussion in Chap. 7, I want to close this chapter with a few suggestive quotations from, or about, serial murderers. There is something in these words, I think, that reveals why it is that these people are evil. The first two come from Bundy and Kemper, respectively.

> He should have recognized that what really fascinated him was the hunt, the adventure of searching out his victims. And, to a degree, possessing them physically, as one would possess a potted plant, a painting or a Porsche. Owning, as it were, this individual.[43]

> It was more or less making a doll out of a human being and carrying out my fantasies with a doll, a living human doll.[44]

Now compare those quotations with the way forensic psychologist Paul Britton describes Fred West, who, with his wife Rosemary, raped, tortured, and murdered at least a dozen young women and girls, some of whom were family members:

> How does Fred West, for example, go from being a child to the sort of person he was? You see someone who wasn't valued as a child, someone who never learnt that other people counted, that learnt people were just playthings.[45]

Or consider how serial killer Robert Berdella once complained in a prison interview, a clip of which is included in a documentary available online,

> The media has so biased my case, portraying me as non-human. And their motivation is no separate from the way I treated my victims. I treated them as something less than human, nothing more than a play object. This is what the media has done to me; it's dehumanized me.[46]

In that same documentary, crime writer James Ellroy had this to say about Berdella:

> I think that he had a long-standing love affair with the male anatomy. And, like a little kid playing with an Erector Set, or playing with one of those

models of the human body, he wanted to find out what was inside. In other words, it's the ultimate objectification of another human being.

Berdella captured several young men and kept them in his basement to be raped, tortured, and eventually killed. He kept detailed logs of his various attempts at torture, their specific effects upon the victim, and so forth. And according to some reports, he claimed to have been inspired by the film adaptation of a certain novel about a young man who collects butterfly specimens as a hobby.

NOTES

1. From Roy Hazelwood's Foreword to Michaud and Aynesworth (1999: 6).
2. Michaud and Aynesworth (1999: 52).
3. Michaud and Aynesworth (1999: 56).
4. Michaud and Aynesworth (1999: 60).
5. Michaud and Aynesworth (1999: 64).
6. Michaud and Aynesworth (1999: 12).
7. Michaud and Aynesworth (1999: 108).
8. Michaud and Aynesworth (1999: 19–20, all italics in original).
9. Federal Bureau of Investigation (2008: 9).
10. Schechter (2003: 216).
11. Michaud and Aynesworth (1999: 19, italics added).
12. Schechter (2003: 216).
13. Fowles (1963: 217–218).
14. Fowles (1963: 101).
15. Blair et al. (2005: 19).
16. There is a long history of psychiatrists associating mental illness with specifically *moral* pathologies, and regarding the practice of psychiatric care in terms of "moral therapy." For an accessible introduction to this history, see Porter (2002). Porter explains, "Moral reformers like the Tukes [William, his son Henry, and grandson Samuel] and [Philippe] Pinel viewed madness as a breakdown of internal, rational discipline on the part of the sufferer. Their moral and psychological faculties needed to be rekindled, so that external coercion could be supplanted by inner self-control. Psychiatry must reanimate reason or conscience" (2002: 105, 107).
17. Blair et al. (2005: 8, 12).
18. Nowadays, researchers of psychopathy tend to divide associated traits into 2- or 3-factor analyses. As Blair et al. explain, "Factor analysis is a means of examining how the items of a given construct hang together. For example, while the PCL-R consists of 20 items that are all thought to contribute

something unique to the set of criteria, overlap will exist among items. Consequently, items that correlate with each other can be grouped together to form a cluster of traits, or a factor, that refers to a more general facet of the disorder" (2005: 7).
19. Even Hare, in places, seems to confuse these two senses of empathy—one in terms of an *awareness* of others' states, and the other in terms of a *concern* for others' states. For instance, when describing the psychopath's lack of empathy, he describes it as "an inability to construct a mental and emotional 'facsimile' of another person" (1993: 44). But the psychopath *can* construct a facsimile of another's mental states, and often uses this for purposes of manipulation and deception. What he apparently does *not* do is to *care* about the facsimile he creates in the appropriate ways. (To his credit, Hare earlier describes the psychopath's lack of empathy as "an inability to *care* about the pain and suffering experienced by others" [1993: 6, italics added].)
20. Blair et al. (2005: 13). Later, Blair et al. explain, "No biologically based disorder other than psychopathy is associated with an increased risk of instrumental aggression" (2005: 155).
21. I also mentioned earlier that, despite the tendency of some to use the terms "psychopath" and "sociopath" interchangeably, psychopathy and sociopathy are not the same thing. They are both forms of ASPD, but they can be distinguished from each other on both biological and behavioral grounds. For one thing, whereas psychopathy has relatively clear neurobiological origins, which I briefly describe in the text, many believe that sociopathy results primarily from environmental factors, and has no neurobiological signature. But there are also important behavioral differences between the two disorders. Sociopaths tend to be more anxious and nervous in social settings than the egocentric and superficially charming psychopath. Psychopaths tend to be more impulsive, deceptive, aggressive, and violent. One suggestion that I find particularly interesting is that sociopaths, as opposed to psychopaths, are often motivated to engage in antisocial behavior by a clear, though warped, sense of right and wrong (see, e.g., Pemment 2013). These are the people who, for example, often write "manifestos" detailing the many reasons for which they were "forced" or driven to act out, such as Norwegian terrorist Anders Breivik and narcissistic spree shooter Elliot Rodger. Psychopaths, by contrast, are "rebels *without* a cause."
22. For the record, there is some evidence of dysfunction in parts of the psychopath's brain other than just the amygdala, such as the orbital frontal cortex (see Blair et al. 2005: 110–140). But most researchers agree that the amygdala is the *primary* source of the psychopath's genetic impairment.

23. Blair et al. (2005: 110–111).
24. Among the documented effects of childhood abuse on the brain are (a) reduced volume in the hippocampus, which is essential to learning and memory; (b) reduced volume in the corpus callosum, which facilitates communication between the two hemispheres of the brain; and (c) reduced volume in the cerebellum, which is important for motor control and executive functioning. For a review, see McCrory et al. (2010).
25. Cleckley (1941: 90).
26. See, e.g., Hare (1993: 129).
27. Blair (1995). Blair's subjects were 10 psychopathic and 10 non-psychopathic patient-inmates at the Broadmoor and Ashworth psychiatric hospitals in England.
28. See Smetana and Braeges (1990).
29. Vargas (2010: 69–74).
30. Vargas (2010: 75).
31. Aharoni et al. (2012: 486).
32. See Cima et al. (2010).
33. For an argument to this effect, see Levy (2007).
34. It is perhaps worth noting that courts almost never find psychopaths not guilty by reason of insanity, and typically, this is because of the psychopaths' apparent proficiency with moral concepts.
35. Of course, some will say that psychopathy is a mental illness, and that this fact is itself a reason to doubt that they are fully morally responsible. I return to this issue in Chap. 5.
36. By his own account, Kemper used to drive the Berkeley area, engaging with hitchhikers and other people, practicing the sorts of skills that he would later need in order to lure would-be victims—for example, gestures, mannerisms, tones of voice, and turns of phrase, all designed to ease tensions and remove any potential suspicion in another's mind that Kemper might intend to harm them.
37. The following account comes from an interview that Kemper gave to French crime writer Stéphane Bourgoin, while Kemper was in prison. Video of the interview is available online at sites such as YouTube.
38. Michaud and Aynesworth (1999: 117).
39. Michaud and Aynesworth (1999: 125).
40. Michaud and Aynesworth (1999: 124, italics added).
41. Michaud and Aynesworth (1999: 131–132). Michaud writes, "*Somewhere, I said to myself, there is an anonymous woman with no idea how lucky she is*" (132, italics in original).
42. See Reavy (2014).
43. Michaud and Aynesworth (1999: 113).
44. Schechter (2003: 216).

45. Cook (1997).
46. The documentary is entitled "Bazaar Bizarre"—directed by Benjamin Meade and hosted by crime writer James Ellroy—and is available online at various video-hosting websites, including YouTube. For the record, during the time of his murders, Berdella owned a store in Kansas City called "Bob's Bazaar Bizarre."

References

Aharoni, Eyal, Walter Sinnott-Armstrong, and Kent A. Kiehl. 2012. Can Psychopathic Offenders Discern Moral Wrongs? A New Look at the Moral/Conventional Distinction. *Journal of Abnormal Psychology* 121(2): 484–497.

Blair, R.J.R. 1995. A Cognitive Developmental Approach to Morality: Investigating the Psychopath. *Cognition* 57: 1–29.

Blair, James, Derek Mitchell, and Karina Blair. 2005. *The Psychopath: Emotion and the Brain*. Oxford: Blackwell.

Cima, Maaike, Franca Tonnaer, and Marc D. Hauser. 2010. Psychopaths Know Right From Wrong but Don't Care. *Social Cognitive and Affective Neuroscience* 5: 59–67.

Cleckley, Hervey. 1941. *The Mask of Sanity*. St. Louis: Mosby.

Cook, Emily. 1997. Cut to Pieces by the Jigsaw Man. *Independent*, May 20. Accessed March 1, 2016. http://www.independent.co.uk/life-style/cut-to-pieces-by-the-jigsaw-man-1262637.html.

Federal Bureau of Investigation. 2008. Serial Murder: Multi-Disciplinary Perspectives for Investigators. Accessed March 1, 2016. https://www.fbi.gov/stats-services/publications/serial-murder/serial-murder-july-2008-pdf/view.

Fowles, John. 1963. *The Collector*. Boston: Little, Brown and Company.

Hare, Robert. 1993. *Without Conscience: The Disturbing World of the Psychopaths among Us*. New York: Guilford Press.

Levy, Neil. 2007. The Responsibility of the Psychopath Revisited. *Philosophy, Psychiatry, & Psychology* 14(2): 129–138.

McCrory, Eamon, Stephane A. De Brito, and Essi Viding. 2010. Research Review: The Neurobiology and Genetics of Maltreatment and Adversity. *The Journal of Child Psychology and Psychiatry* 51(10): 1079–1095.

Michaud, Stephen, and Hugh Aynesworth. 1999. *The Only Living Witness: The True Story of Serial Sex Killer Ted Bundy*. Irving: Authorlink Press.

Pemment, Jack. 2013. Psychopathy versus Sociopathy: Why the Distinction Has Become Crucial. *Aggression and Violent Behavior* 18(5): 458–461.

Porter, Roy. 2002. *Madness: A Brief History*. Oxford: Oxford University Press.

Reavy, Pat. 2014. Officer who killed family had dark side, struggled since childhood. *Deseret News*, July 7. Accessed March 1, 2016. http://www.deseretnews.com/article/865606440/.

Schechter, Harold. 2003. *The Serial Killer Files: The Who, What, Where, How, and Why of the World's Most Terrifying Murderers.* New York: Ballantine Books.
Smetana, J., and J.L. Braeges. 1990. The Development of Toddlers' Moral and Conventional Judgments. *Merrill Palmer Quarterly* 36(3): 329–346.
Vargas, Manuel. 2010. Are Psychopathic Serial Killers Evil? *Are They Blameworthy for What They Do?* In *Serial Killers: Philosophy for Everyone*, ed. S. Waller, 66–77. Malden: Blackwell.

CHAPTER 3

Genocide, Ideology, and Dehumanization

In Chap. 1, I mentioned a survey conducted by Peter Brian Barry in which respondents were asked, of two randomly selected candidates (from a pool of 49), "Who is a better example of an evil person?" To absolutely no one's surprise, Adolf Hitler ranked highest of all—he is widely regarded as the *best* example of an evil person. In fact, in the second iteration of Barry's survey, Nazi leaders make up *half* of the resulting "top 10" best examples of evil people: Hitler, Josef Mengele, Heinrich Himmler, Joseph Goebbels, and Adolf Eichmann. Probably, then, most readers will not need any convincing that, if *anyone* is evil, Hitler and his fellow Nazi leaders were evil. Judging by these results, it is also probably fair to assume that most readers are already very familiar with the events of the Holocaust—specifically, the Nazis' genocide of approximately six million innocent people, most of whom were Jewish.

So rather than reviewing these historical facts in any significant detail, our interest in this chapter will be much like it was in the previous chapter: asking what it is about *genocide* in particular—and especially, what it is about the people who perpetrate genocide—that strikes us as morally evil. Like serial murder, there is something unique, something especially vile or wicked, about genocide, which is able to provoke thoughts about evil. Given the sheer scale of events like the Holocaust and the Rwandan genocide in 1994, it can be easy to think that the relevant factor here—that is, the thing that makes genocide evil—is that there are *so many deaths*. There can be no doubt that these incomprehensible death tolls are hugely morally significant, and that they alone are sufficient for making genocide a deeply tragic and morally awful thing. But this cannot be what makes genocide *evil*. For one thing, most wars are also tragic and morally awful events with very high (and in some cases, much higher) death tolls. But I suspect that even many pacifists will agree that there is something especially heinous about genocide that separates it, morally, from any war. For another thing, it is actually not essential to genocide that there be *any* deaths at all. For example, the forced sterilization of all women in a particular ethnic group might not result in any deaths, strictly speaking, but would still be considered an act of genocide by most. And I suspect that many would agree that this, too, is evil. So we may need to dig a little deeper than such obvious matters as death tolls for an answer to the question, "What makes genocide, and some who perpetrate genocide, *evil*?"

A common metaphor in historical literature on the *Third Reich* is that the Nazi regime was *machine-like* in its subjugation and extermination of victims. This machine operated on three distinct levels. At the top, there were the Nazi leaders: Hitler, Eichmann, and the rest. Next, there were what I will call the Nazi "henchmen": officers of the *Sturmabteilung* (SA), then the *Schutzstaffel* (SS), Nazi doctors, and so forth. Basically, these were the people who, at various ranks and in different capacities, worked to carry out the commands of the Nazi leaders. Finally, there were what I will call Nazi "commoners": ordinary citizens of Germany (and perhaps other Nazi-occupied countries) who, though not actively involved in the genocide, were nonetheless complicit in various ways—by, for example, cheering on the Nazis (even after it became clear what they were doing to the Jews), turning in Jewish neighbors to the SS, and joining Nazi-sympathetic organizations like the National Socialist German Students' League.

This separation between the three "levels" of the Nazi regime is important, since there appear to be significant psychological differences between those acting at one level and those acting at another. It would be very easy to lump all three groups together and to simply say, "They did it because they hated the Jews." But this would be like saying of Ted Bundy that "he did it because he was a sexual sadist." As I suggested in the last chapter, and will defend more fully in Chap. 7, while it is certainly true of many psychopathic serial murderers that they are sexual sadists, the fact about them that makes them *evil* is something deeper than this. Likewise, I will argue, what makes perpetrators of genocide evil is something deeper than their hatred of their victims. So, in order to uncover what that is, I suggest we look more closely at the behavior and motives of those in all three groups, beginning with the so-called commoners and working our way up to the psychologies of genocidal leaders. Along the way, I will draw comparisons not only between the Holocaust and other instances of genocide, but also between genocide and other types of group violence that share similar psychological features.

THE COMMONERS

There is a phenomenon that pervades our moral lives, often without us realizing it, known to philosophers as *moral luck*. Basically, the idea is this: a person is morally *lucky* if it would be appropriate to praise her for something, despite the fact that the thing for which she is praised is to some significant degree beyond her control; a person is morally *unlucky* if it would be appropriate to blame her for something, again, despite the fact that the thing for which she is blamed is to some significant degree beyond her control.

Moral luck is of interest to philosophers—and should be of interest to anyone who cares about such matters—because it appears to run contrary to some of our deepest intuitions about morality: specifically, the intuition that people should not be held responsible for things that are beyond their control. And yet: suppose two people, both very drunk, both drive home along identical routes, and both run their cars off the road and onto the same stretch of sidewalk (just at different times); but unfortunately, for only one of the two drunk drivers, there happens to be a pedestrian walking along that particular stretch of sidewalk at the very moment that the driver runs off the road. One drunk driver makes it home safely; the other strikes and kills a pedestrian. If the *only* relevant difference between the two drivers is something over which neither had any control—namely, whether or not there was a pedestrian on the sidewalk—shouldn't we hold the two drivers *equally* morally responsible? But as a matter of fact, we do *not* hold them equally responsible. And importantly, even if counterintuitively in one respect, it seems *right* to blame the one driver more than the other. So he is morally unlucky.

In his famous essay "Moral Luck," philosopher Thomas Nagel describes four different kinds of moral luck, one of them being "luck in one's circumstances." He writes, "The things we are called upon to do, the moral tests we face, are importantly determined by factors beyond our control."[1] Here is one of his examples of circumstantial moral luck:

> Ordinary citizens of Nazi Germany had an opportunity to behave heroically by opposing the regime. They also had an opportunity to behave badly, and most of them are culpable for having failed this test. But it is a test to which the citizens of other countries were not subjected, with the result that even

if they, or some of them, would have behaved as badly as the Germans in like circumstances, they simply did not and therefore are not similarly culpable.[2]

I mention the issue of moral luck, and Nagel's example of Nazi Germany specifically, to stress two points. First, while it would be easy to write off all Nazi-sympathetic Germans as a bunch of racist sociopaths, the fact of the matter is that most of the people I here refer to as Nazi "commoners" were ordinary folks like you and me, who were simply and terribly unlucky—both historically and morally—to have faced the circumstances that they faced. And if we are being honest with ourselves—and especially if we are familiar with relevant work in social psychology, some of which I will describe later—we may need to admit that it is primarily due to our own dumb moral luck that we do not find ourselves facing similar circumstances. Second, seeking an understanding of the historical and social circumstances of the time, and acknowledging that they contain some element of (bad) moral luck, should not prevent us from recognizing that the beliefs, attitudes, and behavior of many Germans at the time were morally abhorrent—perhaps even morally *evil*. That, again, is supposed to be the point of moral luck: the circumstances may have been to some significant degree beyond their control, but even so, they are rightly blamed for adopting and acting on such morally abhorrent views.

So what, exactly, were the relevant circumstances at the time? And how, ultimately, did they conspire to turn so many decent German people into supporters of—and, in some cases, participants in—one of the greatest moral atrocities in history?

In an episode of Jerry Seinfeld's comedy web series *Comedians in Cars Getting Coffee*, Trevor Noah—South African comedian and new host of *The Daily Show*—recalls some of his family's experiences with apartheid, and then exclaims:

> The whole system was absurd! It doesn't make sense. Racism, all of these things, when you look at them, they don't make sense. You know, Hitler ... when you look now, you go, "How did that craziness happen? It doesn't make sense." There's just a moment in time, if you find the right balance between desperation and fear, you can make people believe anything.

Noah here nicely gives expression to two of the issues we will confront in this chapter, and in this section in particular. First, there may be some sense in which these things—apartheid, the Holocaust, and other evils that unfold across entire societies, and span whole periods of history—are *essentially incomprehensible*. So any attempt to "make sense" of them—as I will attempt here—is bound to fall short, in at least some respects. For now, I am okay with this; we will return to the issue of incomprehensibility in Chap. 5. Second, notice how, immediately after declaring that "all of these things don't make sense," Noah actually makes some sense of them when he notes, "if you find the right balance between desperation and fear, you can make people believe anything." So even if evils like apartheid and the Holocaust are essentially incomprehensible, we might nonetheless be able to gain some understanding of how they come about in the first place, and perhaps also what motivates the relevant perpetrators to take things to such devastating and disturbing lengths. That, at least, is my hope.[3]

Ervin Staub, psychologist and one of the world's foremost experts on the social-psychological origins of genocide and other forms of group violence, agrees with Noah. Of course, there is quite a lot more to it than *just* desperation and fear; however, these two factors figure most prominently in Staub's theory of the origins and causes of genocide. According to the theory, the most significant instigator of group violence is what he refers to as "difficult life conditions and basic human needs."[4] On the one hand, human beings have basic psychological needs for things like security, positive identity, a sense of control over important events in their lives, connections with other people, and a meaningful understanding of the world in which they live. On the other hand, circumstances can arise in which all or most of these needs are threatened—or at least, *perceived* as threatened. The kinds of circumstances that Staub has in mind here include

> economic problems such as extreme inflation, or depression and unemployment, political conflict and violence, war, a decline in the power, prestige, and importance of a nation, usually with attendant economic and political problems, and the chaos and social disorganization these often entail.[5]

When such "difficult life conditions" are perceived by the members of some group as threatening their "basic human needs," the result is a state of desperation and fear.

Now, a little history. In the wake of World War I (1914–1918), a defeated Germany found itself facing many of the difficult life conditions identified by Staub. One of the results of the war was a period of general inflation across all of Europe throughout the 1920s. Additionally, the victorious Allied Powers imposed harsh economic penalties on the

Central Powers, stripping them of various territories and forcing them to pay reparations. In fact, dissatisfied with the rate at which the Germans were making reparation payments, French troops moved in and occupied Germany's Ruhr district in the early 1920s, to the humiliation of many proud German citizens. Things would only get worse later in the decade when Germany began to feel the effects of the Great Depression. So, by the beginning of the 1930s, Germany's economy was in terrible shape, several million workers were unemployed, and in the meantime, its political identity had become devastatingly unstable. Germans were afraid for the future of their nation and desperate for new leadership—specifically, leadership that could offer some glimmer of hope.

Again, according to Staub, this sense of desperation aroused by difficult life conditions, along with a fear that one's basic human needs will not be met, are the two of the most common factors that precipitate group violence. Other such instigators include preexisting conflict between groups, devaluation of rival groups or cultures, high respect for authority figures, and a monolithic culture centered on some set of core values and self-concepts.[6] In the case of Germany, for instance, there was already a long history of hostility between non-Jewish and Jewish residents, the former devaluing the latter significantly. German children were taught from a very young age to have the utmost respect for those in positions of authority. And the German culture was as monolithic as any in modern times, centered on a self-conception of Germany as "superior in character, competence, honor, loyalty, devotion to family, civic organization, and cultural achievements."[7] So, the socio-economic conditions in which Germans found themselves following World War I were not just desperate and scary, but *humiliating* as well.

Some of the same conditions were present in Rwanda in the early 1990s. There was a long history of hostility between the majority Hutus and minority Tutsis. Despite their lower numbers, Tutsis had ruled Rwanda for a while, thanks to a complicated political partnership with German and Belgian colonizers. Over the years, Hutus developed deep feelings of resentment and jealousy of Tutsis. For one thing, Tutsis received preferential treatment from the German and Belgian governments. For another, Tutsis were generally regarded as more physically attractive, due to their more Caucasian features. So in 1959, fed up with their lower political and social status, Hutus revolted, and many Tutsis were either killed or driven out of the country. As a result, Rwanda gained independence, and the Hutus assumed power. Then in 1990, the Rwandan Patriotic Front (RPF)—a group of militant Tutsis who had been driven out of the country as a result of earlier attacks—invaded Rwanda from neighboring Uganda. After a few very violent years, a kind of peace agreement was reached in 1993, which allowed Tutsis some representation in the Rwandan government.

As one might imagine, however, this peace agreement displeased many conservative Hutus, who felt that far too much had been conceded to the RPF. So in 1993 and 1994, these Hutus organized a media campaign that painted Tutsis as violent aggressors who wanted to regain control of Rwanda, and secretly plotted further invasions to take back all of their lost territory. As a result, many Hutus came to regard Tutsis as *inyenzi*, or "cockroaches in need of extermination." So here, too, many of the instigators of group violence identified by Staub are present: perceived threats to basic human needs giving rise to a sense of desperation and fear (e.g., of rumored violent attacks by Tutsis); a long history of conflict between the two groups; devaluation of the rival group; and a relatively monolithic conservative Hutu culture.

When all or most of these conditions are present, Staub's theory continues, they create a kind of breeding ground for violent ideology and scapegoating.

> In the face of persistently difficult life conditions, already devalued outgroups are further devalued and scapegoated. Diminishing others is a way to elevate the self. Scapegoating protects a positive identity by reducing the feeling of responsibility for problems. By providing an explanation for problems, it offers the possibility of effective action or control—unfortunately, mainly in the form of taking action against the scapegoat. It can unite people against the scapegoated other, thereby fulfilling the need for positive connection and support in difficult times.[8]

What Hitler offered to the German people was an ideology that promised to meet many of the "basic human needs" noted above by Staub—for example, security, positive identity, and a meaningful understanding of their world and life conditions. It was also an ideology that simultaneously diminished the Germans' own sense of responsibility for their country's poor state, while scapegoating the Jews and other (perceived) opponents of the Aryan race. This was not simply anti-Semitism, but what Friedländer calls "redemptive anti-Semitism," an entire ideological framework, or worldview, a central component of which was the villainizing and dehumanizing of the Jewish people.[9] As Claudia Koonz explains,

Nazism offered all ethnic Germans [...] a comprehensive system of meaning that was transmitted through powerful symbols and renewed in communal celebrations. It told them how to differentiate between friend and enemy, true believer and heretic, Jew and non-Jew. In offering the faithful a sanctified life in the Volk, it resembled a religion. Its condemnation of egoism and celebration of self-denial had much in common with ethical postulates elsewhere. But in contrast to the optimistic language of international covenants guaranteeing universal rights to all people, Nazi public culture was constructed on the mantra "Not every being with a human face is human."[10]

This Nazi worldview was only confirmed—that is, in the minds of many non-Jewish German citizens—when Hitler and the other leaders actually began to deliver on their promises to reduce unemployment, to return Germany's economy to a state of prosperity, and to restore Germany's status among other world powers.

When Hitler was appointed German Chancellor in January 1933, Melita Maschmann was a passionate and impressionable German teenager, whose parents regularly lamented the state of their once-exalted nation. In her book *Account Rendered: A Dossier on my Former Self*, she gives readers a fascinating firsthand account of her journey from ordinary teenager on a "search for a fundamental purpose" to Nazi commoner—in her case, she began as a proud member of the *Bund Deutscher Mädel* (or BDM, the girls section of the Hitler Youth), later got involved with the Reich Labor Service, and eventually served as a propagandist for the Reich Youth Leadership. At every step along the way, Nazi ideology played a crucial role in shaping not only her motivations, but also the ways in which she viewed other people. Interestingly, the book is actually written in the form of a letter to her closest childhood friend—a Jewish girl—with the hope that she (the friend), and anyone else who reads it, "might gradually be able to understand—not excuse—the wrong and even the evil steps which I took and which I must report, and that such an understanding might form the basis for a lasting dialogue."[11]

As Maschmann recalls, it was very common for non-Jewish citizens at the time to be of two very different—and apparently incompatible—minds about the Jews. Maschmann distinguishes between her Jewish friends and neighbors, on the one hand, and "*the* Jews," on the other.

> *Those* Jews were and remained something mysteriously menacing and anonymous. They were not the sum of all Jewish individuals, who included yourself [her Jewish friend] or old Herr Lewy: they were an evil power, something with the attributes of a spook. One could not see it, but it was there, an active force for evil.[12]

GENOCIDE, IDEOLOGY, AND DEHUMANIZATION   61

For as long as we could remember, the adults had lived in this contradictory way with complete unconcern. One was friendly with individual Jews whom one liked, just as one was friendly as a Protestant with individual Catholics. But while it occurred to nobody to be ideologically hostile to *the* Catholics, one was, utterly, to *the* Jews. In all this no one seemed to worry about the fact that they had no clear idea of who '*the* Jews' were.[13]

This "fatal schizophrenia," as she calls it—that is, the ability to see the humanity in some of the victimized minorities, but to systematically strip the humanity from others—served a necessary function in allowing her to execute her various roles as a Nazi commoner. For instance, at one point, she participated in the forced expulsion of Polish families from their homes, preparing the vacated living spaces for incoming German families to occupy. But by her own admission, had she not "learned to switch off my 'private feelings'" toward the Polish victims by regarding them as something less than human, her participation would not have been possible: "I was bound to consider the Poles 'inferior', otherwise I should have lacked the callousness I needed to help in driving them out."[14]

In a kind of tragically ironic way, Maschmann's participation in driving out these Polish families actually served to confirm (to *her* mind) some of the more dehumanizing elements of Nazism. She and other German schoolchildren had been taught in their "racial science" classes that "*the* Poles" were lazy, simple, and uncivilized brutes. Now, when these Polish families found out that German forces would soon be expelling them from their homes, many of them, understandably resentful, stopped taking care of their homes. So when Maschmann and others came knocking, the filthy conditions of many of these Polish homes seemed only to *verify* what they had been told about "the Poles" all along—after all, only a bunch of lazy, simple, and uncivilized brutes would allow themselves to live in such conditions! Here is an example of how ideology first shapes the way we see things, which then confirms the ideology, which further shapes the way we see things, and so on. This, unfortunately, is how racist and dehumanizing beliefs tend to be self-supporting.

Earlier, I asked: What, exactly, were the relevant circumstances at the time? And how, ultimately, did they conspire to turn so many decent German people into supporters of one of the greatest moral atrocities in history? For even if Nazi commoners like Maschmann did not actively participate in the extermination of several million innocent lives, it seems very likely that the genocide could not have taken place without a generally supportive German populace. We got an answer to the first question from Noah, and then a slightly more detailed one from Staub: primarily desperation and fear, but there are a number of other historical, social, and psychological factors that typically precipitate genocide and other forms of group violence.

The answer to the second question, I submit, has something to do with the aim, spread, and effects of racist and dehumanizing ideology. You cannot get just anybody, at just any time, to be ideologically hostile toward an entire race or ethnic group. But, as Noah puts it, there *is* a moment in time, if you find the right balance of desperation and fear, at which you can make people believe anything. When you consider all of the relevant historical and socio-psychological facts, it makes *perfect sense*—but in a way that still seems *utterly incomprehensible*—that Maschmann and other Nazi commoners would come to see "*the* Jews" and other perceived opponents of the Aryan race as something less than human—as pests, as menaces, as both the cause of their present "difficult life conditions" and potential threat to their "basic human needs."

Does this in any way *excuse* or *justify* them in holding these racist and dehumanizing beliefs? No, of course not. This was one of the points of invoking moral luck earlier. Even if Nazi commoners were morally unlucky to face the circumstances that they faced, and even if others (ourselves included) might also have adopted many of the same racist and dehumanizing beliefs if we had faced those same circumstances, it can nonetheless be perfectly appropriate to *blame* people like Maschmann for what they believed and for what they did. To her credit, Maschmann herself claimed only to want to be *understood*, not *excused*—she, too, seemed to recognize that there is a way to understand an evil without thereby justifying it. The same issue applies just as well to the previous chapter. The point of discussing psychopathy in such detail was, hopefully, to gain some understanding of how psychopathic serial murderers like Bundy and Kemper can do the things they do. But, there as well as here, the understanding we seek is not of a kind that entails anything whatsoever in terms of *moral justification*. (I will say a bit more about this in Chap. 5.)

THE HENCHMEN

Maschmann is rightly ashamed of her participation in such heinous activities as driving innocent Polish families from their homes. But ultimately, the role that she and others like her played in the massacre of several million innocent people was more *enabler* than *perpetrator*. So, what about the actual perpetrators of genocide? What sense might be made of their motivations and behaviors? After all, it is one thing to first adopt and then help spread a racist and dehumanizing ideology. It is quite another thing to consider seriously methods for mass extermination; or to march innocent people into gas chambers, and then to watch in fascination through peepholes as the victims scream, cry, and cling to each other, until falling lifelessly to the floor; or to dump piles of corpses into ditches, and then to shoot the few who still showed signs of life; or to gang-rape women by the thousands, sometimes with spears, gun barrels, or other objects; or to perform gross, invasive, and debilitating medical experiments on innocent and non-consenting men, women, and children; and so on. While it would perhaps be explanatorily convenient to surmise that all perpetrators of genocide suffer from personality disorders like those discussed in Chap. 2, the frightening fact of the matter is that most do not. But then: if they were not just a bunch of psychopaths or sociopaths, then *what is it* about these "henchmen," psychologically, that explains how they could do such things?

One would struggle to make it very far into the literature on the psychology of the Holocaust—particularly, the psychology of its perpetrators—without encountering a discussion of Stanley Milgram's famous obedience experiments. For the original experiment, Milgram recruited 40 adult males between the ages of 20 and 50 to participate in what was advertised as a study of memory and learning.[15] Each of the 40 subjects was assigned the role of "teacher," while a confederate was given the role of "learner"—and importantly, the subjects were unaware that the learner was a confederate. Then the teacher watched as the learner was strapped to an electric chair-like apparatus, and a kind of paste was applied "to avoid blisters and burns." After being given a list of word-pairs to memorize, the teacher's job was to recite one of the words from each pair, and the learner's job was to recall the other word in the pair. Any time the learner recalled incorrectly, the teacher—who by now was seated in a separate room, and could not see the learner, but could hear him through the wall—was supposed to administer an electric shock. Sitting on the table before the teacher was a machine with 30 switches, labeled from 15 to 450 volts (in 15-volt increments). The switches also had labels that ranged from "Slight Shock" to "Danger: Severe Shock," with the highest two voltages labeled simply "XXX."

When Milgram polled 14 of Yale University's senior psychology majors, the consensus was that only about one percent of subjects would ever administer shocks at the highest possible voltage. The vast majority of subjects, everyone assumed, would insist on aborting the experiment at some earlier stage. Milgram's colleagues predicted that most subjects would abort the experiment somewhere in the "Very Strong Shock" stage (195–240 volts). So, the actual results of the experiment came as a surprise to everyone: of the 40 original subjects, two-thirds (26) continued to shock the learner all the way to the highest possible voltage. In fact, the earliest point at which *any* of the subjects aborted the experiment was 300 volts.

These results are made even more remarkable when you consider two additional facts about the experiment. First, the confederates who played the role of learner were instructed to begin complaining of physical pain (due to the shocks) at some point in the early-to-mid stages of the experiment, and the complaining got louder and more intense as the voltage of the shocks increased. Then, at 300 volts, the learner would pound loudly on the wall separating teacher and learner, never to be heard from again. Teachers were instructed to regard silence as an incorrect answer, and to continue shocking the learner regardless. So, apparently, it was not until they believed that the learner had been shocked to the point of being physically incapacitated that any of the subjects insisted on stopping the experiment—and even then, only 5 of the 40 subjects stopped at the 300-volt mark. For all any of the remaining subjects knew, they were administering electric shocks to an unconscious (or worse) body.

Second, none of the subjects were forced or coerced into continuing to participate. They were all free to abort the experiment whenever they wished to do so. And indeed, most of them showed signs of serious psychological distress during the later stages of the experiment. For instance, here is one observer's description of one of the subjects who continued to shock all the way to the highest voltage:

> I observed a mature and initially poised businessman enter the laboratory smiling and confident. Within 20 minutes he was reduced to a twitching, stuttering wreck, who was rapidly approaching a point of nervous collapse. He constantly pulled on his earlobe, and twisted his hands. At one point he pushed his fist into his forehead and muttered: "Oh God, let's stop it."[16]

If it was so psychologically trying, though, why did he continue? After all, no one held a gun to his head. No one barred the door to the room. No one threatened the subjects with any sort of harm or misfortune if they aborted the experiment before completion.

As the standard interpretation of Milgram's experiment goes, human beings have a willingness or tendency to obey those in perceived positions of authority, even if doing so requires that they temporarily abandon or suspend other moral commitments. Sitting in the room with subjects during the experiment was a researcher in a lab coat—thereby giving off an air of authority—who, whenever a subject showed signs of reluctance, would "prod" him by first *requesting* that he continue (e.g., "Please continue," "Please go on"), and eventually *insisting* that he continue (e.g., "It is absolutely essential that you continue"). But, again, subjects could refuse at any time.

Milgram himself saw an obvious connection between the results of his experiments and the events of the Holocaust. He begins his original 1963 report of the study by writing,

> Obedience, as a determinant of behavior, is of particular relevance to our time. It has been reliably established that from 1933-45 millions of innocent persons were systematically slaughtered on command. Gas chambers were built, death camps were guarded, daily quotas of corpses were produced with the same efficiency as the manufacture of appliances. These inhumane policies may have originated in the mind of a single person, but they could only be carried out on a massive scale if a very large number of persons obeyed orders.[17]

Despite recent controversies about the Milgram experiments,[18] there is nonetheless little room for doubting that the studies reveal an underappreciated tendency to obedience lying deep down in human nature (deeper in some than others, perhaps). Importantly, it is a tendency that can apparently overwhelm some of our other moral commitments. Likewise, I think there can be little doubt that this particular feature of human psychology has a role to play in many instances of group violence, including the actions of Nazi officers and other wrongdoers who have occupied "henchmen"-like positions in the perpetration of genocide or other instances of group violence. It is very common for these people to defend themselves after the fact by saying things like, "I was only doing what I was told."

However, despite its frequent association with the Holocaust, there are reasons to wonder about the extent to which Milgram's research on obedience is relevant to understanding the psychology of perpetrators of genocide. For one thing, as many have noted since Milgram first published the study, there are likely other important psychological factors in play, both in the obedience experiments themselves and in historical instances of genocide and other forms of group violence. One such factor that seems particularly salient is what is sometimes called *diffusion of responsibility*. As difficult as it was, psychologically, for subjects to administer higher-voltage shocks, it had to have been made easier by the thought that, at the end of the day, responsibility for any harm would fall not on them, but rather on those in charge (Milgram, his colleagues, and perhaps also the university). Indeed, some subjects later reported thinking this.

Likewise, part of the twisted genius of the Nazi "machine" was that it was designed in such a way that very few perpetrators would ever feel *directly* responsible for any harm or suffering inflicted on the victims. After all was said and done, most Nazi henchmen could defend themselves with claims like, "Hey, I never killed anyone, I just loaded people onto trains," "I never killed anyone, I just got them off the trains," "I never killed anyone, I just assigned them to their barracks," and so forth. In fact, many of the more heinous tasks—for example, filing victims into gas chambers, removing the corpses, and working the crematoria—were assigned to the *Sonderkommandos*. These were groups of *other* Jewish prisoners, whose choice was either to assist in the extermination process or else to be exterminated themselves. In this way, very few of the Nazi henchmen ever had to feel directly responsible for any serious wrongdoing.

Another reason for being skeptical of the relevance of Milgram's obedience studies to understanding the psychology of perpetrators of genocide is this: with few exceptions, perpetrators of genocide do not seem nearly as reluctant to cause harm to their victims as it appears Milgram's subjects were to shock the learner. Here is where the element of dehumanization once again becomes a factor.

In another experiment involving "teaching" by means of electric shock, Albert Bandura and colleagues took subjects in groups of three, and gave them the job of administering shocks to a team of three "decision makers" in another room (who were not actually there).[19] The shocks ranged in intensity from mild (level 1) to painful (level 10), and were meant to punish the decision-makers whenever they proposed an inadequate solution to some bargaining problem. One of the variables Bandura wanted to test was the diffusion of responsibility. He did this by dividing subjects into two conditions. In the *individualized responsibility condition*, subjects were told that they were being matched one-to-one with one of the three decision-makers, and their shocks would be administered directly to the individual decision-maker to whom they had been assigned. In the *diffused responsibility condition*, subjects were told that the researchers would take the average of the three subjects' shock levels, and administer only the average shock level to all three decision-makers. Predictably, when subjects believed that their shock level was being averaged with the shock levels chosen by the other two subjects, they chose higher, more painful shock levels. Once again, when feelings of direct responsibility are diffused, people are more willing to cause greater amounts of harm.

The other variable that Bandura wanted to test was dehumanization. The subjects were set up to "accidentally" overhear an exchange between two of the researchers just before the experiment. In this scripted exchange, the decision-makers were described in one of three ways.

> For subjects in the *humanized condition*, the decision makers were characterized as a perceptive, understanding, and otherwise humanized group. By contrast, in the *dehumanized condition*, the decision makers were described as an animalistic, rotten bunch. In the *neutral condition*, no evaluative references were made as to the characteristics of the group.[20]

What effect, if any, would it have on the shock levels chosen by subjects if, just before administering the shocks, they "accidentally" overheard someone else refer to the decision-makers as animals? The effect was remarkable. On average, the shock levels chosen by subjects in the dehumanized condition were *more than double* those chosen by subjects in the humanized condition. When you take both variables into account, the disparity is even greater. Subjects in both the *individualized responsibility* and *humanized* conditions shocked the decision-makers at an average intensity level of around 1.8; while subjects in both the *diffused responsibility* and *dehumanized* conditions shocked the decision-makers at an average intensity level of nearly 7. In a related study, Bandura and his colleagues found that subjects in the dehumanized condition preferred higher shock levels "even in the face of evidence that weak shocks effectively improved performance [by the decision makers] and thus provided no justification for escalating aggression."[21]

On the basis of these results, Bandura and his colleagues conclude that diffusion of responsibility and dehumanization are two powerful disinhibitors of violent aggression, with dehumanization being the more powerful of the two. The disinhibiting effect of dehumanization is apparently so powerful, in fact, that aggressors will harm dehumanized victims even when there is no purpose to be served by doing so, and apparently also without any of the distress and reluctance exhibited by Milgram's subjects. Now, in light of these studies, let us turn our attention to the words of actual perpetrators of genocide.

For his book *Machete Season: The Killers in Rwanda Speak*, Jean Hatzfeld interviewed ten Rwandan men who participated in the 1994 genocide of several hundred thousand Tutsis and moderate Hutus.[22] One of the killers, after engaging in a bit of confused scapegoating—"Our Tutsi neighbors, we knew they were not guilty of no misdoing [*sic*], but we thought all Tutsis at fault for our constant troubles"—continues,

> We no longer looked at them one by one, we no longer stopped to recognize them as they had been, not even as colleagues. They had become a threat greater than all we had experienced together, more important than our way of seeing things in the community. That's how we reasoned and how we killed at the same time.[23]

Another Hutu "henchman" explains, "We no longer saw a human being when we turned up a Tutsi in the swamps. I mean a person like us, sharing similar thoughts and feelings."[24] Again, they were *inyenzi*—cockroaches, pests, an infestation.

Half a century earlier, and in a completely different moral and political climate, officers of the Imperial Japanese Army were perpetrating war crimes against innocent Chinese civilians during the Second Sino-Japanese War (1937–1945). This war, which ranks among the deadliest in world history, is especially notorious for its genocidal aspects. During the Nanking Massacre—otherwise known as the "Rape of Nanking"—Japanese soldiers invaded the Chinese capital city of Nanking (now Nanjing) and, for a period of six weeks beginning in December 1937, engaged in the mass murder of Chinese civilians and mass rape (and then murder) of Chinese women. While the death toll is highly disputed—unsurprisingly, many Japanese leaders and historians maintain that the actual numbers are much lower than are often reported—most scholars estimate that around 300,000 Chinese men, women, and children were killed during the Nanking Massacre alone.

By the end of the war, many Japanese soldiers had been captured, charged with war crimes, and sent off to do time in a brutal Siberian prison. Remarkably, though, many of these same soldiers were later transferred to the Fushun Prison in China, where, in stark contrast to the way they were treated in Siberia, they were welcomed as guests and treated as dignified persons. Their time in Fushun apparently had quite an effect upon many of these former war criminals, since they eventually formed a group known as the Chukiren—short for "Association of Returnees from China"—whose purpose was to return to Japan, upon being released from prison, to raise awareness of the senseless brutality of war, and to urge Japan to make peace with China.

For his book *Evil Men*, James Dawes interviewed many of these former Japanese soldiers. One of the Chukiren recalls some of the more racist and dehumanizing elements of the Imperial Japanese ideology:

> That is the sort of ideology it is. And from the time we were small, we called Chinese people dirty chinks—made fun of them. We called Russians Russkie pigs. We called Westerners hairy barbarians, you know? And so this meant that when the people of Japan joined the army and went to the front, no matter how many Chinese they killed, they didn't think of it as being much different from killing a dog or a cat.[25]

Dawes also interviewed a former member of the infamous Unit 731, "a now-notorious military unit that conducted research in biological and chemical warfare on human subjects at a secret military installation in Ping Fan."[26] Scientists in Unit 731 infected Chinese civilians with a number of diseases, ranging from pneumonia and whooping cough to epidemic cerebrospinal meningitis; forced victims to ingest contaminated foods; and performed experiments that included forced dehydration, injecting horse urine into victims' kidneys, and intentionally freezing various body parts in order to test methods for healing frostbite. In order to observe the effects of some of these diseases and other conditions upon internal organs, they often performed vivisections on patients, many of whom were insufficiently anesthetized. Here is how one of these former scientists explained himself to Dawes:

> X—— [the scientist] explained that to cultivate the necessary bacteria at highest toxicity, they needed to use living bodies. It was important to begin dissecting people while they were still alive. He also noted that he and his colleagues did not refer to the prisoners as human beings. They referred to them as "logs."[27]

Many of the members of Unit 731 attempted to justify their actions with the following reasoning: if these Chinese prisoners are definitely going to be executed anyway, *why not* use them as instruments for acquiring potentially very useful information? As far as members of Unit 731 were concerned, their victims occupied a kind of state between life and death: their usefulness as experimental subjects depended on their still being alive; but for all other intents and purposes—especially, as far as their status in the moral community was concerned—it was as if they were already dead.

This thought brings us back to the Nazis and, specifically, to their treatment of prisoners in the concentration camps and death camps. Hannah Arendt wrote extensively on this subject, often echoing points made earlier about the moral uniqueness and utter incomprehensibility of the evil that took place in these camps.

> There are no parallels to the life in the concentration camps. Its horror can never be fully embraced by the imagination for the very reason that it stands outside of life and death. It can never be fully reported for the very reason that the survivor returns to the world of the living, which makes it impossible for him to believe fully in his own past experiences.[28]

To support her point about there being no parallels to life in the camps, she goes on to contrast the treatment of concentration camp prisoners with the treatment of slaves and other forced laborers.

> Forced labor as a punishment is limited as to time and intensity. The convict retains his rights over his body; he is not absolutely tortured and he is not absolutely dominated. [...] Throughout history slavery has been an institution within a social order; slaves were not, like concentration-camp inmates, withdrawn from the sight and hence the protection of their fellow-men; as instruments of labor they had a definite price and as property a definite value. The concentration-camp inmate has no price, because he can always be replaced; nobody knows to whom he belongs, because he is never seen. From the point of view of society he is absolutely superfluous.[28]

And finally, making a point very similar to the one made above with respect to the victims of Unit 731, she writes,

> [T]he human masses sealed off in them [concentration camps and death camps] are treated as if they no longer existed, as if what happened to them were no longer of any interest to anybody, as if they were already dead and some evil spirit gone mad were amusing himself by stopping them for a while between life and death before admitting them to eternal peace.[29]

Arendt's characterization of the way in which camp prisoners were regarded—"as if they were already dead," as if they were not persons, but "living corpses"—is interesting not only because of the resemblance that it bears to the way in which Unit 731 scientists regarded their victims, but also because of the resemblance that it bears to what psychologists and criminal profilers often say about the way psychopathic serial murderers regard other people.

We now have answers—or at least, informed things to say in response—to two questions raised earlier in this chapter. First, to begin this particular section, I asked: What is it, psychologically, about those occupying "henchmen"-like roles in the perpetration of genocide that renders them capable of knowingly and willingly participating in such evil behavior? The answer, apparently, is that there are a number of salient psychological factors. For one thing, humans have a tendency to obey those in perceived positions of authority, a tendency that is often powerful enough to override other moral commitments. For another, humans tend to be more aggressive when feelings of personal responsibility are sufficiently diffused. Finally, as Bandura and his colleagues concluded, there is perhaps no more powerful disinhibitor of violent aggression than the dehumanization of one's victims. In every known instance of genocide—not to mention other well-known examples of group violence, such as the mass murder of Native Americans by European settlers or mob lynchings of blacks in the American South[30]—the element of dehumanization figures centrally as a powerful psychological force for evil.

Second, I began the chapter by asking: What is it about genocide in particular—as opposed to other actions or events, like wars, with similarly high death tolls—that makes it seem so *evil*? As I argued earlier, the answer is presumably not that there are so many deaths, though this no doubt bears on its status as an *atrocity*. But then, what is it? According to Claudia Card, one of the essential features of an evil action is that the victims suffer some intolerable harm. In the case of genocide, the relevant intolerable harm is something that she calls "social death"—a term she borrows from Orlando Patterson.[31] As Card construes it, social death occurs when a group of people is utterly (though perhaps not irreparably) cut off from the source, or sources, of their social identity.

> When a group with its own cultural identity is destroyed, its survivors lose their cultural heritage and may even lose their intergenerational connections. To use Orlando Patterson's terminology, in that event, they may become "socially dead" and their descendants *"natally alienated,"* no longer able to pass along and build upon the traditions, cultural developments (including languages), and projects of earlier generations.[32]

But there are at least two problems with thinking that social death, so construed, is what makes genocide evil. First, it is not clear that social death is *always* a consequence of genocide. (Frankly, it is not clear that social death in this sense has *ever* been a consequence of genocide.) As long as a sufficient number of the members of some targeted ethnic group survive a genocide—and as far as I can tell, the number need not be high—these people may very well be able to "pass along and build upon the traditions, cultural developments, and projects of earlier generations," and this may be true even if they are forced to leave their native region. But surely, this would not make the genocide and its perpetrators any less evil. Second, there can apparently be other actions or events—like wars, epidemics, or natural disasters—that similarly threaten a group's social connectedness or vitality without thereby counting as evil.

As I will argue in much more detail in Chap. 7, what makes genocide evil is not the staggering death tolls, nor any particular harm done, like social death, but rather the way in which the victims are *seen*, or *regarded*, by the perpetrators. Sometimes they are seen as pests; sometimes they are seen as animals; sometimes they are seen as abstractions, as living symbols of elements of some hostile ideology; sometimes they are seen as "living corpses," whose biological lives somehow outlasted their moral existence. In all of these ways, and others, victims of genocide are the objects of a kind of *moral disregard*—which, again, I say much more about later in the book.[33]

THE LEADERS

We have already covered a great deal of moral, historical, and sociopsychological ground in this chapter, and all without saying a word (yet) about the *leaders* of the Holocaust and other genocides. Yet, as I began the chapter by noting, these are the people who tend to rank highest as paradigm examples of evil people. So, what is there to say about genocidal leaders—specifically, with respect to their status as evil—that has not already been said about "commoners" like Maschmann or the "henchmen" carrying out the leaders' orders? As a way of approaching an answer to this question, let us first examine and then compare the roles and motives of two very different leaders of two very different genocides: Adolf Eichmann and Pauline Nyiramasuhuko.

Eichmann joined the Nazi Party in 1932, spending the next several years methodically working his way up the ranks of the Party. Throughout his tenure as an officer of the SS, Eichmann's foremost concern was to rid

Germany of any and all Jewish residents. During the mid- to late-1930s, in addition to conducting surveillance operations on a number of Jewish organizations, his position involved negotiating with various Zionist leaders, and even touring Palestine in 1937, all in the hope of coordinating a mass Zionist emigration of Jews out of Germany. Then in the early 1940s, Eichmann was promoted to a directorial position in the Reich Security Main Office, first as the Director of Clearing Activities, and then as the Director of Jewish Affairs. It was from this latter office that Eichmann orchestrated the deportation of millions of Jews from German-occupied lands to concentration camps and death camps.

In 1960, Israeli intelligence officers captured Eichmann in Argentina, where he had fled after the war. Eichmann went to trial in Jerusalem the following year—the first internationally televised trial—and was eventually sentenced to death in December 1961 for his participation in the Holocaust. Hired by *The New Yorker* to report on the proceedings, Arendt actually sat in the Jerusalem courtroom for much of the trial. In 1963, she published her report, entitled *Eichmann in Jerusalem*, with the curious subtitle *A Report on the Banality of Evil*.

Almost immediately after its publication, however, Arendt's characterization of Eichmann became intensely controversial. Understandably, what readers expected was for Arendt to paint Eichmann as a vicious, bloodthirsty, Jew-hating monster. Instead, what they got was a picture of a man who Arendt described as "terribly and terrifyingly normal."[34]

> Except for an extraordinary diligence in looking out for his personal advancement, he had no motives at all. [...] He merely, to put the matter colloquially, never realized what he was doing. [...] He was not stupid. It was sheer thoughtlessness—something by no means identical with stupidity—that predisposed him to become one of the greatest criminals of that period.[35]

Despite her acknowledgement of his criminality, many readers were incensed by this description of Eichmann, thinking that it painted him in a far more sympathetic light than he deserved. But she doubled down in later work, writing in the introduction to *The Life of the Mind* (1978),

> [W]hat I was confronted with was [...] a manifest shallowness in [Eichmann] that made it impossible to trace the uncontestable evil of his deeds to any deeper level of roots or motives. The deeds were monstrous, but the doer—

at least the very effective one now on trial—was quite ordinary, commonplace, and neither demonic nor monstrous. There was no sign in him of firm ideological convictions or of specific evil motives, and the only notable characteristic one could detect [...] was something entirely negative: it was not stupidity but thoughtlessness.[36]

As many have since argued, however, Arendt's characterization of Eichmann is simply not historically accurate. The Adolf Eichmann that Arendt observed in that Jerusalem courtroom was not the *real* Adolf Eichmann.

He was an impressively ambitious and opportunistic man, very much concerned with his own professional advancements, and of course, with all of the power that came with them. On that particular point, Arendt seems to have been right. But it is difficult to understand how someone as "extraordinarily diligent" as she describes could also have "never realized what he was doing." There is simply no denying that Eichmann was firmly committed to the entirety of Nazi ideology, especially its more anti-Semitic elements. As I already mentioned, it was primarily his desire for "a Jew-free Germany" that motivated Eichmann throughout his career as an SS officer. As Clendinnen explains, he had an "obsessive determination to hunt down and destroy every last Jew he could lay his hands on, even when, as the tide of war turned, both the time and power to do so were deserting him."[37] Indeed, during these later stages of the war, when the fall of the Nazi Party was clearly imminent, Eichmann is reported to have often said, "I will jump into my grave laughing, because the fact that I have the death of five million Jews on my conscience gives me extraordinary satisfaction."[38]

Even if Arendt was wrong about Eichmann's motives, though, I wonder if some of her more infamous claims about evil and evil people have simply been misunderstood.[39] Take, for instance, her claims above about Eichmann's thoughtlessness. This is a theme that runs throughout her later work on genocide and evil: those who perpetrate genocide or other great evils are often *thoughtless*, or inconsiderate, in a way that differs from unintelligence, and disposes them to do terrible things to other people. In some places, Arendt goes so far as to suggest that this thoughtlessness is not merely a *lack of thought*, but an *inability to think*. And this is perhaps the cause of the misunderstanding. For instance, while researching for her recent book *Eichmann Before Jerusalem*—meant as a kind of response to Arendt's book—Bettina Stangneth examined thousands of pages of notes, memoirs, testimony, and other writings produced by Eichmann while hiding in

Argentina. Among Eichmann's personal notes is a lengthy critique of the moral philosophy of Immanuel Kant. But, Stangneth wonders, how could someone so thoughtless in his evil, so supposedly "unable to think," interact so thoughtfully with one of history's greatest thinkers (on the topic of morality, no less)?[40]

Unfortunately, it just is not clear what exactly Arendt meant when she described Eichmann as thoughtless. But I wonder if there is an interpretation that explains how Eichmann could be so thoughtless in his participation in the Holocaust, while being so thoughtful in other aspects of his life. This may not have been what Arendt had in mind, but suppose Eichmann's thoughtlessness was a matter of his failing to see his victims as things to which he ought to have *given a thought*. Earlier, I mentioned how Maschmann found that she was able, when necessary, to "switch off" her feelings toward her victims. Perhaps an important difference between commoners like Maschmann and leaders like Eichmann was that Eichmann's own dehumanization of the Jews was not a thing that required him to switch off any genuine feelings of sympathy toward them. There simply were no feelings for him to switch off.

When we read first- and second-hand accounts of Nazi commoners, and even many henchmen, we are often left with the impression that these people suffered from a kind of practical moral schizophrenia, being of two very different and irreconcilable minds about what was going on at the time. But, as blameworthy as these people still might be for their attitudes and behaviors, there is nonetheless something redeeming about the schizophrenia, something recognizably conscientious. One of the frightening things about Nazi leaders like Eichmann is that, except perhaps for a few maudlin displays of feigned remorse during interviews given from prison, they do not seem to have been psychologically *conflicted* in any way in their persecution of the Jews. Eichmann "never realized what he was doing" in the sense that it never occurred—and never would have occurred—to him that "what he was doing" was orchestrating the mass murder of *human persons*. Perhaps this is why Arendt saw fit to repeatedly distinguish between thoughtlessness and stupidity: Eichmann's thoughtlessness consisted not so much in an *inability* to process thoughts, but rather in the conspicuous *absence* of a particularly important thought, namely, that of his victims' humanity. Again, I do not mean to claim that this is actually what Arendt had in mind; but it does explain how Eichmann could be thought-*less* in his actions toward the Jews and thought-*ful* in so many other aspects of his life.

Pauline Nyiramasuhuko was also an ambitious and opportunistic person, driven by a desire to ascend the ranks of political authority, as well as a desire for the all of the power that came with the ascension. Before getting into Rwandan politics, she was a social worker, "roaming the countryside, offering lectures on female empowerment and instruction on child care and AIDS prevention."[41] But after marrying a politician in 1968, Nyiramasuhuko became more interested in political service, and began working with the Rwandan Ministry of Health in 1973. Over the next couple of decades, and partly by exploiting her friendship with the wife of Rwanda's then-President Juvénal Habyarimana, Nyiramasuhuko gradually worked her way up into the higher echelons of Rwandan political power, eventually being named the country's Minister of Family and Women's Development.

Nyiramasuhuko's role in the 1994 genocide is fascinating for a number of reasons. First, she is, to date, the only *woman* ever tried and convicted by an international criminal tribunal for genocide.[42] Second, despite spending the majority of her political career defending women's rights, she is also the only woman ever tried and convicted by an international criminal tribunal for *rape* as a crime against humanity.[43] The mass rape of Tutsi women in Rwanda was a major part of the genocide, and unbelievably, much of it came on the direct orders of Rwanda's Minister of Family and Women's Development.

> [A] U.N. report has concluded that at least 250,000 women were raped during the genocide. Some were penetrated with spears, gun barrels, bottles or the stamens of banana trees. Sexual organs were mutilated with machetes, boiling water and acid; women's breasts were cut off. According to one study, Butare province alone has more than 30,000 rape survivors. Many more women were killed after they were raped.

> These facts are harrowing. More shocking is that so many of these crimes were supposedly inspired and orchestrated by Pauline Nyiramasuhuko, whose very job was the preservation, education and empowerment of Rwanda's women.[44]

And third, as journalist Peter Landesman uncovered while interviewing Nyiramasuhuko's mother for a 2002 *New York Times Magazine* story, there is some reason to think that Nyiramasuhuko is actually a Tutsi herself, and knew it all along. In Rwanda, kinship is defined patrilineally, and Nyiramasuhuko's great-grandfather was a Tutsi.

I asked Theresa [Nyiramasuhuko's mother] if that didn't mean that Pauline was a Tutsi. "Yes, of course," she said eagerly. And would Pauline have known that she came from Tutsi lineage? Theresa pursed her lips and gave a firm, affirmative nod.[45]

So here is a woman *génocidaire*—a rarity in itself—presumably aware of her own Tutsi heritage, serving as Rwanda's Minister of Family and Women's Development, commanding the mass rape of Tutsi women, as well as the mass murder of Tutsi men, women, and children throughout Rwanda.

How could someone in Nyiramasuhuko's position possibly do the things that she did? What sense can be made of her actions and motivations? As Drumbl notes, "other than the Landesman article, few media or academic reports endeavor to grapple with—or even explore—what fueled Nyiramasuhuko's violence in the first place."[46] Probably, as was the case with Eichmann, she was partly motivated to perpetrate these crimes by an insatiable professional ambition and an opportunistic desire for power. Indeed, these psychological forces may have been even more powerful in her case than in Eichmann's, given that she likely felt additional pressure to prove herself as deserving of her rank in a government made up of mostly authoritarian men.

At most, though, Nyiramasuhuko's political and professional ambitions could only have served to amplify dispositions to violence that were already present. After all, what could her general desire for political power and respect among peers have had to do with the particular ferocity that she apparently reserved for Tutsi women? In his own effort to explain Nyiramasuhuko's peculiar motivations and participation in the genocide, Landesman returns us once again to the matter of dehumanization.

> Unlike the Nazis, who were fueled by myths of Aryan superiority, the Hutus were driven by an accumulated rage over their lower status and by resentment of supposed Tutsi beauty and arrogance. "The propaganda made Tutsi women powerful, desirable—and therefore something to be destroyed," Rhonda Copelon told me. "When you make the woman the threat, you enhance the idea that violence against them is permitted."

This pernicious idea, of course, came to full fruition during the genocide. The collective belief of Hutu women that Tutsi women were shamelessly trying to steal their husbands granted Hutu men permission to rape their supposed competitors out of existence. Seen through this warped lens, the men who raped were engaged not only in an act of sexual transgression but also in a purifying ritual. "Once women are defiled as a group, anything one does to them is done in some kind of higher purpose," Robert Jay Lifton said. "It becomes a profound, shared motivation of eliminating evil. Tutsis must be killed down to the last person in order to bring about utopia. They are seen, in a sense, as already dead."[47]

One cannot help but recall Dawes' account of how the scientists at Unit 731 regarded their victims as if they were already dead, or Arendt's description of how concentration camp prisoners were treated "as if they no longer existed, as if what happened to them were no longer of any interest to anybody, as if they were already dead." Landesman continues, "This explanation conformed with my sense of Pauline's view of the Tutsis; like many of her countrymen, she seemed able to view individual Tutsis as abstractions."[48]

For Nyiramasuhuko, her victims were not human—especially not the Tutsi women. They were abstractions, or symbols, living representations of things she wished to eradicate. But in her case, the dehumanization was oddly *personal*. Every Tutsi woman was a reminder to her of *both* (a) the elevated status and attractiveness often associated with Tutsi women, which she felt she lacked, and (b) her own Tutsi heritage, which she understandably kept secret, and which, due to intense social pressures which she herself had helped to propagate, had become a source of haunting shame for her. Nyiramasuhuko occupied a profoundly confused psychological state, and it drove her to evil. But despite her confused psychological state, she was apparently no more *conflicted* when ordering mass rape and murder than Eichmann was when orchestrating the mass deportation of Jews to camps to be exterminated. She was not in any way acting out-of-character. She was obeying no one. Her attitudes toward her victims were not "put on" for any reason; they were genuinely hers. This was simply, even if incomprehensibly, the kind of person that she was.

If genocide is evil because of the utter moral disregard shown for the victims' humanity, then leaders of genocide are evil—unlike their supportive commoners and perhaps also their obedient henchmen—because the dehumanization of others is not merely a *thing that they do*; rather, it is a *way that they are*. Far from being an *exception* to their moral characters, it is a *feature* of their moral characters. This, at least, is what I will argue in greater detail in Chap. 7. But there is still much ground to cover before then.

Concluding Thoughts

In Chap. 5, I discuss three philosophical puzzles related to the notion of moral evil. The first puzzle, which I briefly mentioned near the beginning of this chapter, concerns the idea that evil is in some sense essentially incomprehensible. The second puzzle concerns the appropriateness of moral labels, especially negative labels like "evil," as they are applied to people whose bad behavior may be rooted in things like brain malfunction, personality disorder, childhood trauma, and the like. And the third puzzle concerns the psychological reality and explanatory power of traits of character. To conclude *this* chapter, however, I want to briefly address two other puzzles related to evil—or maybe it would be better to think of them as *paradoxes*—one theoretical, the other practical.

The first paradox arises out of two intuitions that people often have about evil, but which appear at first glance to conflict with one another. On the one hand, people often have the intuition that evil, if it exists at all, is *very rare*. Indeed, part of what makes evil so fascinating is just that it is so foreign to our ordinary, everyday experience with morality. We see wrongdoing all the time, and we often have to deal with people who we might describe as jerks or scumbags. But we rarely witness evil firsthand. On the other hand, people also often have the intuition that the capacity for evil is inside all of us. This is implied by Nagel's discussion of moral luck, described above, as well as a host of studies in social psychology, some of which I discussed in this chapter (others will be discussed in Chap. 5). Alison Des Forges was a human rights activist whose work focused primarily on the African continent, where she eventually became a senior advisor for Human Rights Watch. She was at one point the world's foremost expert on the Rwandan genocide. Referring to the Hutu perpetrators, she once said,

> This behavior lies just under the surface of any of us. [...] The simplified accounts of genocide allow distance between us and the perpetrators of genocide. They are so evil we couldn't ever see ourselves doing the same thing. But if you consider the terrible pressure under which people were operating, then you automatically reassert their humanity—and that becomes alarming. You are forced to look at these situations and say, "What would I have done?" Sometimes the answer is not encouraging.[49]

Assuming that Des Forges is right about this, evil is apparently paradoxical in at least this one respect: in one sense, it is very rare; but in another sense, it is also frighteningly and depressingly common. If a philosophical theory of evil is to remain faithful to our intuitions about the subject matter, then, it will have to be able to explain and accommodate this paradoxical feature of evil. I will return to this issue later in the book, when it comes time to evaluate theories of evil, and then to develop and defend a theory of my own.

The second paradox has to do with the notion of dehumanization. On the one hand, our discussion of genocide and its perpetrators has revealed an apparent relationship of some sort between evil and dehumanization. I expound on this relationship in Chap. 7. On the other hand, in order to explain how it is that someone could engage in such despicable behavior, we often resort to dehumanizing those who dehumanize—by, for example, calling them "inhuman monsters," "devils," "fiends," "barbarians," and the like. Now, of course, to some degree, this is understandable. For one thing, it is very hard for us to imagine how a human being *just like you and me* could do such a thing. For another thing, these dehumanizing labels, like "inhuman" and "monster," are useful as devices for expressing our serious disapproval of evildoers and their actions.

However, as much as evildoers and evil people may *deserve* these labels, we nonetheless ought to resist using them, for a couple of reasons. First, while it certainly is not itself an evil action to dehumanize dehumanizers in this way, it does represent a kind of stooping *toward* their level. If we think it is wrong for perpetrators of genocide to regard their victims as less than fully human, then perhaps we ought not answer in kind. Second, somewhat ironically, describing evildoers as inhuman monsters may inadvertently let them off the hook a bit. After all, who can really blame a monster for doing a monstrous thing? So the paradox here is more practical, and goes something like this: in order to adequately condemn evildoers and evil people, we often resort to dehumanizing them; but for us to be *able* to adequately condemn them, we must resist the urge to dehumanize.

Notes

1. Nagel (1979: 33).
2. Nagel (1979: 34).
3. Historian Inga Clendinnen begins her book *Reading the Holocaust*—a collection of essays about Nazi Germany—by first acknowledging how utterly baffling the topic is for most people, and then explaining, "The primary aim of these essays is to challenge that bafflement, and the demoralisation

which attends it. [...] This is not a matter of arriving at some 'Aha! now I comprehend everything!' theory or moment. The understanding I seek comes from framing sufficiently precise questions to be able to see exactly what is before us, whether persons or processes. It is both cumulative, and never complete" (1999: 4). This is a nice way of describing the kind of understanding that I seek in this chapter.

4. Staub (2003: 293).
5. Staub (2003: 293).
6. Staub (2003: 293–299).
7. Staub (2003: 297).
8. Staub (2003: 299).
9. See Friedländer (1997).
10. Koonz (2003: 173).
11. Maschmann (1964: 6).
12. Maschmann (1964: 40, italics in original).
13. Maschmann (1964: 40–41, italics in original).
14. Maschmann (1964: 125). Throughout her memoir, Maschmann talks repeatedly about this ability to "switch off her feelings" toward her victims.
15. Milgram (1963).
16. Milgram (1963: 377).
17. Milgram (1963: 371).
18. See Perry (2013).
19. Bandura et al. (1975).
20. Bandura et al. (1975: 258).
21. Bandura et al. (1975: 266).
22. As is always the case with these things, the actual death toll of the Rwandan genocide is a matter of some dispute. Estimates range from 300,000–500,000 on the low end, up to a million or more on the high end.
23. Hatzfeld (2005: 121).
24. Hatzfeld (2005: 47).
25. Dawes (2013: 49).
26. Dawes (2013: 39–40).
27. Dawes (2013: 40).
28. Arendt (1951 [1973]: 444).
29. Arendt (1951 [1973]: 445).
30. Fittingly, Staub discusses these and other forms or instances of group violence in the course of developing and defending his theory of the sociopsychological origins of genocide (Staub 2003: 360ff.).
31. Card (2003). See Patterson (1982).
32. Card (2003: 73).

33. For the record, Patterson's own use of the term "social death"—which, again, he coined, and uses primarily in relation to slavery—reflects more of an element of *dehumanization* than Card's (see Patterson 1982). Here is how Card herself characterizes Patterson's view:

> Slaves who are treated as nonpersons have (practically) no socially supported ties not only to a cultural heritage but even to immediate kin (parents, children, siblings) and peers. As a consequence of being cut off from kin and community, they also lose their cultural heritage. But the first step was to destroy existing social ties with family and community, to "ex-communicate them from society," as Patterson puts it. (Card 2003: 74)

But even by her own description of the view, the first step is not to destroy slaves' social ties to family and community, but rather to treat them as nonpersons—or, to dehumanize them. In other words, slaves end up "socially dead" because they are first treated as things that could never have been "socially alive" to begin with.

34. Arendt (1963 [1977]: 276).
35. Arendt (1963 [1977]: 287–288).
36. Arendt (1978b: 3–4).
37. Clendinnen (1999: 103).
38. Clendinnen (1999: 112).
39. I here focus only on Arendt's claims about a connection between evil and *thoughtlessness*. Her most infamous claim about evil, however, is the one that she makes in the subtitle of the Eichmann book (and then only once inside the book), namely, that there is some sense in which evil is *banal*. I address this matter in detail in Chap. 7. (For the record, while taking issue with Arendt's depiction of Eichmann, Clendinnen mentions the so-called banality of evil, and asks critically, "[W]hat does it mean to call a man 'banal'?" (1999: 102). But, Arendt did not say that Eichmann was banal; she said that *evil* is banal.)
40. Stangneth (2014: 217–221).
41. Landesman (2002).
42. Drumbl (2013: 562).
43. As one might imagine, genocide and other forms of group violence are often—indeed, *typically*—accompanied by mass rape. In addition to figuring prominently in the Rwandan genocide, for instance, it was also a major part of the Japanese attacks on Chinese civilians during the Second Sino-Japanese War. In fact, historically speaking, the Holocaust is somewhat unique in that rape does *not* appear to have been especially common. For more on the connection between genocide and rape, see Dawes (2013: 98–99).

44. Landesman (2002). Nyiramasuhuko's actions during the genocide have since earned her the unfortunate, but fitting, nickname "The Minister of Rape."
45. Landesman (2002).
46. Drumbl (2013: 569).
47. Landesman (2002).
48. Landesman (2002).
49. Landesman (2002).

REFERENCES

Arendt, Hannah. 1951 [1973]. *The Origins of Totalitarianism*. San Diego: Harcourt, Inc.
———. 1963 [1977]. *Eichmann in Jerusalem: A Report on the Banality of Evil*. New York: Penguin Books.
———. 1978b. *The Life of the Mind*. New York: Harcourt Brace Jovanovich.
Bandura, Albert, Bill Underwood, and Michael E. Fromson. 1975. Disinhibition of Aggression through Diffusion of Responsibility and Dehumanization of Victims. *Journal of Research in Personality* 9: 253–269.
Card, Claudia. 2003. Genocide and Social Death. *Hypatia* 18(1): 63–79.
Clendinnen, Inga. 1999. *Reading the Holocaust*. Cambridge: Cambridge University Press.
Dawes, James. 2013. *Evil Men*. Cambridge: Harvard University Press.
Drumbl, Mark A. 2013. She Makes Me Ashamed to Be a Woman: The Genocide Conviction of Pauline Nyiramasuhuko, 2011. *Michigan Journal of International Law* 34(3): 559–603.
Friedländer, Saul. 1997. *Nazi Germany and the Jews: Volume 1: The Years of Persecution 1933–1939*. New York: HarperCollins.
Hatzfeld, Jean. 2005. *Machete Season: The Killers in Rwanda Speak*. Translated by Linda Coverdale. New York: Farrar, Straus, and Giroux, LLC.
Koonz, Claudia. 2003. *The Nazi Conscience*. Cambridge: Harvard University Press.
Landesman, Peter. 2002. A Woman's Work. *The New York Times*, September 15. Accessed March 1, 2016. http://www.nytimes.com/2002/09/15/magazine/a-woman-s-work.html?pagewanted=all.
Maschmann, Melita. 1964. *Account Rendered: A Dossier on my Former Self*. Translated by Geoffrey Strachen. London: Abelard-Schuman.
Milgram, Stanley. 1963. Behavioral Study of Obedience. *Journal of Abnormal and Social Psychology* 67(4): 371–378.
Nagel, Thomas. 1979. Moral Luck. In *Mortal Questions*, 24–38. Cambridge: Cambridge University Press.

Patterson, Orlando. 1982. *Slavery and Social Death*. Cambridge: Harvard University Press.
Perry, Gina. 2013. *Behind the Shock Machine: The Untold Story of the Notorious Milgram Psychology Experiments*. New York: The New Press.
Stangneth, Bettina. 2014. *Eichmann Before Jerusalem: The Unexamined Life of a Mass Murderer*. New York: Alfred A. Knopf.
Staub, Ervin. 2003. *The Psychology of Good and Evil: Why Children, Adults, and Groups Help and Harm Others*. Cambridge: Cambridge University Press.

CHAPTER 4

Money, Greed, and Commodification

In his first letter to Timothy, the Apostle Paul famously declares, "The love of money is the root of all kinds of evil" (6:10). But people are often surprised to learn that these words come from the Bible. Not because of any preconceived notions about the Bible, mind you, but rather because versions of the same expression have become, over time, a kind of moral *commonplace*, a proverb shared every bit as often in non-religious settings as in religious settings. Most people, it seems, believe that there is some kind of connection between (the love of) money and evil.

So it comes as a bit of a surprise to me to find so little discussion of the supposed relationship between money and evil in the philosophical and psychological literature on moral evil. Philosophers and psychologists tend to focus almost entirely on the types of characters discussed in Chaps. 2 and 3, namely, psychopathic serial murderers and perpetrators of genocide. But in doing so, one runs the risk of defining too narrowly the terms of one's theory of evil, since it only has to accommodate these two kinds of cases, and not others. For instance, most philosophers and psychologists associate evildoing with the causing of some sort of extreme or significant *harm* to one's victims. And if one's theory were based solely on the kinds of cases we encountered in the previous two chapters, it would be easy to assume that the relevant *form* of harm is *violent* in nature. After all, what do Ted Bundy and Pauline Nyiramasuhuko have in common, except that they were both responsible for the brutal and dehumanizing deaths of others?

But what about someone like Bernie Madoff? He surely harmed many people, but the harm was of a very different nature than that discussed in Chaps. 2 and 3. Madoff never tortured or killed anyone, though a few of his victims have since killed themselves. Nor did he orchestrate or command the torture or murder of anyone, though he did orchestrate their destruction in another sense. And yet, when sentencing Madoff to the maximum allowable 150 years in prison (an official "life" sentence was not permitted by law), Judge Denny Chin insisted that such a punishment was justified since Madoff's actions were not just *wrong*, nor *very* wrong, but "extraordinarily evil."[1] As I said in the introductory chapter, even if someone like Madoff would not rank *as highly* on anyone's list of the most plausible candidates for an evil person, the extremity of his crimes, especially in light of our common intuitions about a connection between money and evil, suggests that he at least belongs in the discussion.

So the purpose of this chapter is twofold. First, I want to explore just what sort of connection there might be between money and evil. What is it, exactly, about money—or the love of money, or the unscrupulous pursuit of wealth, or whatever—that disposes a person to evil? Whereas the previous two chapters were relatively narrow in terms of the diversity of characters studied, with Chap. 2 focusing entirely upon psychopathic serial killers, and Chap. 3 focusing almost entirely upon people involved in the perpetration of genocide, this chapter will be intentionally broad in its review of cases. If there *is* an interesting connection to be found between money and evil, I think the best way to uncover that connection will be to examine a relatively diverse set of cases. Those cases will be (a) Madoff's execution of the largest Ponzi scheme in history, (b) the human trafficking industry, and (c) intensive animal farming. In light of the worry expressed in the previous paragraph, another purpose of this chapter is to bring new and important information to bear upon the discussions of Chaps. 6 and 7, wherein I critique several prevailing philosophical theories of evil (Chap. 6), before developing and defending a theory of my own (Chap. 7).

The suggestion at the end of Chap. 2 was that evil as it manifests itself in psychopathic serial killers and their crimes is a matter of *objectification*—that is, the way in which victims are utterly objectified, regarded as specimens, or collectibles, or playthings, and so on. In Chap. 3, the suggestion was that evil as it manifests itself in genocide and its perpetrators is a matter of *dehumanization*, that is, the way in which victims are regarded not as living human individuals, but rather as insects, or medical logs, or living corpses, as if they were already dead. The suggestion in this chapter is that evil can manifest itself in another way. As it appears in the cases discussed below, evil is more a matter of the *monetization* or *commodification* of members of the moral community, that is, the way in which victims are regarded not as creatures with some moral status, but rather as products, commodities, or even as forms of currency themselves.

THE *REAL* "WOLF OF WALL STREET"

If Jordan Belfort's $110 million fraud was enough to earn him the nickname "the Wolf of Wall Street," what does that make Bernie Madoff? Known for executing the largest Ponzi scheme in history, the total value of Madoff's fraud is estimated to be in the neighborhood of $65 billion—almost 600 times the size of Belfort's. Some compare him to psychopathic serial killers, like those discussed in Chap. 2, as when Vanity Fair columnist Marie Brenner referred to Madoff as "this century's financial Jeffrey Dahmer."[2] Others have even put him in the company of Nazi leaders, discussed in the previous chapter, as when one of Madoff's victims exclaimed (referring to his tendency to target Jewish businesspeople, retirees, and organizations), "What Hitler didn't finish, he did!"[3] But to his new friends—fellow prison inmates—Madoff is "a hero arguably the greatest con of all time."[4]

Madoff's promise to investors was not outrageous; in many cases, he promised only 10–12 % return on the year, significantly less than what some others were promising at the time, and this was part of what contributed to the success of his scheme. He had already made a name for himself as someone with an unparalleled sense of the market, and here he was making what seemed like a relatively modest and realistic proposal. By the time word got around that he was apparently delivering on his promise to early investors, people from all over the world—from foreign aristocrats to grandparents living in retirement communities in Florida—were practically begging him to take their money. But as we now know, what Madoff was *actually* delivering to those early investors was money given to him by later investors—a classic Ponzi scheme.

In the early days of the fraud, Madoff knew most of his clients by name; in fact, he recruited many of them in face-to-face meetings, over dinners on the yacht, sharing cigars, and so forth. But before long, there were so many feeder funds, investment partnerships, family trusts, and other pooled accounts, all sending money to Madoff, that it would have been impossible for him to have the kind of relationship with these people that he had with those on the ground floor. In the end, the distance between Madoff and many of the thousands who had sent him money was immense, and not just in terms of geography.

While Madoff still insists, in interviews that he now gives from prison, that most of his clients will avoid a net loss, this is apparently not the case for the vast majority of his victims. According to a recent story in the *New York Times*, those who dealt *directly* with Madoff can expect to get back about 54 cents for every dollar they invested. But these "eligible victims" make up only 15 % of the tens of thousands of Madoff-related claims, and each claim might itself represent hundreds or thousands of investors at a time.[5] Many of these people had their life's savings invested with Madoff, and will not get a dime of it back. As a result, some have been forced to sell their homes, to come out of retirement, and in some cases, to beg friends and family for assistance. At least a few of Madoff's victims—including one of his two sons—have chosen to commit suicide rather than to deal with the effects of his crimes.

As I mentioned above, the judge at Madoff's sentencing described his actions as "extraordinarily evil." But some find it difficult to call Madoff's actions evil *at all*. After all, many of his victims were among the very same privileged "top 1 %" of society as Madoff himself, and it is much harder to sympathize with these people than it is to sympathize with the poor and destitute—or even just anyone who is *not* exceedingly wealthy. In fact, many will think that his victims got what they deserved, since, it is assumed, part of what motivated them to invest with Madoff in the first place was their own greed. But this would be to paint in strokes that are way too broad. After all, Madoff advertised himself not as a "high return guy," but as someone who could deliver *consistent* returns. As a result, he tended to attract investors who were driven less by greed and more by a desire for security. Many of his clients were retirees planning to live—albeit very comfortably—off of the returns from their investments, and then to pass along whatever was left to their children and grandchildren. Perhaps even worse, among the list of victims there are a number of different charities and other non-profit organizations, all gutted by Madoff's fraud.

Theories abound as to what motivated Madoff to perpetrate one of the largest financial crimes in history. Of course, greed likely did play a role. But probably not as significant a role as one might think. For one thing, as Madoff is always eager to point out, not *all* of his business was fraudulent, and he was making enough from the legitimate trades, investments, and so forth, to live as comfortably as he desired. And for another thing, had greed been the primary motivator, he likely would have conducted the fraud differently, more to his own advantage. As Fishman reports, "It isn't clear that the fraud was even designed to make money. 'He left millions and millions on the table,' one of the trustee's lawyers said, implying that if it had been about the money, he could have taken more."[6] But then, if not simply greed, what else explains Madoff's actions?

One popular theory is that Madoff was motivated to a significant degree by deep feelings of insecurity and inadequacy. Early in his life, he had to watch as his father's once-successful sporting goods business failed, which had an effect not only upon Madoff's opportunities, but also upon his attitude toward those he perceived as having an easier way in life.

> His father's collapse also affected Madoff in an immediate and practical way. He headed to Wall Street without the pedigree, connections, or capital that ease a young man's way. "Of course my father was not in a position to offer me that," Madoff told me. To the young Bernie Madoff, Wall Street was an exclusive club that barred the door against the likes of him. "I was upset with the whole idea of not being in the club. I was this little Jewish guy from Brooklyn," he said.[7]

Madoff spent his freshman year of college at the University of Alabama, before transferring to Hofstra University, where he earned a degree in political science. Then, after a brief stint in law school, Madoff borrowed office space from his father-in-law, and began his own investment business with all the money he had been able to save to that point—a meager $500. He founded Bernard L. Madoff Investment Securities in 1960, and by the late 1980s, he was making up to $100 million per year—and perfectly legally, by most accounts. However, for Madoff, just as important as the money itself—if not more so—was the status that came with it. He had gone from being "this little Jewish guy from Brooklyn" to being one of the most prominent members of the very Wall Street "club" that once excluded him. The Ponzi scheme, then, was likely fueled by Madoff's fear of being exposed as *a fraud himself*. This explains not only why he did it, but also why he was not especially interested in profiting *financially* from it.

To some degree, at least, this should sound relatively familiar. After all, people tell lies every day and often in order to avoid being exposed to others as some kind of imposter. But surely something is still missing from this explanation. People may tell lies every day, but what they do *not* do every day is destroy thousands of lives in order to maintain a particular social status and self-image. Madoff's actions were hardly just the desperate attempts of a man afraid of being found out. For instance, he liked very much to play the so-called con of exclusivity, initially turning most prospective investors away, as if their money was not good enough for him. This, of course, often had the effect of making them beg even harder for him to take their money. At one point, after apparently forcing a friend of his to "pull on his heartstrings," he accepted $7.3 million from a recently widowed elderly woman—everything she had at the time—knowing that she would likely never see a penny of it ever again.

These are not the actions of someone who is merely insecure, and hoping to be accepted among his Wall Street companions. These are the actions of a psychopath. In fact, the similarities between Madoff and psychopathic serial killers like Ted Bundy and Edmund Kemper are remarkable. For one thing, as we saw in Chap. 2, some of the hallmark traits of a psychopath include superficial charm, a tendency to manipulate and deceive, and egotism and over-confidence. Every single one of these traits appears to have played a pivotal role in enabling Madoff to perpetrate his fraud.

> [S]ome analysts say that a more complex and layered observation of his actions involves linking the world of white-collar finance to the world of serial criminals. […]

> "Some of the characteristics you see in psychopaths are lying, manipulation, the ability to deceive, feelings of grandiosity and callousness toward their victims," says Gregg O. McCrary, a former special agent with the F.B.I. who spent years constructing criminal behavioral profiles.

> McCrary cautions that he has never met Mr. Madoff, so he can't make a diagnosis, but he says Mr. Madoff appears to share many of the destructive traits typically seen in a psychopath. That is why, he says, so many who came into contact with Mr. Madoff have been left reeling and in confusion about his motives.

> "People like him become sort of like chameleons. They are very good at impression management," Mr. McCrary says. "They manage the impression you receive of them. They know what people want, and they give it to them."[8]

This explains why, on the one hand, his therapy sessions are apparently "often teary." "He feels misunderstood. He can't bear the thought that people think he's evil. 'I'm not the kind of person I'm being portrayed as,' he told me."[9] But on the other hand, back in prison, where "he doesn't have to hide his lack of conscience," he once proudly declared to his adoring fellow inmates, "Fuck my victims. I carried them for twenty years, and now I'm doing 150 years."[10]

Due in part to their extreme over-confidence—specifically, the belief that they can get away with anything—psychopathic serial criminals often flirt with danger by fraternizing with local police, federal investigators, or other legal authorities during the period of their crimes. Kemper, for instance, regularly visited bars known to be favorites among local law enforcement officers, befriended several cops, and even—according to some reports—discussed his own case with a few of them. Here, too, Madoff behaved similarly.

[L]ike a burglar who knows the patrol routes of the police and can listen in on their radio scanners, he also actively wooed regulators who monitored his business. [...]

"He was very smart in understanding very early on that the more involved you were with regulators, you could shape regulation," this individual [someone who knew Madoff for years, but wished not to be identified] adds. "But, if we find out that the Ponzi scheme goes back that far, then he was doing something much smarter. If you're very close with regulators, they're not going [to] be looking over your shoulders that much. Very smart."[11]

But in addition to being smart for Madoff to keep his friends close, and these "enemies" closer, former FBI criminal profiler McCrary suggests that it was also likely a "heady, intoxicating" experience for Madoff to remain so close to federal authorities during the time of his crimes—much as it was for Kemper.

So while Madoff's first few fraudulent decisions were likely *motivated* to some degree by a kind of insecurity—in particular, a fear of being exposed as not completely deserving of the status he had achieved—what *enabled* him to make those decisions, and the thousands of fraudulent acts that followed, was a personality that, while never officially diagnosed, strongly resembles that of a psychopath. As I explained in Chap. 2, while most of us are psychologically inhibited from engaging in instrumental forms of violence, psychopaths lack these inhibitions. As a result, behaviors that most would consider *unthinkable*—like rape, murder, and theft—are nonetheless live options for people like Bundy, Kemper, and Madoff. "[W]hereas Mr. Bundy murdered people," Creswell and Thomas Jr. write, "Mr. Madoff murdered wallets, bank accounts and people's sense of financial trust and security."[12]

Given the topic of the chapter, however, we might still wonder: What role, if any, could *the money itself* have played in either motivating or enabling Madoff's behavior?

WHEN YOUR MIND IS ON MONEY, AND MONEY IS ON YOUR MIND

One of the hotter topics in moral psychology these days is the impact of money, wealth, and socio-economic status (SES) upon people's beliefs, attitudes, and moral decision-making. While on the one hand I want to avoid inspiring any simple-minded conclusions to the effect that all wealthy people are bad, not only because such claims are clearly false, but also because they are irrelevant to the topic of the book; on the other hand, the evidence *does* suggest a positive correlation between SES and immoral behavior. From field studies of people's driving habits (where a vehicle's make and model are taken as signs of SES) to laboratory studies of people's performances in economic games and surveys of people's attitudes toward greed, a growing body of research seems to indicate that the higher is one's SES, the more likely one will be to think and to act immorally.[13] But given my aims in this book—specifically, the particular theory of evil that I defend in Chap. 7—I am especially interested here in studies of the effects of money, wealth, and SES upon people's attitudes toward or about other people.

One of the major underlying premises of the moral psychological literature on SES is that with *limited* access to socio-economic resources like wealth, education, and job opportunities comes a sense of *dependence* upon other people for one's own well-being; and with *increased* access to such resources comes a corresponding sense of *independence*. Kraus and Keltner hypothesized that this sense of dependence or independence will manifest itself publicly in various ways, one of which has to do with people's nonverbal behavior when interacting with strangers.

[W]e predicted that upper SES would be associated with a disengaged style of nonverbal behavior (e.g., self-grooming and doodling) in an interaction with a stranger. We expected lower SES, in contrast, to be associated with increased engaged behaviors (e.g., head nods, eyebrow raises).[14]

Basically, the idea is this: the more dependent you are, or feel, on others, the more likely you are to give them your attention; whereas, the more independent you are, or feel, the less likely you are to attend to other people. For their study, Kraus and Keltner took two individuals who were strangers to one another, sat them in chairs facing each other in a laboratory room, and had them engage in "a videotaped get-acquainted interaction" for five minutes. After the get-acquainted interaction, the two subjects then engaged in mock job interviews, under the pretense that they were helping to determine effective interview strategies. Finally, the two subjects were brought to separate tables, "where they independently decided how to split a signing bonus of $5000 on the basis of their perceptions of their performance during the interview."[15] After the nonverbal behavior was coded and rated, the results confirmed the researchers' predictions:

> As predicted, actor SES was significantly and positively associated with disengagement cues [...] Upper-SES individuals were more likely than lower-SES individuals to self-groom, fidget with nearby objects, and doodle during the 60-s slice of their conversation with their interaction partners. [... Likewise, a]ctor SES was significantly and negatively associated with engagement cues [...] Upper-SES individuals were less likely than lower-SES individuals to look at their partners, laugh, nod their heads, and raise their eyebrows.[16]

Another underlying premise of the moral psychological literature on SES is that individuals with lower SES face harsher living environments than those with higher SES, and this partly explains the fact that individuals with lower SES are more likely than those with higher SES to experience negative emotional states like anxiety, sadness, and anger.[17] However, the harsher living environments of individuals with lower SES may also contribute to an increased tendency to feel some *positive* emotions, like compassion. To test this, Stellar et al. had 148 undergraduates (78 female, 70 male) at a large public university complete a survey designed to relate a subject's self-reported SES-rank to his or her "trait-like tendency to feel several distinct positive emotions including joy, contentment, pride, love, compassion, amusement, and awe."[18] First, subjects were asked to identify which socio-economic class they most identified with: lower, lower-middle, middle, upper-middle, or upper. Then, they completed The Dispositional Positive Emotion Scale, which asks subjects to rank their agreement or disagreement (on a 7-point Likert scale) with statements like "I am a very compassionate person," "When I see someone hurt or in need, I feel a powerful urge to take care of them," and "It's important to take care of people who are vulnerable." As predicted,

> participants who reported lower levels of social class [...] reported higher levels of the trait-like tendency to feel compassion, controlling for gender, ethnicity, and spirituality [...] Moreover, using similar regressions controlling for gender, ethnicity, and spirituality, social class did not predict scores for dispositional joy, contentment, pride, love, amusement, and awe.[19]

This is perhaps less surprising in light of the data on social engagement and disengagement. After all, you are less likely to *notice* when another is suffering or in need if your attention is directed inwardly.

In a related study, Kraus, Côté, and Keltner examined the effect of SES upon an individual's "empathic accuracy," that is, "the ability to accurately infer the emotions of other individuals."[20] Following up on Kraus and Keltner's earlier study of SES and (dis)engagement, the researchers predicted that "lower-class individuals should exhibit higher empathic accuracy than their upper-class counterparts," given that "the elevated rank and resources of upper-class individuals leads them to be relatively self-focused."[21] To test this, the researchers asked 200 employees at a public university (67.7 % female, 32.3 % male) to complete the Mayer-Salovey-Caruso Emotional Intelligence Test, part of which is designed to test a subject's ability to identify emotions in human facial expressions. For this study, SES was operationalized in terms of the educational attainment of participants: subjects were divided according to whether they had or had not received a 4-year college degree, since "high-school- and college-educated individuals differ considerably in life outcomes such as job stability and occupational prestige."[22] As predicted, subjects who had not received a 4-year college degree had higher empathic-accuracy scores than college-educated participants.[23] These results were then extended in various ways. For example, the researchers ran a separate study that tested empathic accuracy during face-to-face interactions. Again, the basic prediction was confirmed: "lower-class actors were more accurate than their upper-class counterparts in judging the spontaneous emotions of their interaction partner."[24]

What are we to make of this research? Kraus nicely summarizes the findings of his own and others' studies of SES by suggesting that the individuals with lower SES had limited access to material resources, which creates what he calls a *contextualized self*: a self that is greatly attuned to the socio-moral context in which one finds oneself, including changes both in the environment and in the behaviors of others.

The contextualized selves allow individuals from lower-class backgrounds to respond more quickly and accurately to significant environmental challenges. As such, we find that people from these backgrounds tend to be more aware of and accurate in reading others' emotions during interactions than their upper-class counterparts.[25]

If I may extend Kraus' explanation a bit, it seems as if an individual with lower SES will be more inclined than an individual with higher SES to recognize that *he is but one person among many*, and that the thoughts, attitudes, and behaviors of other people *matter* in a way that demands his attention. By contrast, the increased access to such resources enjoyed by individuals with higher SES creates what Kraus calls a *solipsistic self*: "a self that is less aware of the external environment and more attuned to internal goals, thoughts, and motivations."[26] In other words, an individual with higher SES likely will *not* see himself as but one person among many, but rather, will be more inclined to see himself as *the only one in his environment whose interests really matter*.

Assuming all of this is on point, it should not be surprising that the incredible wealth and status that Madoff accrued over the years of his apparently legitimate investment business might *itself* have played a role in enabling him to perpetrate such a heinous crime. Apparently, being on the higher end of the SES spectrum not only makes a person more likely to engage in generally unethical behavior—for example, cutting off other drivers on the road—but also, and more significantly for my purposes, affects the way a person perceives others, making him less likely to see others as appropriate objects of moral concern. But SES is a complicated matter, involving not just monetary wealth, but also things like education and occupational prestige. So, it is still hard to tell, from studies like those just described, what role, if any, *the money itself* might occasionally play in blunting a person's moral sensibilities.

In that light, I want to mention another study. Kouchaki et al. sought to explore the possible effects of "exposure to the construct of money" upon moral decision-making.[27] In other words, what effect might it have upon the likelihood that people—regardless of SES—will engage in unethical behavior if we *simply get them to think about money* ahead of time? The researchers began the study by having 50 undergraduates at a university in the United States complete a descrambling task "in which words were arranged to make sentences that either referenced money or did not." For those participants who were randomly assigned to the money condition, half of the descrambled sentences referenced money (e.g., "She spends money liberally"), and half were neutral (e.g., "She walked on grass"). For participants assigned to the control condition, all of the descrambled sentences were neutral. After completing the descrambling task, participants were then given a series of 13 scenarios, and asked to rate on a scale of 1 ("not at all likely") to 7 ("highly likely") how likely it is that they would engage in the behavior described in the scenario. Several of the scenarios describe behavior commonly deemed unethical. Here is one such scenario:

> You work as an office assistant for a department at a University. You're alone in the office making copies and realize you're out of copy paper at home. You therefore slip a ream of paper into your backpack.[28]

Participants in the money condition—people who were merely primed to *think* about money ahead of time—indicated that they were more likely than those in the control condition to engage in unethical behavior. Another study had subjects participate in a deception game, and found that money-primed participants were significantly more likely than their neutral counterparts to lie for personal benefit.[29]

So money priming apparently makes subjects more likely to engage in unethical behavior. But why? The researchers hypothesized that money priming has the effect of placing subjects into a particular frame of mind, and that people are more likely to engage in selfish behavior while in this frame of mind. They call it a "business decision frame":

> Along these lines, we assume that the mere presence of money can elicit a business decision frame [...] which prompts the objectification of others (either those who stand to be directly harmed, or others more broadly construed) in a cost-benefit analysis in which self-interest is pursued over others' interests.[30]

To test whether money priming really does elicit a business decision frame, the researchers ran another study, priming participants either by using the same word-descrambling task or by showing them images of money-related or neutral subject matter (e.g., pictures of currency or landscapes, respectively). Participants then engaged in a word-completion task in which they were given some, but not all, of the letters of some word, and then asked to complete the word on their own. The basic idea was that participants' choice of words would reveal implicit thought processes—specifically, it would reveal whether or not subjects in the money condition had been primed to think "business related thoughts." So, for instance, if a participant chose to complete "M A R _ _ _" by spelling "market" instead of things like "marble," "marine," or "marvel," that was taken as an indication that he or she was thinking in business-related terms. Sure enough, "the only significant predictor of number of business related words was prime."[31]

What are we to make of these studies? As the researchers themselves put it, "money may be a more insidious corrupting factor than previously appreciated, going well beyond the often lamented 'love of money' to touch even those not overtly motivated by greed."[32] And importantly, for my purposes, money's insidious effect goes beyond simply making people more likely to engage in selfish, or otherwise unethical, behavior. Apparently, the introduction of money into some socio-moral context can have the effect of placing people into a business-like frame of mind. From this frame of mind, other people come to be regarded either as means to, or as obstacles in the way of, the satisfaction of our own interests. In other words, from the business decision frame, we are more likely to objectify—or, as I prefer to put it in this context, *commodify* other people.

I began this chapter by asking: What connection, if any, might there be between money and evil? What is it, exactly, about money that disposes a person to evil? A full answer to these questions will have to wait until Chap. 7, wherein I explain what evil is. But for now, I can foreshadow a bit by saying that, if there *is* an interesting relationship between money and evil, it is a matter of how money can change the way we see others—not as people whose interests matter just like our own, but rather as objects, or commodities, to be used (even *used up*) in the pursuit of our own interests.

We can see now that Bernie Madoff was a kind of "perfect storm" of psychological influences. For one thing, he was motivated by very deep insecurities and an obsessive desire to feel as though he belonged to the "exclusive club" of Wall Street, which had once excluded him. For another, his personality strongly resembles that of a psychopath. Finally, the personal wealth and socio-economic status that he acquired over the course of his career had the effect of making his moral universe even more solipsistic, and of making other people out to be mere commodities. One wonders if there was ever a moment when Madoff was *not* in a "business decision frame."

HUMAN TRAFFICKING: MODERN-DAY SLAVERY

There is no better example of the commodification of persons than that of human trafficking, but understanding why this is the case requires that we first understand why "human trafficking" is such an unfortunate term for the practice—or rather, practices—to which it refers. Probably due in no small part to its association with the *drug* trafficking industry, people often assume that human trafficking is mostly a matter of the illegal *movement* and *sale* of humans. This is unfortunate for a couple of reasons. First, as a simple conceptual point, to the degree to which we think of trafficking as primarily a matter of *moving* humans from one location to another, it will be difficult to distinguish between trafficking and *smuggling*. But as Siddharth Kara explains, there are important differences between these two activities.

> Most Mexicans who cross illegally into the Unites States are smuggled rather than trafficked. The difference is subtle but important. Smuggling involves an individual who chooses to cross the border illegally, alone or with the help of an expert. Whereas smuggled individuals are technically on their own once they cross the border, a trafficking victim's ordeal is just beginning, as the trafficker sells the victim to an exploiter or exploits the victim himself. Trafficking is thus smuggling with coercion or fraud at the beginning of the process and exploitation at the end.[33]

The second reason it is unfortunate that people think of trafficking in terms of movement is that it misses out on what, *morally*, is surely a more significant aspect of human trafficking—namely, the conditions into which victims are trafficked, which typically involve violent and degrading forms of exploitation, and often last for years at a time. Kara states:

> [T]rafficking is not about movement; it is about slavery. The transatlantic slave trade from the sixteenth to the eighteenth centuries involved the trafficking of eleven million Africans across thousands of miles to work as slaves

on plantations. Why is this historical practice termed a slave trade and the same practice today termed trafficking?[34]

Human trafficking is thus a prime example of the commodification of persons because it is really just slavery with a different name.

From a business perspective, drug trafficking and human trafficking are the first and second most successful criminal enterprises in the world, respectively. On the one hand, in terms of annual revenue, the gap between these two crimes is actually quite large. For instance, in 2004 alone, the drug industry generated revenues of $322 billion, compared to just $152.3 billion of annual revenues from the trafficking and exploitation of slaves.[35] But on the other hand, as Kara explains, human trafficking may nonetheless be *more profitable* than drug trafficking, since, "[u]nlike a drug, a human female does not have to be grown, cultivated, distilled, or packaged. Unlike a drug, a human female can be used by the customer again and again."[36] Among forms of human trafficking and exploitation, sex slavery is by far the most profitable.

> Only 4.2 percent of the world's slaves are trafficked sex slaves, but they generate 39.1 percent of slaveholders' profits. To benchmark the astounding profits generated by the exploiters of sex slaves, one need look no further than the fact that the global weighted average net profit margin of almost 70 percent makes it one of the most profitable enterprises in the world. By comparison, Google's net profit margin in 2006 was 29.0 percent, and it is one of the most profitable companies in the United States. The same figure for Microsoft was 28.5 percent; for Intel, 14.3 percent. General Electric posted a 12.8 percent profit margin; AT&T, 11.7 percent; and Exxon Mobil, 10.8 percent.[37]

In addition to having lower *costs* than the drug industry—allowing for greater profits—the *risks* associated with human trafficking and exploitation are lower as well. In India, for instance, the Narcotic Drugs and Psychotropic Substances Act of 1985 stipulates a financial penalty of up to 200,000 INR (rupees) for drug trafficking, which is 100 times more severe than the financial penalty currently levied against sex traffickers.[38] And unfortunately, unlike laws against drug trafficking, laws against human trafficking and exploitation are rarely enforced, since it is commonplace in almost every country in which slavery exists for law enforcement officials to be complicit in the crime—by, for example, turning a blind eye, regularly accepting bribes from exploiters, or even abusing the slaves themselves. The United Nations Office on Drugs and Crime (UNODC) released a report in 2009 based on criminal justice and victim assistance data from 155 countries. According to the report, as of 2007–2008, only 60 % of the countries covered by the report had recorded a single human trafficking-related conviction.

The human trafficking industry is incredibly large, but determining its exact size (or even a trustworthy approximation) is also incredibly difficult. In 2004, the United States government estimated that between 600,000 and 800,000 people are illegally trafficked across international borders each year, and these are still the numbers most often quoted by governments and nongovernmental organizations (NGOs) across the globe.[39] But in 2006, the United States Government Accountability Office issued a statement alleging that these numbers are questionable, due to "methodological weaknesses, gaps in data, and numerical discrepancies."[40] For instance, the 2004 numbers do not take into account victims of internal trafficking, that is, trafficking from one location to another within the same country. Since 2006, the UNODC has assumed primary responsibility for assessing trafficking data for the United Nations; but in that same year, the UNODC ceased offering estimates of the numbers of trafficking victims until more analysis of the relevant data could be conducted. As of today, there are no "official" estimates of the size and scope of human trafficking. But, taking into account both inter- and intra-national trafficking, Kara's calculations put the total number of annual trafficking victims between 1.5 and 1.8 million, almost half of which are trafficked for commercial sexual exploitation.[41] Of the total number of trafficking victims each year, about 80 % are women or girls, most of whom are trafficked into sex slavery. Men and boys are typically trafficked into conditions of either forced labor or forced begging.[42] Occasionally, children are trafficked for purposes of either adoption or—perhaps most despicably—organ harvesting.

While circumstances may differ greatly, depending upon such factors as the conditions out of which victims are taken and the purposes for which they are trafficked, there is nonetheless a recognizable "pattern" to most instances of sex trafficking. To begin, the victims almost always come from conditions of extreme poverty. The women and girls, especially, are typically not only very poor, but also live in cultures in which their rights are regularly neglected or abused, even by their own husbands and fathers. This makes them especially vulnerable to traffickers who promise either well-paying jobs or marriage to wealthy businessmen in other countries.

[I]t was not difficult to see why Sindhupalchok was a breeding ground for sex slaves. When women were not being raped or abused, they were unable to survive due to a lack of education, job opportunities, and basic rights. Who could blame them for fleeing? If you were a beaten, starving woman in Sindhupalchok and an agent offered you a job in a carpet factory or marriage to a fine Indian businessman, you would take the first bus out of town. [...] Nothing could possibly be worse than the life you were already living.[43]

Most sex trafficking begins with an act of deception, but victims are also acquired via coercion, abduction, or sale; sometimes, desperate parents sell their children to traffickers on the condition that some fraction of their earnings will be sent back to the family.

The next step is for the traffickers to "break the spirits" of their victims. For victims of sex trafficking, this often involves a brief stay at an intermediate location—for example, a room in a hotel en route to their final destination—where they are starved and drugged, and repeatedly beaten and raped, for anywhere from a few days to several weeks. This mistreatment seems to be specifically designed in order to destroy the victims' wills, to remove whatever remains of their autonomy, and to transform them into unresisting automatons. After being beaten, starved, and drugged in a similar "spirit-breaking" effort, Albanian children trafficked into Greece for forced begging developed a name for themselves: *robots*. "In the town of Fier, a man told me the children adopted this name because this is how they felt when they were forced to take drugs to beg day and night with no sleep."[44]

Eventually, trafficked women and girls are sold either to street pimps or to owners of brothels, massage parlors, or dance clubs, and told that they will have to work in order to pay off this "debt" to the slaveholders—which immediately begins to grow with interest. And of course, in most cases, this "work" consists in forced prostitution. Some brothels are quite large, like those of India's two notorious red-light districts—Kamathipura and Falkland Road—which house up to a few hundred prostitutes at a time, half of which are usually minors and slaves. Brothels in Thailand typically hold a few dozen slaves, who often await selection behind a pane of glass in a room known as an "aquarium." These women and children usually work every day of the week, for 12–18 hours per day. They are often raped up to 30–40 times per day.

Karla Jacinto became a victim of sex trafficking at the age of 12. Sexually abused and neglected from a young age, Jacinto was lured into sex slavery by a 22-year-old man who promised her a better life. But after a few months of showing her the affection that she craved, showering her with gifts, and so forth, he forced her into sex work. For the next four years, Jacinto was raped every day of the week, by up to 30 men per day. At one point during her captivity, police raided the hotel where she was working.

> She thought it was her lucky day—a police operation to rescue her and the other girls.

Her relief quickly turned to horror when the officers, about 30 she says, took the girls to several rooms and started shooting video of them in compromising positions. The girls were told the videos would be sent to their families if they didn't do everything they asked.

> "I thought they were disgusting. They knew we were minors. We were not even developed. We had sad faces. There were girls who were only 10 years old. There were girls who were crying. They told the officers they were minors and nobody paid attention," Karla says. She was 13 years old at the time.[45]

Jacinto was finally rescued at the age of 16—after she had been raped, by her count, more than 43,000 times.

As sex slaves grow older, they become less desirable to customers, many of whom are taking advantage of the industry in order to satisfy pedophilic desires. So, often times, when a woman is no longer deemed sufficiently profitable by a pimp or brothel owner, she will either be killed or "promoted" to a position from which she can recruit younger girls. In fact, as the UNODC reports, there is a remarkably high rate of participation of women in the trafficking industry: "In Europe, for example, women make up a larger share of those convicted for human trafficking offenses than for most other forms of crime."[46] But it is worth noting that many of these women are former victims themselves. In India, these sex-slaves-turned-madams are known as *gharwalis*. On a research trip to Kamathipura—one of the aforementioned red-light districts in India—Kara spoke with a *gharwali* named Silpa, who had herself been trafficked out of the Nepalese district of Sindhupalchok 16 years earlier.

> I asked Silpa if it concerned her that young Nepalese girls like Urmila were performing sex work in her brothel.

"These girls are safer here than their homes where their father will beat them and their uncle will make sex with them. Here, no harm can come to them unless they misbehave. You see, men are weak. We can take what we want if we give them the prize in our legs. This is the lesson I teach my girls."[47]

And so the cycle repeats itself, with commodified victims commodifying other victims. Silpa's understanding of her own moral status—and consequently, that of the younger victims now under her "care"—had been so warped by years of mistreatment that she apparently believed rape can be harmless depending on where it occurs.

In a recent story for their "Freedom Project," a coordinated investigative project aimed at "shining a spotlight on the horrors of modern-day slavery," CNN interviewed both a former sex slave, named Patricia, and also the man who enslaved her, who asked not to be identified (the story refers to him as "Gustavo").[48] Gustavo grew up in a relatively modest household—his father a schoolteacher, his mother a housewife. He was never abused, abandoned, or neglected. But by his own admission, and from a very early age, Gustavo was obsessed with wealth and power. "What they [his parents] were able to give me was never enough," he says. In fact, at one point, Gustavo migrated illegally into the United States, and for three months, earned as much as $700 a week—a fortune compared to the average income of those in his hometown. "Still, Gustavo says, it was not enough."

It was his own greed and lust for power that drove Gustavo into the sex trafficking industry. At age 18, he began traveling to various Mexican cities and towns, approaching young, vulnerable girls, and promising them love, gifts, and a better life. Then, almost immediately after they agreed to leave their hometowns with him, he would force them into prostitution by threats, coercion, and abuse. "The faster they fall in love and leave with you," Gustavo explains, "the faster the business starts making money and the less cash you have to spend showering them with gifts and going out. To me, the girls meant a source of income, merchandise you can buy, trade or sell."[49] Worlds apart from Bernie Madoff, here we have another person acting from a "business decision frame," from which others come to be regarded as mere commodities to be used for personal gain.

Like Karla Jacinto, Patricia—one of Gustavo's victims, who bravely testified against him in court—was trafficked through the Mexican town of Tenancingo. Despite its small population of about 13,000, Tenancingo is known internationally as a major sex trafficking hub. For the aforementioned story, CNN correspondent Rafael Romo showed Patricia video of a festival that takes place in Tenancingo, during which hundreds of young men, dressed as pimps, whip each other in a show of strength and dominance. After showing her the video, Romo asks Patricia, "What does Tenancingo mean to you?" She smiles, uncomfortably, and responds, "Evil. Evil. And, I think, people without a heart."[50]

Intensive Animal Farming

Before concluding this chapter and moving on to the more straightforwardly philosophical second part of the book, I want to briefly consider another plausible candidate for a money-related evil: intensive animal farming, or "factory farming," as it is perhaps more commonly known. To be clear, I will not here defend the claim that intensive animal farming *is* evil. Nor am I claiming that intensive animal farmers are evil people. For reasons I take to be obvious, I want to put off any such claims until after I have explained exactly what I think it means for an action, institution, person, or whatever, to be evil—which I do in Chap. 7.

Ultimately, as far as my thoughts about evil are concerned, whether or not intensive animal farming counts as an evil will depend primarily upon the place or status of animals in the moral community—which I define as the set of things whose interests matter morally—and I do not intend to take a stance on that issue anywhere in this book. My reason for briefly discussing intensive animal farming is this: there are many, philosophers and non-philosophers alike, who—primarily due to their views about the moral status of animals—*do* regard this practice as not merely morally wrong, but evil, and the theory of evil that I defend in Chap. 7 implies that they may be right about this. To begin to see why, let us here attend to the relevant details.

Perhaps the first thing to say about the conditions of intensive animal farming is that they are getting much better. The contemporary debate about the humaneness of animal farming is widely thought to have originated with Ruth Harrison's 1964 book *Animal Machines*. Twenty years later, M.W. Fox of the Humane Society of the United States wrote that most intensively farmed animals were still "being treated inhumanely or with indifference," and that one of the reasons for this was that "we lack objective, scientific knowledge about the behavioral requirements and emotional, subjective world of animals."[51] But much has changed since the mid-1980s, and we have advanced quite far in our knowledge of animals' needs. For instance, as von Keyserlingk et al. report, "considerable progress has been made in understanding and measuring animal pain, and a large and rapidly developing body of scientific literature on pain assessment and prevention [is] now available for farm animals."[52]

As an example of the usefulness of this research on animal pain, consider the practices of dehorning and disbudding in cows and calves. Unlike tail docking, which arguably provides no real benefit to the animal, dehorning and disbudding are widely regarded as crucial to keeping farmed cattle safe—for example, by reducing risk of injury from displays of aggression. But the evidence makes plainly clear that these procedures cause pain to the animals. And thanks to advancements in animal pain research, we now also know that local anesthetics neither fully mitigate the pain nor provide adequate postoperative pain relief. However, also due to these advancements in research, farmers, veterinarians, and other caretakers have been able to determine which methods for dehorning and disbudding cause the least and most controllable types of pain, and also which combinations of medication and treatment are most effective for pain prevention and relief. Unfortunately, many farmers both within the United States and around the world still dehorn and disbud cattle with little-to-no regard for the welfare of the animals, for example, by neglecting to provide any pain-relieving medication at all. However, this does not change the fact that, due to a large and growing body of "objective, scientific knowledge about the behavioral requirements and emotional, subjective world of animals," gained mostly in order to improve the living conditions of animals, intensive animal farming has undergone significant moral progress over the past few decades. Interestingly, though controversially, scientists are now able to use gene-editing technologies to breed hornless cattle, thereby eliminating any need to engage in dehorning practices.[53]

According to the EU's Animal Welfare Quality Program, there are four basic criteria for assessing the well-being of a farm animal: (1) *good feeding*: the animal should be free from hunger and thirst; (2) *good housing*: the animal should be free from dangerously high or low temperatures, and should be free to move around and rest in comfort; (3) *good health*: the animal should be free from illness and injury; and (4) *appropriate behavior*. What is appropriate behavior? Basically, this general criterion stipulates that animals should be free to engage in behavior deemed "natural" to their species—for example, cows ought to be free to graze, since they are grazing animals—as long as the behavior is not harmful to themselves or other animals. The "appropriate behavior" criterion also includes more specific criteria for healthy animal–human relations, and also for the absence of living conditions that might induce fear, frustration, or other forms of emotional distress in the animal.[54]

By nearly all accounts, most animal farms in the United States are doing at least a minimally decent job at satisfying the first three criteria. But, according to a recent Pew Commission report, "In the United States, the 'Appropriate Behavior' criteria seem to be the hardest to satisfy and generally are not met for food animals."[55] Some might defend farmers on this point by citing the inherent difficulties of determining the "naturalness" of certain animal behaviors. For instance, as von Keyserlingk et al. explain, "given the genetic changes that have occurred among cattle because of artificial selection, there is great difficulty in deciding what their natural life is."[56] And of course, in many ways, farm animals would be worse off in more natural living conditions, due to increased exposure to harsh weather, predators, and diseases.

Ultimately, though, the reason that intensive animal farms in the USA so often fail to meet the conditions stipulated by the *appropriate behavior* criterion is pretty simple: of the four criteria for animal well-being, it contributes the least to the profitability of the animals. It is obviously good *for the animals* that they are well fed, sheltered, and protected against disease and injury. But all of these things are also good *for the farmers*, since they directly contribute to the overall productivity of the farm. On the other hand, it is significantly less clear how an animal's being free to engage in "natural" behaviors, or how an animal's being free from conditions that might induce fear or frustration, could have a significant enough impact on a farmer's bottom line in order to justify (financially) his taking measures to ensure that these criteria are met. In other words, in order for the various conditions laid out by the *appropriate behavior* criterion to matter to an intensive animal farmer, one of two things would have to be the case. Either (a) he would have to be convinced that satisfying these conditions would make the farm more profitable, or (b) he would have to come to see the animals as things whose interests matter independently of their financial value. But alas, as much as things have improved since Harrison published *Animal Machines* back in 1964, it seems many of these farms are still run by what she then called "a generation of men who see in the animal they rear only its conversion to human food."[57]

What I have not done in this section is to detail the many specific harms and horrors that unfold on a daily basis on intensive animal farms around the world. But to be clear, I have avoided these details not because I think them morally unimportant, but because I think them ultimately irrelevant to the matter of whether or not intensive animal farming is *evil*. Let me briefly explain before moving on.

At the beginning of Chap. 3, I made the claim that, *if* genocide is evil, what *makes* it evil cannot be the number of deaths, or even the amount of physical harm done to the victims—for we can imagine actions that many would deem genocidal, but that do not involve any deaths, or even great amounts of serious physical harm, such as the forced sterilization of all of the women of a particular race or ethnic group. Surely things like massive death counts and immeasurable amounts of serious harm are relevant to genocide's status as a deeply tragic and morally heinous crime. But what makes it *evil* will have to be some other feature. Likewise, on the assumption that intensive animal farming is evil—which, again, is not a claim to which I intend to commit myself here—it would be very easy to think that the relevant evil-making feature has something to do with the unimaginable physical harms done to the animals. But, as with genocide, while observations about extreme harm are surely relevant to the *wrongness* of intensive animal farming, I nonetheless think they are irrelevant to its status as *evil*. Rather, if intensive animal farming *is* evil, its status as evil has more to do with the peculiar way in which the victims are seen or regarded by the perpetrators—in this case, as with human trafficking, the perpetrators apparently see the victims as mere commodities. Or, to borrow the words of "Gustavo" from the previous section, intensive animal farmers typically see the animals as nothing more than "a source of income, merchandise you can buy, trade or sell."

Concluding Thoughts

As I noted at the outset, it is very common for people to claim—even in non-religious settings—that money, or the love of money, is the root of at least many forms or instances of evil. Now, to be sure, when people make this claim, probably most times, they mean only to be denouncing greed, which is still a far cry from making any substantive claims about a relationship between money, or greed, and the kind of evil at issue in this book. On the other hand, there seem to be good reasons for at least suspecting that there *is* such a relationship. For one thing, as I noted in Chap. 1, there are some actions or events whose moral gravity just cannot be fully captured by terms like "bad" or "wrong." As Haybron puts it, "Prefix your adjectives ['wrong' and 'bad'] with as many 'verys' as you like; you still fall short. Only 'evil', it seems, will do."[58] As I understand his point here, this is not to say that things like serial murder and genocide are *not* very wrong. They are. Rather, it is to say that, even after we denounce these actions as very bad or very wrong, there is a kind of moral remainder—something warranting the language of "evil." Plausibly, the same is true of some of the actions described in this chapter. They *are* very wrong. But, that is not *all* they are, morally.

Furthermore, while it may seem as if Bernie Madoff could have nothing of significance in common with sex traffickers and intensive animal farmers, I think they actually do resemble each other in at least one respect, which has emerged as a kind of theme throughout this chapter. As the empirical literature described earlier suggests, thinking in money-related terms can have the effect that we come to regard others as commodities—things to be used for the purpose of improving our financial lot. Now, it is one thing to see others as commodities, where "commodity" simply refers to a useful or valuable thing. If Rachel is an excellent salesperson, then her boss will likely regard her as something of a commodity in this sense: her excellence as a salesperson is good for the business. It is another thing, however, to see others as *nothing but* commodities, that is, to see them as if their value were exhausted by their usefulness or profitability.[59] This seems to be the way in which Madoff regarded many of his investors. It also seems to be the way in which human traffickers regard the people they traffic. It also seems to be the way in which many intensive animal farmers regard the animals on their farms. And if my arguments in Chaps. 6 and 7 are on point, then this may place Madoff, human traffickers, and (depending upon one's views about animals' status in the moral community) intensive animal farmers squarely in the discussion of moral evil.

We are now at a turning point in the book. As I explained in the introductory chapter, the purpose of Part I is to survey a variety of case studies (Chaps. 2–4) in order to gather information on which to base the more theoretical discussions of Part II. This has taken us through literature on the nature and implications of psychopathy, the social and psychological origins of genocide, and from Wall Street to the streets of India's red-light districts. Now, in Part II of the book, I turn to philosophical issues related to moral evil. In the next chapter, I address a few puzzles or problems that threaten to undermine philosophical theories of evil. Then, in Chap. 6, I critique a number of prominent theories of evil, holding these theories accountable to the psychological data gathered from Part I. Finally, in Chap. 7, I offer my own theory of evil, defending it, in part, by showing how well it can accommodate the cases discussed in Part I.

NOTES

1. Weiser (2011).
2. Brenner (2008).
3. Seal (2009).
4. These words come from Robert Rosso, a convicted drug trafficker who for a while was serving his life sentence at the same federal prison as Madoff (Fishman 2010).
5. Henriques (2013).
6. Fishman (2011).
7. Fishman (2011).
8. Creswell and Thomas Jr. (2009).
9. Fishman (2011).
10. Fishman (2010).
11. Creswell and Thomas Jr. (2009).
12. Creswell and Thomas Jr. (2009). In Blair et al. (2005), the authors explain that, while psychopathy is equally common at all socio-economic levels, violent antisocial behavior is significantly more common at lower socio-economic levels (especially among psychopaths). Part of the explanation, they suggest, is that psychopaths at higher socio-economic levels are afforded greater resources, in terms of education, upbringing, vocational options, etc., than those at lower socio-economic levels. So while we should not be surprised to find wealthy psychopaths engaging in antisocial behavior—they are, after all, psychopaths, and as such, lack certain psychological inhibitions against such behavior—it also should not come as a surprise that their instrumental aggression is often aimed at things other than victims' bodies (e.g., wallets, bank accounts).
13. See Piff et al. (2012) for brief descriptions of several such studies. See also Kraus and Keltner (2009); Kraus, Côté, and Keltner (2010); and Kraus, Piff, and Keltner (2011).
14. Kraus and Keltner (2009: 100).
15. Kraus and Keltner (2009: 101).
16. Kraus and Keltner (2009: 102). For the record, gender also predicted social engagement to a significant degree, with women being generally more engaged than men.

17. See Gallo and Matthews (2003) for a review.
18. Stellar et al. (2012).
19. Stellar et al. (2012: 452). Spirituality was also a significant predictor of compassion. So was gender, even if less significantly. Ethnicity was not a significant predictor.
20. Kraus, Côté, and Keltner (2010). For the record, there has been some movement lately—especially among philosophers—toward conceiving "empathic accuracy" in less explicitly *inferential* terms. According to some, for instance, we are sometimes able to *directly perceive* (and thereby to *know*, non-inferentially) the emotions of others in the expressive displays of those emotions, for example, facial expressions and vocalizations. See, for example, Abell and Smith (2016), especially Sias and Bar-On, "Emotions and Their Expressions."
21. Kraus et al. (2010: 1717).
22. Kraus et al. (2010: 1718).
23. Kraus et al. (2010: 1718).
24. Kraus et al. (2010: 1720).
25. Kraus (2014).
26. Kraus (2014).
27. Kouchaki et al. (2013).
28. Kouchaki et al. (2013: 56).
29. Kouchaki et al. (2013): 57.
30. Kouchaki et al. (2013: 55).
31. Kouchaki et al. (2013: 56).
32. Kouchaki et al. (2013: 53–54).
33. Kara (2009: 189).
34. Kara (2009: 4–5). In the same context, Kara suggests another reason for thinking it unfortunate that so many focus on the *movement* aspect of trafficking: as a consequence of this, most abolitionist policies and programs focus more on "thwarting movement across borders than on shutting down the modern plantations to which those individuals are being moved. Such tactics have proved overwhelmingly futile because the modes of transport are numerous (by ship, vehicle, plane, train, foot), the costs of transport are miniscule, and the sources of potential slave labor are nearly limitless" (2009: 5).
35. Kara (2009: 222).
36. Kara (2009: x).
37. Kara (2009: 19).
38. Kara (2009: 209).
39. See Kara (2009: 17) and Shelley (2010: 5).
40. U.S. Government Accountability Office (2006: 2).

41. Unlike officials in the United States Department of State, who declined to explain their methodology to Kara when he reached out to them in 2006, Kara provides a lengthy explanation of the method by which he reached his own numbers (2009: 264–266).
42. United Nations Office on Drugs and Crime (2009: 10–11).
43. Kara (2009: 78).
44. Kara (2009: 148).
45. Romo (2015a).
46. United Nations Office on Drugs and Crime (2009: 10).
47. Kara (2009: 52).
48. Romo (2015b).
49. Romo (2015b).
50. Romo (2015b).
51. Fox (1984: 65).
52. von Keyserlingk et al. (2009: 4105). The authors here refer readers to Weary et al. (2006) for a review of the scientific literature on animal pain assessment and prevention.
53. Interestingly, though controversially, scientists are now able to use gene-editing technologies to breed hornless cattle, thereby eliminating any need to engage in dehorning practices..
54. Pew Commission on Industrial Farm Animal Production (2008: 37).
55. Pew Commission on Industrial Farm Animal Production (2008: 35).
56. von Keyserlingk (2009: 4106).
57. Harrison (1964: 1).
58. Haybron (2002: 260).
59. The distinction here is very similar to one made by Kant in his famous Principle of Humanity, one of the formulations of the Categorical Imperative. Kant distinguishes between (a) treating another as a means to some end, and (b) treating another *simply* as a means, or as a *mere* means. According to Kant, while there is nothing wrong with treating another as a means, it is always wrong to treat, or regard, another person as a mere means. I discuss these issues at greater length in Chap. 7, in the service of developing my theory of evil.

References

Abell, Catharine, and Joel Smith, eds. 2016. *The Expression of Emotion: Philosophical, Psychological and Legal Perspectives.* Cambridge: Cambridge University Press.

Blair, James, Derek Mitchell, and Karina Blair. 2005. *The Psychopath: Emotion and the Brain.* Oxford: Blackwell.

Brenner, Marie. 2008. Madoff in Manhattan. *Vanity Fair*, December 31. Accessed October 21, 2015. http://www.vanityfair.com/style/2009/01/madoff200901.

Creswell, Julia and Landon Thomas Jr. 2009. The Talented Mr. Madoff. *The New York Times*, January 24. Accessed October 21, 2015. http://www.nytimes.com/2009/01/25/business/25bernie.html.

Fishman, Steve. 2010. Bernie Madoff, Free at Last. *New York Magazine*, June 6. Accessed November 4, 2015. http://nymag.com/news/crimelaw/66468/.

———. 2011.The Madoff Tapes. *New York Magazine*, February 27. Accessed November 3, 2015. http://nymag.com/nymag/rss/all/berniemadoff-2011-3/.

Fox, M.W. 1984. Empathy, Humaneness, and Animal Welfare. In *Advances in Animal Welfare Science*, eds. M.W. Fox and L.D. Mickley, 61–73. Washington, DC: The Humane Society of the United States.

Gallo, L.C., and K.A. Matthews. 2003. Understanding the Association between Socioeconomic Status and Physical Health: Do Negative Emotions Play a Role? *Psychological Bulletin* 29: 10–51.

Harrison, Ruth. 1964. *Animal Machines: The New Factory Farming Industry*. London: Vincent Stuart Publishers.

Haybron, Daniel. 2002. Moral Monsters and Saints. *The Monist* 85(2): 260–284.

Henriques, Diana B. 2013. Madoff Victims, Five Years the Wiser. *The New York Times*, December 7. Accessed November 4, 2015. http://www.nytimes.com/2013/12/08/business/madoff-victims-five-years-the-wiser.html.

Kara, Siddharth. 2009. *Sex Trafficking: Inside the Business of Modern Slavery*. New York: Columbia University Press.

Kouchaki, M., K. Smith-Crowe, A.P. Brief, and C. Sousa. 2013. Seeing Green: Mere Exposure to Money Triggers a Business Decision Frame and Unethical Outcomes. *Organizational Behavior and Human Decision Processes* 121: 53–61.

Kraus, Michael W. 2014. How the Rich are Different from the Poor. *Psychology Times*, Summer 2014. Department of Psychology, University of Illinois at Urbana-Champaign.

Kraus, Michael W., and Dacher Keltner. 2009. Signs of Socioeconomic Status. *Psychological Science* 20(1): 99–106.

Kraus, Michael W., Stéphane Côté, and Dacher Keltner. 2010. Social Class, Contextualism, and Empathic Accuracy. *Psychological Science* 21(11): 1716–1723.

Kraus, Michael W., Paul K. Piff, and Dacher Keltner. 2011. Social Class as Culture: The Convergence of Resources and Rank in the Social Realm. *Current Directions in Psychological Science* 20(4): 246–250.

Pew Commission on Industrial Farm Animal Production. 2008. Putting Meat on the Table: Industrial Farm Animal Production in America. http://www.ncifap.org/.

Piff, Paul K., Daniel M. Stancato, Stéphane Côté, Rodolfo Mendoza-Denton, and Dacher Keltner. 2012. Higher Social Status Predicts Increased Unethical Behavior. *Proceedings of the National Academy of Sciences* 109(11): 4086–4091.

Romo, Raphael. 2015a. Human trafficking survivor: I was raped 43,200 times. *CNN.com*, November 10. Accessed November 12, 2015. http://www.cnn.com/2015/11/10/americas/freedom-project-mexico-trafficking-survivor/.

———. 2015b. Jailed trafficker meets victim who put him away. *CNN.com*, November 12. Accessed December 9, 2015. http://www.cnn.com/2015/11/12/americas/freedom-project-mexico-jailed-trafficker/.

Seal, Mark. 2009. Madoff's World. *Vanity Fair*, March 31. Accessed October 21, 2015. http://www.vanityfair.com/news/2009/04/bernard-madoff-friends-family-profile.

Shelley, Louise. 2010. *Human Trafficking: A Global Perspective*. Cambridge: Cambridge University Press.

Stellar, Jennifer E., Vida M. Manzo, Michael W. Kraus, and Dacher Keltner. 2012. Class and Compassion: Socioeconomic Factors Predict Responses to Suffering. Emotion 12(3): 449–459.

U.S. Government Accountability Office. 2006. Human Trafficking: Better Data, Strategy, and Reporting Needed to Enhance U.S. Antitrafficking Efforts Abroad [GAO-06-825]. Accessed December 13, 2015. http://www.gao.gov/new.items/d06825.pdf.

United Nations Office on Drugs and Crime. 2009. Global Report on Trafficking in Persons. http://www.unodc.org/documents/Global_Report_on_TIP.pdf.

von Keyserlingk, M.A.G., J. Rushen, A.M. de Passillé, and D.M. Weary. 2009. *Invited Review*: The welfare of dairy cattle—Key concepts and the role of science. *Journal of Dairy Science* 92: 4101–4111.

Weary, D.M., L. Niel, F.C. Flower, and D. Fraser. 2006. Identifying and preventing pain in animals. *Applied Animal Behavior Science* 100: 64–76.

Weiser, Benjamin. 2011. Judge Explains 150-Year Sentence for Madoff. *The New York Times*, June 28. Accessed October 21, 2015. http://www.nytimes.com/2011/06/29/nyregion/judge-denny-chin-recounts-his-thoughts-in-bernard-madoff-sentencing.html?_r=0.

PART II

The Philosophy of Evil: Puzzles, Problems, and Theories

CHAPTER 5

Three Puzzles about Evil

For the past few decades, philosophers have given more and more attention to the nature of moral evil. What began in the early parts of the second half of the twentieth century as a suspicion that people like Hannah Arendt might be right in thinking that evil exists as a separate moral category, in need of its own analysis, has since blossomed into its own subgenre of moral philosophy, with new theories of evil springing up left and right. But as interesting and exciting as this theoretical work can be, it risks being completely undermined by a number of similarly interesting challenges. In this chapter, I wrestle with three of the most significant of these challenges.

The first of the three challenges, or puzzles, goes something like this: Isn't evil fundamentally *incomprehensible*? And if so, what hope could there be for a useful or insightful *theory* of evil, if one of the central purposes of such a theory is to help us to comprehend it? Many believe that the term "evil" refers primarily to those wrongdoers or wrongful acts of which sense cannot be made. We call things "evil" only when, and because, they defy our understanding. But if that is right, then anyone attempting to offer a theory of *what evil is*—like those I critique in the next chapter, and my own in Chap. 7—is bound to fail. For if the theory succeeds in making sense of its subject matter, then the subject matter must not have been evil all along, since evil is something of which sense cannot be made. So even if the theory succeeds, it fails that is, as long as people are right to assume that evil is fundamentally or essentially incomprehensible.

The second puzzle is related to the first. As you may recall, I began the book by recounting an experience I recently had while teaching a course on moral psychology. Before starting a unit on psychopathy, I had my students write down their responses to the following questions: Can a person be genuinely morally evil? If no, why not? And if yes, what would it take for someone to count as genuinely morally evil? And of the 13 students in the class, 11 answered that, no, there is no such thing as a genuinely evil person. I will say more about their explanations below, but for many of them, the gist was this: people who commit especially heinous moral crimes, like serial murder or genocide, must have some sort of mental illness—like, perhaps, psychopathy; and if they are mentally ill, then it would be either incorrect or unfair (or both) to consider them morally evil. In short, these people are not *evil*, they are *sick*.

This second puzzle is related to the first in that it is essentially another way of saying that once something can be understood—in this case, once a person's mental health status is sufficiently understood—it ceases to be a plausible candidate for evil. But the implication of this second puzzle is a bit different. If the first puzzle implied that there cannot even be theory of evil, this second puzzle implies only that no such theory could ever be *useful*, at least insofar as it is supposed to apply to persons. For even if an evil person exists as a kind of theoretical posit, this does not help us to understand any part of the actual moral universe, since no person has ever actually been evil, but only sick.

Finally, the third puzzle arises out of some work done in social psychology over the past half-century or so. In light of hundreds of psychological studies, some of which will be described later in this chapter, there appears to be little room for doubting that we are often guilty of what psychologists call "the fundamental attribution error." Basically, when it comes to explaining or predicting people's behavior, we tend to overestimate the importance of their traits (of character or personality) and to underestimate the importance of factors in the environment or situation in which the behavior occurs. In other words, we attribute too much causal significance to the person, and do not attribute enough to the situation—hence, the attribution error.

Some philosophers have used this social psychological research as evidence for a much more startling claim. Contrary to a very long tradition in moral philosophy, often associated with Aristotle, according to which the ethical life is a matter of developing and exercising virtuous traits of character, these philosophers argue that the psychological evidence suggests that there really are no such things as virtuous traits of character.

Gilbert Harman, for instance, with some of this research in mind, writes, "Empirical studies designed to test whether people behave differently in ways that might reflect their having different character traits have failed to find relevant differences."[1] From this, he concludes,

> [O]rdinary attributions of character traits to people may be deeply misguided, and it may even be the case that there is no such thing as character. [...] Since it is possible to explain our ordinary belief in character traits as deriving from certain illusions, we must conclude that there is no empirical basis for the existence of character traits.[2]

Even if Harman and other so-called situationists would go too far to deny the reality of moral character altogether, there may nonetheless be empirical grounds for denying the reality of a particular trait, or feature, of moral character—namely, *evil*. Indeed, this is one very natural way of interpreting some recent work by psychologist Philip Zimbardo. If Zimbardo is right, there are no evil *persons*. Rather, there are evil *situations*—that is, situations whose influence is such as to compel (otherwise decent) people to perform evil actions. This is what he calls "the Lucifer effect."

I think situationists are mistaken. Moral character is real. And unfortunately, some people's characters are evil. So in the third and final substantive section of this chapter, I will analyze and respond to some of the evidence and arguments offered by those who would suggest otherwise (especially Zimbardo).

Evil and Incomprehensibility

Perhaps understandably, the association of incomprehensibility with evil is often based upon the way people typically *react* to instances of purportedly evil actions, events, persons, or whatever. As Feinberg nicely explains,

> Our strong tendency, I think, is to reserve the word "evil" for wrongdoing and harm causing that we cannot understand. [...] The apparent evil person is one whose conduct not only shocks and angers us but also puzzles us. "How could such a thing have happened?" is often our first question in response to evil, and before we begin to search for an answer, we fear that no explanation is possible.[3]

Feinberg goes on to say that one of the hallmarks of evil behavior is that it is "done for no intelligible reason," and that "people understandably find [it] extremely perplexing."[4] Likewise, Stephen de Wijze suggests that part of what separates evil behavior from behavior that is merely wrong or bad is that the former is able to evoke "horror, disgust, and incomprehension."[5] Lance Morrow insists that, while evil is "distinctly *real*," and while "it is possible to *describe* evil," nonetheless, "it is ultimately not possible to *understand* evil."[6]

In his book *Evil Men*, Dawes describes a couple of paradoxes associated specifically with the task of writing about evil, one of which has to do with the trauma suffered by victims of evil actions or events. As Dawes puts the paradox, "[the trauma] is unspeakable, but must be spoken."[7] Here he references Cathy Caruth, who argues that something important gets lost in translation when people try to write about evil, especially when the purpose of writing about evil is to make some sense of it. "Beyond the loss of precision," she writes, "there is another, more profound, disappearance: the loss, precisely, of the event's essential incomprehensibility, the force of its affront to understanding."[8] Since the whole second half of my own book is aimed at making sense of the category of moral evil, I want to examine this claim that evil is essentially incomprehensible. What, exactly, is meant by this?

To say that evil is incomprehensible is to say that it cannot be understood, but there are at least two different senses of "cannot" that might be at work in such a claim. My two-year-old son cannot understand what it is like to be married. He also cannot understand what it is like to be a married bachelor. But his inability to understand these things is rooted in two very different phenomena. In the first case, the "cannot" is a *psychological* matter: he cannot understand what it is like to be married because marriage—and all that marriage involves—goes too far beyond his current conceptual resources. He just does not "get it," and there is nothing he can do—aside from growing older and getting married—to change this. In the second case, the "cannot" is a *logical* matter: he cannot understand what it is like to be a married bachelor because, as a matter of logical necessity, there can be no such thing. In the first case, it is something *about my son* that inhibits his understanding; in the second case, it is something *about the subject matter* that inhibits his understanding (or anyone's, for that matter). Likewise, when people claim that evil is incomprehensible, that it cannot be understood, the "cannot" here might be either psychological or logical—in other words, it is either something *about us* that inhibits our understanding, or else it is something *about evil*. I will address these two points in reverse order, starting with the logical point.

It is relatively common for people to think that evil is somehow a matter of perverse motivational states: evil actions are those that are perversely motivated, evil people are those with perverse motives, or whatever. A motivational state is perverse when it involves or represents a kind of reversal of the way rational moral agents are *supposed* to be motivated—as, for example, when Milton's Satan says, "Evil be thou my good." An agent acts perversely, then, if he pursues something bad *because it is bad*, or if he does something wrong *because it is wrong*. In his own discussion of evil, Kant refers to such an agent as a "diabolical being," and then suggests that this label could never apply to rational agents like us.[9] Sussman explains,

> Kant takes the moral law to be a basic principle of practical reason, and so truly diabolical motivation would involve an agent performing an act simply because he sees there to be a particularly strong if not conclusive reason against so acting. Acting diabolically would be analogous to adopting a belief just because it was self-contradictory, decisively disproven, or in some other way manifestly absurd.[10]

In other words, just as it is contained in the concept of *belief* that belief aims at the truth—so that one cannot genuinely believe what one also takes to be either self-contradictory or decisively disproven—many also believe that it is contained in the concept of *intentional action* that it is rational, or reasons-responsive, and aims at the good. In other words, anyone who acts intentionally does so because he believes there are good reasons for so acting. But, presumably, to think that an action is *bad* or *wrong* is to think there is "a particularly strong if not conclusive reason *against* so acting." So how could it even be possible to intentionally act perversely?

This is perhaps why Cole thinks that the "pursuit of the suffering and destruction of others for its own sake," the supposed hallmark of pure evil, "verges on the incomprehensible."[11] After all, suffering is universally regarded as a bad thing *in itself*. It would be one thing to pursue suffering for the sake of something further, something that one takes to be good, like some personal benefit. But it would be another thing entirely to intentionally pursue a bad thing like suffering for the sake of nothing but the bad thing itself. (Even sadists and masochists pursue suffering for the sake of something good—namely, pleasure.) If the above assumptions about *intentional action* and *thinking x is bad* are correct, then Cole's notion of a "purely" evil action sounds incomprehensible in virtue of being conceptually incoherent: pure evil would be a matter of acting for reasons that one thinks are reasons for acting otherwise. This, again, is like believing something for reasons that one thinks are reasons for believing otherwise, such as that the proposition is to be believed self-contradictory or has been decisively disproven. It is hard to know what that could even mean.

If all of this is right, then evil cannot be understood for basically the same reason that my two-year-old son cannot understand what it is like to be a married bachelor: because in each case, the thing to be understood involves a kind of conceptual incoherence. Understanding is barred not by our own intellectual or psychological shortcomings, but by the logic of the concepts themselves.

Even if one does not accept the above assumptions about *intentional action* and *thinking x is bad*, though, one might still think that evil is incomprehensible for a different reason. That is, one might think that perverse motivational states, while involving no logical or conceptual confusion at all, are nonetheless too foreign from our ordinary, human ways of thinking for us to be able to understand them. After applying the label "diabolical being" to anyone perversely motivated, Kant assures his readers that the label is not "applicable to the human being."[12] Sussman picks up on this, noting,

> Yet if Kant holds that the very idea of doing evil for its own sake is incoherent, why would he claim that a diabolical will is not a possibility for *the human being* in particular? This qualification suggests that Kant may not be ruling out the logical possibility of a diabolical will, even though he denies that such a will could ever be present in creatures like us.[13]

Immediately after claiming that the perverse motivational state involved in pure evil "verges on the incomprehensible," Cole goes on to say,

> [It verges on the incomprehensible] to such an extent that many thinkers have argued that mere human beings are incapable of it. Human agents can only be evil in the impure sense, while pure evil, if it exists at all, belongs to the supernatural.[14]

So perhaps, like Sussman's alternative reading of Kant, Cole means only to be saying that evil is incomprehensible in virtue of being too far removed from ordinary human psychology. We cannot understand evil for basically the same reason that my two-year-old son cannot understand marriage: because in each case, the thing to be understood lies sufficiently far outside the subject's knowledge, experience, and available concepts. As long as my son is a two-year-old child, he will never understand something so complicated as marriage. And as long as we are human, we will never understand something so strange as evil.

For my own part, I reject any claim to the effect that evil is literally incomprehensible. Evil may be difficult to understand, but it is a mistake to think that it *cannot* be understood—in either of the above two senses of "cannot." For one thing, I am not convinced that there is anything conceptually incoherent about perverse motivation, but pursuing the relevant issues any further would take us too far afield into the philosophy of action.[15] Besides, close attention to human behavior seems to reveal that perverse motivation is actually a quite common psychological phenomenon. I quote Sussman at length:

> In discussing perversity, philosophers have tended to focus on its more dramatic moral forms, such as spite, malice, and *Schadenfreude*. Yet perversity is not confined to the ethical. Kitsch is appealing because of its conspicuous aesthetic flaws, and movies such as *Showgirls* and the remake of *The Wicker Man* have become minor classics by dint of their exquisite and unrelenting awfulness. In winter, it is hard to see the fragile beauty of icicles or a freshly frozen pond without having some urge to smash them. We smell or taste spoiled food just because we expect it to be disgusting, or find ourselves attracted by someone's ugliness (the "*jolie-laide*"). We are fascinated precisely by what we consider repellent about corpses, deformities, and grisly accidents. Perfectly sane and happy people sometimes have inexplicable but very real urges "to throw themselves from high places or under approaching tube-trains." We may even court physical pain out of a vivid and immediate appreciation of its unpleasantness. Even apart from the complex dynamics of sexual masochism, most of us know what it is like to pick at a scab or worry a loose tooth simply because of the peculiar way in which doing so hurts.[16]

In all of these ways and others, it seems as if human beings are regularly motivated in perverse ways. We may not be fully diabolical in the Kantian sense, but it would nonetheless be a mistake to claim that perverse motivation is too far removed from ordinary human psychology to even be comprehensible.[17] As a matter of fact, human beings are *often* attracted to things that are bad *because* they are bad. So evil, insofar as it involves perversity, is apparently not incomprehensible in the psychological sense either.

More importantly, however, the assumption that evil is somehow related to perverse motivational states is itself a mistake. As I explained in Chap. 1, this idea that evil is a matter of causing suffering for the sake of suffering, or of pursuing the bad because it is bad, or of doing wrong for no other reason than that it is wrong, may make for a plausible *religious* conception of evil—hence, the appropriateness of referencing Milton's Satan. But this book aims to shed light on a thoroughly *secular*, thoroughly *public*, conception of moral evil. To that end, theorists would do well to take Haybron's advice:

> [T]he concept [of evil] has its home, not in moral theory, but in ordinary moral discourse. [...] Theorists of evil ought not to treat the term as if it were up for grabs, to be defined however it suits our moral theories. If we wish to take the moral phenomena seriously, we need to take the ordinary notion seriously.[18]

One way to "take the ordinary notion seriously" is to attend closely to the kinds of persons, actions, events, or whatever, that people ordinarily consider evil. This is precisely why I chose to organize the book in the way that I have. Psychopathic serial murderers like Ted Bundy and genocidal leaders like Adolf Eichmann are widely regarded as evil people, but they are certainly *not* people whose motivational states were perverse in exactly the sense described above. So either these people are not *really* evil, since their motivational states were not perverse in the above sense or they *are* evil, and evil is apparently not a matter of perversion. If we really are to "take the ordinary notion [of evil] seriously"—by, for example, taking for granted that those people most widely regarded as evil really are instances of the ordinary notion—then it seems we have to accept that evil is not a matter of perversion, but of something else.

Isn't there still some sense, though, in which serial murder, genocide, human trafficking, and other instances and figures of evil are incomprehensible? After all, while people do ordinarily regard people like Bundy and Eichmann evil, they also ordinarily describe the actions of these men as if they were incomprehensible. So if we really are going to "take the ordinary notion seriously," it seems we have to accommodate *some* sense in which evil is incomprehensible.

Ultimately, what I suspect underlies the common assumption that evil is incomprehensible is a confusion of two different kinds of understanding. To get a sense of the difference, consider two cases in which a person might say, "I understand." In the first case, someone explains to Bob how photosynthesis works, and after thinking about it for a moment, he says, "I understand." In the second case, Bob's close friend Mary apologizes to him for missing his birthday party, explains her reasons for being absent, expresses her regret, and after thinking about it for a moment, he says, "I understand." In the first case, Bob *understands* in what might be called the *epistemic* sense of understanding—he now knows how photosynthesis works. But in the second case, while he does understand his friend's absence in the epistemic sense (he now knows why she was absent), this is apparently not the *only* sense in which he understands.

Oftentimes, when we say of another person's actions that we "understand" them, we imply not only that their reasons for acting are knowable, or intelligible, but even further that their reasons are *good*, or *good enough*. By saying, "I understand," we issue a kind of hypothetical endorsement of a person's actions or reasons for acting; that is, we agree that their reasons "pass rational muster," as it were, when compared with the significance of whatever they are supposed to be reasons *for*. To understand, in this sense, is to allow that the other person's behavior is justified to some degree, which is not the same thing as saying or implying that *we* would do the same thing in the same circumstances. For example, suppose that Mary missed the party because she was not feeling well, and the party itself was not especially important. In this case, it is easy to imagine Bob replying, "I understand," even if he also believes that he would not have behaved in the same way as Mary—maybe Bob is someone who takes birthday parties very seriously, so much so that he would not let a little illness keep him from attending, but he also recognizes that others might perfectly reasonably prioritize birthday parties lower than he does.

On the other hand, if Bob and Mary were very close friends, and both knew that Bob would be leaving the country permanently on the morning after the party, then he likely would not reply, "I understand," on learning that she missed the party only because she was not feeling well. For in this case, even allowing for idiosyncratic priorities, preferences, and so forth, Mary's reasons are not good enough. When presented with another person's reasons, we try to imagine ourselves doing the same thing *for those reasons*—again, leaving room for idiosyncrasies and personal preferences—and when we cannot even imagine ourselves sharing the other person's reasons or motives, we cannot understand why they would do such a thing, even if we know what their reasons are or were. Call this further sense of understanding the *empathetic* sense of understanding. Empathetic understanding implies epistemic understanding, but not vice versa.

If evil is incomprehensible, it is incomprehensible because it cannot be understood in the empathetic sense. We cannot understand the actions of Ted Bundy or those who perpetrate genocide or engage in human trafficking, because we cannot imagine ourselves ever being motivated to do those things. Feinberg says as much when he attempts to clarify his own use of the term "incomprehensible":

> The puzzlement that is part of the natural response to evil is of the same kind, though more intense and disturbing, as that of a jealous lover, who says, "I cannot understand what she sees in him." In both cases the speaker puts himself imaginatively in the other person's shoes and finds that his experiences in those shoes are quite different from those of others. Killing children has no more appeal to our imagination than it has influence on our motives, and one cannot easily conceive of any people being otherwise. If there are such people (and, alas, it appears that there are), then most of us cannot identify with them.[19]

But this does not mean that evil cannot be understood in the epistemic sense of understanding. For it surely can. We can know what motivates serial murderers, perpetrators of genocide, and human traffickers—indeed, criminal profilers, forensic psychologists, and other aides or agents of law enforcement make a living out of knowing a wrongdoer's motives or reasons for acting.

Primo Levi—Jewish Italian chemist, writer, and Holocaust survivor—once urged that we not even try to understand the Nazi leaders. For, as he explained,

> To understand a proposal or human behavior means to 'contain' it, contain its author, put oneself in his place, identify with him. [... But] no normal human being will ever be able to identify with Hitler, Himmler, Goebbels, Eichmann, and endless others.[20]

In the same context, Levi warns, "Perhaps one cannot, what is more one must not, understand what happened, because to understand is almost to justify."[21] But surely this is only correct if we are referring to understanding in the empathetic sense. Again, forensic psychologists are in the business of *understanding* the actions of serial murderers and other criminals, in the epistemic sense of understanding; but surely they are not thereby also in the business of *justifying* such actions, even a little bit. Why not think that the same sort of understanding (without justifying)—that is, understanding in the epistemic sense—is also possible even with respect to supporters and perpetrators of genocide?[22]

A more interesting—not to mention haunting—question is this: Is it really the case that we cannot understand evil in the empathetic sense of understanding? Is Levi right to suggest that "no normal human being will ever be able to identify with" perpetrators of evil? Recall (from Chap. 3) Alison Des Forges' remarks about the actions of the Hutu murderers:

> This behavior lies just under the surface of any of us. [...] The simplified accounts of genocide allow distance between us and the perpetrators of genocide. They are so evil we couldn't ever see ourselves doing the same thing. But if you consider the terrible pressure under which people were operating, then you automatically reassert their humanity—and that becomes alarming. You are forced to look at these situations and say, "What would I have done?" Sometimes the answer is not encouraging.[23]

As we will see below, there is actually some evidence from social psychology to support her claim here. But for now, I will say only this: if there is any truth to what Des Forges says—about evil behavior lying just under the surface of any of us, ready to be revealed by just the right amount or type of pressure, temptation, or other situational influence—then we might reasonably wonder whether evil really is impossible to understand in the empathetic sense.

Evil is not essentially incomprehensible. It *can* be understood, at least in the epistemic sense of understanding. Although I will not defend the claim here, it may even be understandable, to some degree, in the empathetic sense as well. When we say that evil is incomprehensible, I think this is best understood as hyperbole. It is not that evil actions are literally *unintelligible*, or that the motives of evil persons *cannot be known*. Rather, it is only that we find it *incredibly difficult* to imagine ourselves ever doing such things, or sharing such reasons or motives.

Evil and Moral Agency

As I mentioned earlier, when asked whether or not a person can be genuinely morally evil, most of my students answered that, while perhaps there can be evil *actions*, there cannot be evil *persons*. Here is a sampling of their responses and explanations:

> "No evil people, just evil acts. For example, murder is evil, but if the murderer has paranoid schizophrenia and believed he had to murder, is he evil? Or just mentally ill?"

"This person would need to be completely self-caused in his actions. Genetic or social factors (upbringing, current social climate) cannot play a role. [...] It is likely that we would categorize such a person as a psychopath and tell either a physiological or psychological exculpating story."

"No, I do not think a person can be genuinely morally evil, because I believe that people are good. [...] I believe that people are a product of their environment. Thus, if someone constantly performs 'evil' acts, I believe it stems from their upbringing or environment."

"No. A person is simply a result of his/her upbringing, life experiences, and genetics. [...] If a person does possess the attributes typically associated with being evil, it is only because external factors in their life forced them to be that way."

"No [...] I don't think there are evil people, but there are evil actions. I think people's choices are ultimately affected too greatly by external experiences and biological factors, such that the choices a person makes that may be evil are not caused by some intrinsic 'evil-ness'."

Now, let me try to translate my students' concerns—which, I should say, are both legitimate and likely shared by many others—into some language that will be easier to use in the discussion to follow. Philosophers sometimes distinguish between *moral agents* and *moral patients*. Basically, something counts as a moral patient as long as it has interests that matter morally, or as long as it can be (morally) *wronged*. Most adult humans are moral patients, but so are very young children and at least some nonhuman animals. If I were to abuse my neighbor's pet dog, there might be some sense in which I thereby wrong my neighbor, but there is also an obvious sense in which I wrong the dog. This is because both my neighbor and his dog are moral patients. Moral agents, on the other hand, are things that can legitimately be held morally responsible for their actions. Here again, most adult humans are moral agents, but many think that very young children and nonhuman animals are not. If my neighbor's dog were to dig up my lawn, I might blame the neighbor (for his failure to supervise the animal), but I would not blame the dog.

Moral agents are legitimate candidates for moral responsibility, but this does not mean that moral agents are always morally responsible. I am a moral agent, and as such, I am prima facie morally responsible for my behavior. But we can easily imagine an episode in which I might be temporarily excused from moral responsibility: suppose, for example, unbeknownst to me, someone slips a psychotropic drug into my drink; the drug has the effect of inducing a psychotic episode during which I hallucinate that the person sitting next to me is trying to kill me; and in self-defense, I strike the person. The drug does not remove me from the set of things called moral agents, but it does seem right to say that the drug subverts or compromises my moral agency, such that the violent act was not really an *exercise* of my moral agency. And for that reason, most will agree that I should not be held morally responsible for that particular act. Being a moral agent makes you a candidate for moral responsibility; exercising moral agency makes you morally responsible.

Presumably, my students (and the many others who share similar concerns) think it is either incorrect or unfair (or both) to consider people like those discussed in Chaps. 2–4 morally evil because they believe either (a) that these people are not *moral agents*—for example, maybe psychopaths belong in the same category with very young children and nonhuman animals—or (b) that, even if they *are* moral agents, they were not really *exercising moral agency* when they performed their evil actions—for example, maybe paranoid schizophrenia has the same effect upon a person's capacity to exercise moral agency as the psychotropic drug. So, ultimately, what I want to explore in this section is whether or not there is any truth to these beliefs as they might apply specifically to people like Bundy, Eichmann, Madoff, and the others.

Before going any further, though, we need to address one potential source of confusion or misunderstanding. Some of the above remarks from my students could be interpreted as implying something to the effect that, as long as there *are* genetic, socio-environmental, or biochemical explanations of a person's behavior, then that person cannot be a moral agent—or at least, that person was apparently not *exercising* moral agency when performing the action or actions in question. But if this is right, then no humans are moral agents—or have ever exercised moral agency—since there are genetic, socio-environmental, or biochemical explanations of *all* human behavior. So, presumably, just as Bundy and Eichmann ought not to be condemned as evil, people like Martin Luther King Jr. and Susan

B. Anthony ought not to be praised as good. (Indeed, one of the other students, not quoted above, insisted that there are no genuinely evil people because moral labels like "good" and "evil" are not appropriately applied to *people* at all.) But I will proceed on the assumption, which I take to be a bit of moral commonsense, that there *are* good people, and that their status as good is not threatened in any way by the fact that their behavior can be explained in genetic, socio-environmental, or biochemical terms. So it cannot be the bare fact that Bundy's actions, for instance, can be explained in similar terms that makes an evaluative label like "evil" inappropriate when applied to him. Rather, there must be something peculiar *about* the genetic, socio-environmental, or biochemical explanations of his actions, something that does not apply just as well to people like Martin Luther King Jr. and Susan B. Anthony. For instance, maybe the actions of purportedly evil people are best explained in terms of their moral agency being subverted or compromised by mental illness. Bundy was, after all, a psychopath.

What *is* moral agency, then, that it could be subverted or compromised by something like mental illness? Unfortunately, there simply is not enough space here to offer a complete account of moral agency, which would require discussion of too many aspects of human psychology, including things like intention, emotional intelligence, a capacity to regulate mood, and so forth. It would also require interaction with some of the literature on moral character, which I would rather put off for the next section. So, instead, I shall focus here upon two capacities in particular that many people take to be necessary for moral agency. (Indeed, many take them to be mutually sufficient for moral agency, so that anyone exhibiting both of these capacities is prima facie morally responsible for his or her behavior. But I will not defend that claim here.)

The first is a capacity for moral knowledge.[24] This, presumably, is why very young children and nonhuman animals are so often excluded from the category of moral agents, that is, not because they *do not* know what things are right, wrong, and so forth, but rather because they *cannot* know such things. Having a capacity for general moral knowledge, that is, knowledge of general moral truths, such as that it is wrong to punish the innocent, good to help people in need, and so forth, is required for counting as a moral agent. But *exercising* moral agency seems to require a more specific capacity: a particular action counts as an exercise of moral agency only if the agent could reasonably be expected to know whatever truths—moral or otherwise—are relevant to the moral status of that particular action. So, for instance, in the above scenario with the psychotropic drug, while I may still count as a moral agent during the episode, the effect of the drug is to interfere with my ability to know all of the truths relevant to the moral status of my action, such as that the person sitting next to me is not really trying to kill me.

Notice that moral agency depends only upon a capacity to know, and not upon actual possession of the relevant knowledge. This is to accommodate the commonsense intuition that it is sometimes okay to hold people morally responsible as long as they *could have* and *should have* known better, that is, as long as they could reasonably have been expected to know that their actions were morally wrong, morally required, or whatever. Granted, it is sometimes very difficult to know when such expectations are in fact reasonable. But any plausible theory of moral responsibility or moral agency has to allow for the possibility of *culpable ignorance* if it is to accord with our everyday practice of holding people responsible. This commonsense intuition even has a role to play in the practice of law, in principles like *ignorantia juris non excusat* ("ignorance of the law does not excuse") and *ignorantia juris neminem excusat* ("ignorance of the law excuses no one").

Can mental illness subvert or compromise a person's capacity for moral knowledge? Surely it can. Some mental disorders, like schizophrenia and dementia, wreak havoc on a person's ability to see things as they are in reality. The symptoms of these disorders are typically characterized as "psychotic," where psychosis, even in clinical contexts, is understood in terms of being out-of-touch with reality. Patients with schizophrenia are especially prone to hallucinations and delusional beliefs, that is, beliefs that are typically false, diverge significantly from what most others believe, and are held with great conviction even in the face of strong counter-evidence.[25] It seems fair to conclude, then, that schizophrenia likely interferes with a person's capacity to exercise moral agency, in much the same way as the psychotropic drug in the above example. So there may be some truth to the first student's comment: if a person murders in the midst of a hallucinatory or delusional schizophrenic state, it may be a mistake to consider him evil—since doing so implies blameworthiness, but people should not be blamed for actions that were not exercises of their moral agency.

For this reason, I think a distinction ought to be made between *psychopathic* serial murderers like Ted Bundy and *schizophrenic* serial murderers like Richard Trenton Chase. In the mid-1970s, Chase was involuntarily committed to a mental hospital, where he was diagnosed with paranoid schizophrenia. Not long after his release, Chase killed six people, raping and cannibalizing some of the victims. Horrific as his actions were, there is nonetheless some reason to think that he was unable to know that they were morally wrong—for example, as he later explained to a criminal profiler for the FBI, he was convinced at the time of the murders that his life was under constant threat from Nazi UFOs, and that he had to kill others in order to save himself. If this is true, then perhaps Chase is no more blameworthy for his terrible actions than I am for striking the person sitting next to me while under the influence of the psychotropic drug. And if he is not even blameworthy, then presumably, he also is not evil.

There are important differences, however, between *psychosis* and *psychopathy*, differences that are directly relevant to moral agency. Psychosis is the result of malfunctioning cognitive faculties—faculties whose function, loosely put, is to put the mind in touch with reality. Psychopathy, on the other hand, is a disorder of the personality. Psychopaths are not prone to hallucinations or delusional beliefs. They are able to see things, and to form true beliefs about the things they see, just as well as anyone else. Indeed, as we saw in Chap. 2, when forced to do so, they are able to discern moral right and wrong almost as reliably as a typical college student. So while there may be good reasons for thinking that Chase's murders were not genuine exercises of moral agency, the same reasons do not apply to psychopathic serial killers like Bundy. When it comes to the relationship between mental illness and moral agency, we have to resist the temptation to treat all mental illnesses alike.[26]

We also must resist the temptation to infer from someone's apparently deviant or false moral beliefs that his or her capacity for moral knowledge has been somehow subverted or compromised. For it is also possible that his or her capacity for moral knowledge has simply been *incorrectly or poorly used*. We assume that, if someone has a capacity for knowledge about x, then, as long as he or she is of sound mind, that capacity will actually produce knowledge about x. So, when someone has seriously deviant or badly mistaken beliefs about x, we infer either that she never had a capacity for knowledge about x in the first place, or else that she is not of sound mind—in other words, we assume that her capacity for knowledge has been subverted or compromised by some temporary or permanent mental condition or disorder. But the initial assumption and associated inference are both incorrect. Some people still believe the earth is flat; most others believe it is round. Some believe there are alien species living on other planets; many others do not. Some believe the universe is only six or seven thousand years old; others believe it is much, much older. For any of these debates, if one side is right, then the other side is badly mistaken, and, depending upon the case, perhaps also seriously deviant. But, tempting as it may be, we cannot infer from this either that they are unable to know better or that their capacity to know has been compromised by mental illness. Maybe they are just being culpably irresponsible with their own epistemic capacities—by, for example, ignoring known counter-evidence, demonizing those with opposing beliefs, refusing to consider other points of view, treating nonexperts as experts, and jumping hastily to conclusions that suit their own interests.

Genocidal leaders like Adolf Eichmann and Pauline Nyiramasuhuko had moral beliefs—whole ideologies, even—that were badly mistaken, and, depending upon the point of reference, also seriously deviant. But we are no more licensed in this case than we were in the above cases to infer that either Eichmann or Nyiramasuhuko was actually *unable* to know better—either because they lacked a capacity for moral knowledge or because their capacity for moral knowledge had been subverted or compromised by mental illness. Here, too, the deviant and false beliefs are just as likely to be the results of culpable epistemic irresponsibility. As "crazy" or "insane" as their beliefs may seem to the rest of us, we cannot assume they are literally the effects of some mental illness or disorder.

Nomy Arpaly complains about a scarcity of what she calls "moral imagination" in the world today, writing,

> In contemporary interpersonal interaction, psychiatric categories—including scientifically legitimate ones—are often used as awkward substitutes for moral imagination [...] or as an awkward cover for lack thereof [...] I think there is a lot to say, morally speaking, for moral imagination: specifically, I think there is a lot to say for being conscious of the fact that the other person's inner world is not only (as Kant would remind us) as real or as important as our own, but potentially very, very different from our own—and not an iota less real or important for that.[27]

The person who lacks moral imagination assumes that psychiatric categories must be relevant whenever he cannot imagine how others would believe or behave in the ways that they believe or behave, because, deep down, the person who lacks moral imagination assumes that every person's "inner world" is basically the same, barring some disruptive or debilitating mental illness. I echo Arpaly's call for greater moral imagination, and note that a morally imaginative person will resist making hasty inferences from the presence of very deviant and false moral beliefs to conclusions to the effect that the believer's capacity for moral knowledge has been subverted or compromised in some way.

Earlier, I said that I would be focusing on two capacities widely regarded as necessary for moral agency. The first was a capacity for moral knowledge. And to this point, I have argued that there are no good reasons either for thinking that the people discussed in Chaps. 2–4 did not have a capacity for moral knowledge, or for thinking that their capacity for moral knowledge had been subverted or compromised by something like mental illness. Thus far, then, there do not appear to be any good reasons for withholding moral responsibility from these evildoers. So let us turn now to the second capacity that many take to be necessary for moral agency: the ability to do otherwise.[28]

Even if Bundy, or Eichmann, or Madoff, was fully capable of knowing that his actions were seriously morally wrong, if for some reason he was *unable to do anything but* commit such evil actions, then most would agree he should not be held morally responsible for them. After all, agency seems to require that the agent has a genuine choice between two or more actions, both (or all) of which he is equally *capable* of performing, even if he is not equally *likely* to perform each action. So, are there any reasons for thinking that the people discussed in Chaps. 2–4 were actually *unable* to do otherwise, and not simply *unlikely* to do otherwise? Of course, one reason would be if causal determinism were true. This is the idea that every action or event that occurs is necessitated by a combination of antecedent actions, events, or conditions and the laws of nature. If Bundy's actions were completely causally determined, then there is an obvious sense in which it was no longer open to him, at the time of a particular murder, to refrain from murdering.

For my own part, I would rather avoid the thorny debate about causal determinism and its compatibility (or not) with free will, or the ability to do otherwise. So, instead, I will say only this: if your reason for denying that Bundy was able to do otherwise is that you think causal determinism is true, then you will also have to deny that people like Martin Luther King Jr. and Susan B. Anthony could have done anything other than what they did. And so, once again, your grounds for denying that Bundy and others are evil will force you also to deny the moral commonsense that some people are genuinely good. I suspect that, for most readers, that will be too big a pill to swallow. (For the record, none of the students quoted above clearly endorses anything quite as strong as causal determinism, but they do say things to which the same basic point applies. For instance, they say that "external factors in their life *forced* them to be that way," or that "people's choices are ultimately *affected too greatly* by external experiences and biological factors." But it is hard to see how these concerns would not cut equally well in both directions, rendering people like Martin Luther King Jr. and Susan B. Anthony not moral heroes to be praised, admired, and emulated, but mere amoral socio-biological outcomes.)

Short of causal determinism, then, what reason could there be for thinking the people discussed in Chaps. 2–4 could not have done otherwise? Here again, it seems we are led back into a discussion of mental illness and its effect upon a person's moral agency. And, perhaps, even more so than before, we need to be very careful here. As I said above, when it comes to the relationship between mental illness and moral agency, it is imperative that we not treat all illnesses alike. In some cases, it does seem as if an illness or disorder has the effect of subverting or compromising a person's ability to do otherwise. This is perhaps clearest in the case of something like Tourette syndrome. As far as agency is concerned, Tourettic outbursts are akin to things like seizures or nervous twitches: the person suffering from these conditions has little-to-no control over when the relevant behavior occurs. It would not make sense to say something like, "She shouldn't have had the seizure right in the middle of the ceremony"—because, presumably, the seizure victim could not have done otherwise. Likewise, it would not make sense to say of a person that you know has Tourette syndrome, "He shouldn't have shouted those obscenities so close to the children"—since, again, it presumably was not within his power to refrain from the outburst. In this case, the person's agency is *bypassed* by the disorder, so that it seems fair to say that *the disorder caused the behavior, not the agent.*

The same is not true, however, with respect to other disorders, like psychopathy. Psychopaths may be more likely to engage in violent behavior, but it would nonetheless be a mistake to say that psychopathy *causes* violent behavior. Bundy was a known psychopath, and his psychopathic personality certainly made it easier for him to brutalize so many victims, for example, by desensitizing him to their suffering and by enabling him to be convinced of his own ability to escape capture. But, the psychopathy did not *make him do it*. After all, while *all* people with Tourette syndrome engage in some sort of motor or vocal tics, only an exceedingly small percentage of psychopaths engage in serial murder.[29] Indeed, the majority of psychopaths live relatively normal and successful lives. So, if the disorder somehow *bypassed* Bundy's agency, effectively *forcing* him to commit serial murder, why does it not do the same for other psychopaths? As we saw in Chap. 2, psychopaths show an increased propensity to both reactive and instrumental forms of violence or aggression. But as I explained there, psychopathy—rooted as it is in amygdala dysfunction—does not *cause* this behavior. Rather, it only removes a kind of behavioral inhibitor that typically keeps the rest of us from acting this way. In simpler terms, psychopathy leaves open a door that is usually shut for the rest of us, but it is still up to the psychopath to walk through it.

In a similar context, Arpaly argues that, in chalking a particular action or behavior up to a mental disorder, we risk undermining the meaningfulness of the fact that the person engaged in *that* sort of behavior and not others.

> Imagine an artist who spends long, excited nights in a state of inspiration which results in good art. Imagine this artist being told that his state of inspiration is actually a mild form of mania known as 'hypomania' and that hypomania is a symptom of a disease, just like a diabetes-induced seizure or the ravings of Tourettic person. [...] If his art is central to the life or identity of the artist, [...] such statements are likely to make [him] feel either insulted or devastated: a natural reaction to being told that the meaningful activities and concerns of your life are like sneezes. [...] But there is no reason for [him] to be devastated, and there is good reason for [him] to be insulted. While the fact that one is prone to hypomanic episodes is a brute "hard-ware" fact, it is probably no accident that the artist spends his hypomanic times creating rather than doing things that other hypomanics do: shopping, gambling, or having sex. It is probably also not an accident that he produces a certain kind of art and not another, and that his art is good rather than bad.[30]

Even if the hypomania is *part of the explanation* of how he is able to create good art, it is not the hypomania that chooses to create; it is not the hypomania moving the brush or molding the clay; it is not the hypomania that knows to alter the tone of a patch of color in order to suggest a difference of light; and so forth. These things are only even meaningful insofar as they are credited to the artist, and not to the disorder. The same is true of Bundy: psychopathy may be part of the explanation of how he was able to commit such heinous acts, but it was still Bundy who chose to commit them, to commit them in the way that he did, and so forth.

Besides, if there were really any question about a psychopathic serial murderer's ability to do otherwise, we need look no further than the accounts of the killers themselves. Near the end of Chap. 2, I recounted two stories—one from Kemper, the other from Bundy—in which a psychopathic serial murderer made a decision to try to refrain from murder, and was successful in doing so. I concluded then,

> If these accounts are to be believed [...] they imply that both Bundy and Kemper actually had a remarkable capacity for exerting higher-order control over their own violent and sadistic impulses, and could use this capacity either to spare potential victims or to ensure their demise.

Psychopathy does not remove a person from the class of things called moral agents. Nor does it subvert or compromise a person's agency by rendering him or her unable to do otherwise. Again, it may make certain sorts of antisocial behavior *more likely*. But it does not make that behavior *inevitable*. Barring further evidence, then, that any of the people we discussed in Chaps. 2–4 suffered from illnesses or conditions that effectively forced them to commit evil acts by bypassing their agency in Tourette-like fashion, I cannot see any good reason for believing that they were unable to do otherwise than what they did.

There is much more that could be said and explored in this section. For instance, I have said nothing about the effect that a particularly bad upbringing is supposed to have on a person's candidacy for evil: if a serial rapist or murderer was neglected, abused, and tortured as a child, would it then be inappropriate to consider him evil? For the record, I think similar things can be said about bad upbringings as were said here about psychopathy. Again, the question is not whether or not the upbringing is *relevant* to his actions later in life. (It surely is.) Rather, the question is more complicated than that: what, exactly, is the causal connection between the upbringing and the later evil behavior? Did the upbringing *make him do it*? Or did it simply make it more likely that he would exercise his own agency in *that* way and not others?

In the end, my students raise some very legitimate concerns. As we have seen, there *are* some genetic, socio-environmental, or biochemical explanations of behavior according to which the actor's moral agency is subverted or compromised in ways that make it inappropriate to hold him morally responsible, and, therefore, similarly inappropriate to consider him evil. This is clearly the case when the relevant explanations involve disorders like schizophrenia, dementia, and Tourette syndrome. And as we will see starkly and uncomfortably in the next section, there is a real sense in which our behavior *is* sometimes strongly influenced by external situational factors. But still, there do not seem to be any good reasons for denying that the people discussed in Part I were moral agents, or for believing that their moral agency was subverted or compromised in any way while they were engaging in behavior so widely regarded as evil. So, while we do not yet have an answer to the book's central question—what makes someone an evil person?—I see no reason here for ruling Bundy, Eichmann, Madoff, and the others out as potential candidates.

Evil and Moral Character

Imagine that someone is using a payphone in a shopping mall. After hanging up the phone, the person turns to walk away, when a nearby stranger stumbles and drops a bunch of papers on the floor. Will the person stop to help the stranger pick up the papers? And more importantly for our purposes here, how best do we account for the difference between someone who does stop to help and someone who does not? More often than not, it seems, we assume the difference between people who help and people who do not is a matter of personality or moral character. John Doris captures this assumption when he writes,

> Perhaps it depends on the person: Jeff, an entrepreneur incessantly scheming about fattening his real estate holdings, probably won't [stop to help pick up the papers], while Nina, a political activist who takes in stray cats, probably will. Nina is the compassionate type; Jeff isn't.[31]

As with *predicting* people's behavior, we also naturally assume that differences in personality or character best *explain* people's behavior as well. When we see Nina stop to help a stranger pick up some dropped papers, we explain her behavior (even if only to ourselves) by attributing to her qualities like helpfulness and compassion. After all, helpful people help, right?

For a now-famous study reported in 1972, Alice Isen and Paula Levin set up an experiment featuring precisely the above scenario: subjects leaving a payphone, where they are met by an experimental confederate who "accidentally" drops a stack of papers.[32] The study, however, sought to determine the effects—if any—of good feelings on people's willingness to engage in helpful behavior. So, in order to induce good feelings in their subjects, the researchers planted a dime in the coin-return slot of the payphone—since, as those of us who have actually used a payphone (a shrinking number, I have found) can attest, it is very common for people to check the coin-return slot at some point before, during, or after making a call, just in case someone else's misfortune or the machine's malfunction happened to result in there being an unclaimed coin or two. And, of course, it feels good to find money—even if only a dime.

The results of the experiment are shocking. Of the 41 subjects (24 female, 17 male) who checked the coin-return slot, 16 found a dime, and 25 did not. Of the 25 subjects who did not find a dime, only one stopped to help. But of the 16 subjects who did find a dime, 14 stopped to help.[33]

Unless, by some remarkable coincidence, the dime-finding subjects happen also to be people that others regard as helpful (and those who did not find a dime happen also to be unhelpful people), it looks as if even a small boost of positive affect, from something as seemingly insignificant as finding a dime, can have a very pronounced effect upon people's willingness to engage in helpful behavior. As Doris explains, "If greedy Jeff finds the dime, he'll likely help; if caring Nina doesn't, she very likely won't."[34] So what, *really*, explains why some people help and others do not? Is it a matter of their personality or moral character—composed of such traits as helpfulness and compassion, or unhelpfulness and greed—as is typically assumed? Or is it instead a matter of the subtle influence of various situational factors, sometimes, as in this case, factors that have little or nothing to do with the behavior in question?

You may have heard of the social psychological phenomenon known as "bystander effect." At the most general level, this refers to the effect had upon people's behavior by the presence (or assumed presence) of other people. Inspired by the 1964 murder of Kitty Genovese—wherein dozens of Genovese's neighbors heard her cries for help, but none intervened or even bothered to call the police, because they all assumed someone else would do so—psychologists John Darley and Bibb Latané conducted a number of studies over the next several years to explore this puzzling and underappreciated feature of human psychology.

In one study, for instance, they sat college students alone in a room, where they could communicate anonymously over an intercom system with what they assumed were other college students—but were, in fact, just recordings—about "personal problems associated with college life."[35] Early in the discussion, one of the other "students"—again, just a recording—explained that one of his "personal problems" was that he was prone to seizures. Then, at some point later in the discussion, the subject would hear over the intercom what sounded very much like a person having a seizure. So, to be clear, as far as the experimental subject is concerned, there is another college student in another room, on the same hallway of this building, taking part in the same experiment, currently having what sounds like a life-threatening seizure. (In the recording of the seizure, the victim even says, through sounds of choking, "I'm gonna die-er-er-I'm gonna die-er-help-er-er-seizure-er-[chokes, then quiet]."[36]) And importantly, the subjects are told ahead of time that the experimenters will not actually hear their discussion until after the experiment is over. This way, the subjects must assume it is the responsibility of the students participating in the intercom discussion to intervene in case of such an emergency. How many will intervene? How long will it take for them to intervene? And importantly, what effect will be had by the (assumed) presence of others?

To answer this latter question, the experimenters varied the size of the group. Some subjects were told that there were only two students taking part in the discussion (only the subject and the would-be seizure victim). Some were told that there were three students (the subject, the seizure victim, and another student). The rest were told that it was a six-person discussion (the subject, the seizure victim, and four others). Of the subjects who assumed they were the only ones witnessing the seizure, 85 % made an attempt to intervene by leaving their room and reporting the incident to the experimental assistant at the end of the hall. And they did so relatively quickly, at an average of just 52 seconds. Of the subjects who assumed there were four others witnessing the seizure, only 31 % made an attempt to intervene, and they took an average of 166 seconds (almost 3 minutes) to do so.

In another study, subjects were led to a waiting room that was separated from another room by only a curtain. Some subjects sat in the waiting room alone, some sat with a stranger, some sat with a friend, and some sat with a passive confederate (i.e., someone whose role in the experiment was simply to remain inactive during the staged "emergency"). After leading the subject to the waiting room, a female experimenter would leave the room by walking around to the other side of the curtain divider, and soon after this, the experimenters played a recording that sounded very much like the female researcher took a nasty fall, and was moaning and complaining about an injured leg. So again, to be clear, as far as the subjects are concerned, the same person who led them to this waiting room has just fallen on the other side of the curtain, and sounds seriously hurt. How many will intervene? What effect will be had by the presence of others in the waiting room? Of the subjects who were alone in the waiting room, 70 % attempted to intervene. Of the subjects who sat in the waiting room with a confederate, many "seemed upset or confused during the emergency and frequently glanced at the passive confederate," but only 7 % of them attempted to intervene.[37]

In fact, the bystander effect is so potent that it apparently can even cause people to endanger themselves. In a third study, Darley and Latané had subjects sit in a waiting room and fill out a questionnaire. Some subjects sat in the room alone, some sat with two other naïve subjects, and some sat with two passive confederates. The confederates were instructed ahead of time to notice the emergency, but to remain indifferent. While the subjects filled out the questionnaire, the experimenters slowly began filling the room with smoke (it entered through a wall vent). So as far as the subjects are concerned, they are in a potentially very dangerous situation, as there could be a serious fire somewhere in the building. How many subjects will get up to investigate, report the fire, or even just attempt to get to safety? Here again, the presence of others has a dramatic effect upon people's behavior. Of the subjects sitting alone, 75 % reported the smoke, and usually within a couple minutes of noticing it. Of the 10 subjects sitting with passive confederates, only one reported the smoke.

> The other nine stayed in the waiting room as it filled up with smoke, doggedly working on their questionnaires and waving the fumes away from their faces. They coughed, rubbed their eyes, and opened the window—but they did not report the smoke.[38]

Even without the passive confederates, the response rate from the groups of three naïve subjects was surprisingly low. "Of the twenty-four people run in these eight groups, only one person reported the smoke within the first four minutes before the room got noticeably unpleasant."[39]

Situational influences can affect our judgments as well. Moral psychologists have long been interested in the role of emotions—or affect, more generally—in moral judgment. One of the ways they have tested this is by placing subjects into situations likely to induce some sort of affective response. Just as *feeling good* can lead people to engage in helpful behavior, it can also lead people to be more lenient than they otherwise would have been in their moral judgment of others. In one study, for example, subjects who had just watched a humorous video clip—which, it seems likely, produced a positive affective response—were significantly *less* harsh in their responses to a moral judgment survey than subjects who watched an affectively neutral video clip.[40] When situational influences induce a *negative* affective response, the effect can be even more striking, but in the opposite direction. Subjects who completed a moral judgment survey either at a filthy desk or near an odorous dumpster—both areas designed to induce a disgust response—were significantly *more* harsh in their responses than were subjects who completed the same survey at a clean workspace.[41] We might like to think that our moral judgments are based only on things like beliefs and personal values, but this research suggests that they can also be influenced by things like the cleanliness of our surroundings and the smell of the room.

Psychologists distinguish between two views of the causes of people's behavior. According to a view known as *dispositionism*, our behavior—here taken to include both action and judgment—is typically caused by some internal psychological factor or factors, such as our beliefs, values, or traits of personality or character. As I mentioned above, dispositionism is the view assumed by most, if not all, laypeople. When we see people behave in helpful, brave, dishonest, or cowardly ways, we typically explain the behavior (even if only to ourselves) by assuming that the people themselves are helpful, brave, dishonest, or cowardly. Once we assume that people have certain traits, we then use this assumption to predict future behaviors. We expect our reliable friends to arrive somewhere on time, and are unsurprised when our unreliable friends are running late. Opposite dispositionism is a view known as *situationism*, according to which our behavior is typically caused by external factors—usually features of the situation in which the behavior occurs.

Here is the rub, though. If situationism is the correct view of the causes of human behavior, what reason is there to continue believing in the reality of these supposed traits of personality or character? Presumably, what warranted this belief in the first place was the apparently indispensable role that such traits have to play in explanations and predictions of people's behavior. But what studies like those described above seem to suggest—and, for the record, the above studies represent only the smallest tip of the situationist iceberg—is that, for purposes of explaining and predicting people's behavior, we might actually be better off attending closely to features of their situations. For instance, when people are made to feel good (by finding a dime, perhaps), we can predict that they will engage in helpful behavior—and, unsettling as it may be, such a prediction might actually be *better* than one made on the basis of assumptions about whether or not they are helpful people. But then, if assumptions about people's traits no longer play the role they used to play in explaining and predicting behavior, why even continue making the assumption that people have such traits? If situationism is right, then perhaps everything we think we know about people and their personalities or characters (ourselves included) is mistaken. Maybe Harman is right—maybe there is no such thing as character.

Two of the most famous social psychological studies of the twentieth century—both of which are also taken as evidence in favor of situationism—are Milgram's obedience study (discussed in Chap. 3) and Zimbardo's Stanford Prison Experiment (hereafter, SPE). Ostensibly, the SPE was designed to investigate the effects of a prison environment on the behavior of both prisoners and guards. To that end, Zimbardo converted the basement of Stanford's psychology department building into a makeshift prison, and recruited the help of Carlo Prescott, an ex-con who served 17 years at San Quentin Prison for attempted murder. Before the start of the experiment, 24 students were selected to participate from a pool of several dozen candidates, after being prescreened for psychological health and stability; 12 were randomly assigned the role of prisoners (nine to start the experiment, and three to stand by as alternates); and 12 were randomly assigned the role of guards (again, three of whom were alternates). On the day before the experiment began, Zimbardo and Prescott together led a kind of orientation session for the guards. According to Zimbardo—who played the role of prison warden throughout the experiment—the guards were given their uniforms and told that their jobs would simply be "to maintain law and order, not allow prisoners to escape, and never to use physical force against the prisoners."[42] The next day—a Sunday—the prisoners were "arrested."

Here is a timeline of how the experiment unraveled:

SUNDAY (day)
   Prisoners are taken from their homes in simulated arrests, booked, assigned numbers (by which they would be known during the experiment), and transferred to the makeshift prison. The guards then conduct their first counts—during which prisoners are taken out of their cells, and forced to stand at attention and call out their numbers—accompanied by laughter from the prisoners, and even some reluctance and awkwardness from guards.

SUNDAY (night)

This is the first night shift of the experiment. Already, the guards are getting more aggressive during prisoner counts, issuing arbitrary and manipulative commands—like, for example, forcing prisoners to shout or sing their numbers. And prisoners are already showing signs of resentment of the guards, as well as a willingness to rebel.

MONDAY (day)

The guards take the prisoners' blankets outdoors and drag them through bushes and brush, so the blankets are filled with pine needles and other prickly objects. Prisoners in Cell 1 barricade the door with their beds. Prisoners in Cell 2 attempt to incite a rebellion. There is a failed escape attempt. And Zimbardo invites the prisoners to participate in a grievance committee, during which Prisoner 8612 has an emotional breakdown.

MONDAY (night)

A couple of the night shift guards are apparently trying to "one-up" each other with their abusive behavior toward the prisoners. Prisoner 8612 is released, and almost immediately, there are rumors that he will attempt to return and break the others out.

TUESDAY (day)

Family and friends of prisoners are allowed to visit, but guards stand over the prisoners' shoulders in order to discourage them from opening up to the visitors about abuses taking place in the prison. Rumors of 8612's return are apparently false.

TUESDAY (night)

The night shift guards step up their abuse a bit more, apparently taking out some frustration from the stress of the day. But now, the prisoners are starting to accept the abuse without resistance.

WEDNESDAY (day)

Another prisoner breaks down, and is released by Zimbardo. His replacement, Prisoner 416, is admitted into the prison, and is immediately shocked by the behavior that he witnesses from both guards and fellow prisoners. In response, he begins a hunger strike, for which the guards punish him severely.

WEDNESDAY (night)
There is an intense power struggle between two of the night shift guards (Guard Hellman and Guard Landry) and two of the prisoners (the newly admitted Prisoner 416 and Prisoner 2093, who, up to this point, had been mostly cooperative).

THURSDAY (day)
Zimbardo conducts a number of "Parole Board" meetings, during which a couple more prisoners experience intense emotional breakdowns and are "granted parole." (Carlo Prescott is the chair of the Parole Board.) Zimbardo's love interest at the time—Christina Maslach, then a graduate student of psychology who had recently accepted a tenure-track position at the University of California, Berkeley—attended the Parole Board meetings, and was later appalled by some of the things she saw take place in the prison, such as prisoners being led to the bathroom in degrading fashion, with bags over their heads, and so forth. This causes her to erupt in anger at Zimbardo. The two argue for a while, and eventually, by Zimbardo's own admission, he comes to his senses and realizes that he must put an end to the experiment.

THURSDAY (night)
Almost simultaneous with Zimbardo's decision to terminate the experiment, the most abusive of the night shift guards, Guard Hellman, forces the five remaining prisoners to simulate acts of sodomy with each other during a particularly terrible prisoner count.

FRIDAY (day)
Zimbardo conducts a series of "encounter groups" (i.e., debriefing sessions), first with all of the guards, then with all of the prisoners, and finally with guards and prisoners together. Eventually, all participants are released to their homes. The plan was for the experiment to last for two weeks, but it concluded after just six days.

According to Zimbardo, the abusive behavior of the guards went way beyond what they had been instructed to do. Indeed, it apparently even shocked some of the guards themselves. One of the guards reflected after the experiment, "I was surprised—no, I was dismayed—to find out that I could really be a—uh—that I could act in a manner so absolutely unaccustomed to anything I would really dream of doing."[43] This is a prime example of what Zimbardo has since been calling "the Lucifer effect"—that is, the ability of particularly evocative situations, such as prison environments, to cause otherwise decent people to behave in cruel, dehumanizing, and abusive ways toward others. Boiling the entire experiment down to a single sentence, he writes, "Good dispositions were pitted against a bad situation."[44]

Situationists often cite this experiment as further evidence that people's behavior is determined more by the influence of situational factors than by internal traits or dispositions. The assumption is that Zimbardo could have placed just about *anyone* into the role of prison guard, even someone you might otherwise regard as kind and compassionate, and eventually, the power of the situation would take hold and cause this same person to engage in cruel and abusive behavior toward other people. And if that is right, then what explanatory or predictive work is really being done by our attribution of such traits to people? For his own part, Zimbardo draws a somewhat more specific conclusion from the study. As he sees things, what the SPE shows us is that there are no evil people, but there are evil situations—situations with the power to influence people to perform evil acts. Indeed, even people who occupy "henchmen"-like positions in genocidal regimes, he thinks, are compelled to commit such heinous acts by the corrupting influence of their situations.[45] Zimbardo puts his own situationist spin on the haunting lesson above from Alison Des Forges, about evil behavior lying "just under the surface of any of us," when he writes,

> Any deed that any human being has ever committed, however horrible, is possible for any one of us—under the right or wrong situational circumstances. That knowledge does not excuse evil; rather, it democratizes it, sharing its blame among ordinary actors rather than declaring it the province only of deviants and despots—of Them but not Us.[46]

The studies described in this section should be concerning to anyone who believes in the reality of moral character, and especially to those of us who believe in the reality of *evil* character. So what can we say in response either to situationism in general or to Zimbardo in particular?

The response to situationism from those who defend the reality of moral character has been two-pronged. First, they argue that situationist arguments depend upon a conception of character traits as *direct* dispositions to certain stereotypical behaviors, but this is not the correct view of such traits. For instance, Rachana Kamtekar complains,

> [T]he experiments which find character traits to correlate poorly with behavior rely on a very particular conception of a character trait: as an isolable and nonrational disposition to manifest a given stereotypical behavior that differs from the behavior of others and is fairly situation insensitive.[47]

And Robert Adams echoes,

> I consider it a weakness of situationist writing about traits of character, both in philosophy and in psychology, that it tends to assume that all traits of character must be what I shall call *direct behavioral dispositions.*[48]

In place of the overly simplistic situationist conception of character—which, to be fair, seems likely to be shared by many—Kamtekar defends an Aristotelian view according to which traits of virtue are not direct behavioral dispositions, but rather dispositions to *appropriate response*, where one can respond appropriately to something in both *judgment* and *feeling*, as well as action.[49] Adams defends a view according to which character traits are both modular and probabilistic (rather than direct) in disposing their possessor to certain behaviors.[50] And Miller defends a view according to which "human beings do have robust traits of character which play an important explanatory and predictive role, but which are triggered by certain situational variables that preclude them from counting as genuine Aristotelian virtues."[51]

The second part of the two-pronged response to situationists has been to insist that character consists of more than just *behavioral* dispositions. This is contained in Kamtekar's view, which includes dispositions to judgment and feeling as traits of character. But Adams goes even further to include values, concerns, motives, ways of caring about things, ways of seeing things, and even social roles and affiliations as all partly constitutive of a person's moral character.[52] Emphasizing the importance of motive to virtue, for instance, he writes,

> It is very doubtful that a direct behavioral disposition is sufficient to constitute a virtue. At a minimum, we may think, one must have a good motive for the behavior in question if the disposition is to count as a virtue. It seems possible to have a direct disposition to behave honestly out of fear of social consequences of dishonest behavior without caring much at all about honesty and other people's rights for their own sake. Such a disposition, badly motivated though it be, will still be socially *useful*, [...] but few will think it is *excellent* enough to be a virtue.[53]

As soon as one adopts this more holistic approach to the constitution of moral character, it becomes hard to see how the reality of moral character ever would have been significantly threatened by empirical studies like the ones described above. Are we not as reliably helpful as we might like to think we are? Sadly, it seems we are not. But is this any evidence against the existence of a character that is made up of things like emotional dispositions, enduring cares and concerns, habits of perception, roles and affiliations? Obviously not. Nor is it any evidence against the reality of virtuous (or vicious) behavioral dispositions, as long as those dispositions are properly understood.

In response to Zimbardo's arguments in particular, I have three things to say. First, despite his insistence that the guards' cruel and abusive behavior "was emitted simply as a 'natural' consequence of being in the uniform of a 'guard' and asserting the power inherent in that role,"[54] there is some evidence that Zimbardo actually had an influential role to play in prodding the guards into behaving that way. For one thing, Zimbardo himself admits that, when guards were not perceived as "tough enough," either he or one of his assistants would say things like,

> We need you to act in a certain way. For the time being, we need you to play the role of 'tough guard'. We need you to react as you imagine the 'pigs' would. We're trying to set up the stereotype guard—your individual style has been a little too soft.[55]

But more damning than any of Zimbardo's admissions are the subsequent testimonies of others who participated in the experiment—especially that of Carlo Prescott. Zimbardo is coy about the role played by Prescott, admitting only that "intense monitoring by Carlo helped to infuse our little experiment with a kind of situational savvy."[56] But Prescott himself is more explicit. In a 2005 op-ed for *The Stanford Daily* entitled "The Lie of the Stanford Prison Experiment," he writes,

> [I]deas such as bags being placed over the heads of prisoners, inmates being bound together with chains and buckets being used in place of toilets in their cells were all experiences of mine at the old "Spanish Jail" section of San Quentin and which I dutifully shared with the Stanford Prison Experiment braintrust months before the experiment started. To allege that all these carefully tested, psychologically solid, upper-middle-class Caucasian "guards" dreamed this up on their own is absurd.

> How can Zimbardo [...] express horror at the behavior of the "guards" when they were merely doing what Zimbardo and others, myself included, encouraged them to do at the outset or frankly established as ground rules?[57]

And indeed, since the conclusion of the experiment, some of the guards have insisted that they were merely doing (often reluctantly) what they were told to do.[58] If this is true, then while *the situation itself* might still have had *some* influence on their behavior, it would be hard to say whether this influence was really significant enough for the experiment to count as evidence in favor of situationism. After all, even most dispositionist accounts of human behavior allow for some situational influence.

A second thing to say in response to Zimbardo is that his own brand of situationism is deeply inconsistent. In the first chapter of his book, he introduces the distinction between dispositionist and situationist accounts of behavior, making his own skepticism of dispositionism very clear. But throughout the book, his description of the so-called Lucifer effect is that of evil situations corrupting what are essentially *good dispositions*. You saw this above when Zimbardo says of the experiment, "Good dispositions were pitted against a bad situation."[59] Elsewhere, he explains the reluctance of some of the guards to participate in cruel and abusive behavior in terms of their possessing good dispositions: "In our study, being a good guard who did his job reluctantly meant 'goodness by default'."[60] But what could a term like "default" be referring to here, except for something like *character*? According to Zimbardo, even the prisoners divided guards into three categories—"good," "bad," and "by the book"—where the *good* guards were those "who had done little favors for them [the prisoners] or who had never been so fully immersed in their role that they forgot that the prisoners were human beings."[61]

Judging from context, it seems Zimbardo is more than willing to allow that the behavior of the good guards is explained by their having good dispositions, or good traits of character, that enabled them to resist the influence of the situation. (Indeed, he devotes the entire final chapter of the book to a discussion of "resisting situational influences and celebrating heroism.") But first of all, such an explanation is only available to dispositionists, who believe that there are such things as robust traits of character with important roles to play in explaining and predicting behavior. Second, at no point does Zimbardo address the following question: once you *allow* that there can be *good* dispositions, what reason is there to *disallow* that there can be *bad* dispositions as well, as he apparently is inclined to do? His inconsistency on this point is actually contained in the very subtitle of the book, *Understanding How Good People Turn Evil*. Apparently, in Zimbardo's moral taxonomy, there are *good people* and (presumably also) *good actions*. But like some of my students mentioned above, he thinks there can be *evil actions*, but not *evil people*. Except for some perhaps understandable, but nonetheless empirically baseless, optimism about human nature, what reason could there be for accepting this curiously asymmetric view of the moral landscape?

Finally, while Zimbardo's study may nonetheless offer some valuable insight into the psychology of "henchmen"-like perpetrators of evil—for example, the way in which negative attitudes toward the prisoners spread among the guards, as well as the "one-upmanship" that drove some of the guards to try to out-perform each other's cruelty, are both reminiscent of some of the accounts of officers of both the Imperial Japanese Army and the Hutu militia—it is frankly very difficult to see what relevance, if any, the SPE could have to such figures of evil as Ted Bundy, Adolf Eichmann, or Bernie Madoff. (As you may recall, I briefly noted this complaint about Zimbardo in Chap. 1.) Worries about methodology aside, it is relatively easy to imagine even artificial prison settings having a somewhat profound influence on the behavior of those contained therein. After all, Zimbardo is surely right when he says, "Prisons can be brutalizing places that invoke what is worst in human nature."[62] But such obvious situational influences are simply not nearly as present or prominent in accounts of the lives and decisions of Bundy, Eichmann, Madoff, and many others. Indeed, Zimbardo's own explanation of the Holocaust—which he describes as a system of situations created by the Nazi "power elite" and maintained by means of propaganda—leaves *unexplained* the behavior of the very "power elite" to which Eichmann belonged. The actions of Nazi henchmen are explained in straightforwardly situationist terms, but Zimbardo describes the Nazi leaders as occupying positions that enabled them to "transcend" the situation. Might *their* behavior, then, be better explained in terms of their being evil?

Concluding Thoughts

In this chapter, I addressed three puzzles that threaten to undermine any attempt to analyze the concept of evil philosophically. The first puzzle assumes that evil is, in some sense, essentially incomprehensible. If this assumption is correct, then it may be hard to see how a philosophical theory of evil could ever be successful, if success is to be understood in terms of its making sense of the relevant phenomena. But in response, I argued that there is no sense in which evil is literally incomprehensible. If it is incomprehensible at all, it is only so in the sense that it is very difficult for us to empathize with evildoers. But that is no problem for a philosophical theory of evil.

According to the second puzzle, all purported candidates for evil personhood are likely, on further examination, to be ruled out as deserving of the title, in virtue of their apparently being afflicted with some kind of mental illness or disorder. For instance, psychopaths, it is commonly assumed, either do not know any better or, even if they do, lack the sort of behavioral control required for them to refrain from misbehavior. If this is right, then while a philosophical theory of evil personhood may be possible, it will not be particularly useful or insightful, since it will not actually apply to any person in our world. In response, I argued both (a) that we should resist the temptation to infer from seriously deviant or immoral beliefs or behaviors that the person must therefore be mentally ill, and (b) that we should resist the common assumption that all forms of mental illness or disorder have similar effects on a person's status as a moral agent, or ability to exercise his or her moral agency.

Finally, according to the third puzzle, theories of evil personhood or character are bound to fail, since there is no such thing as evil character—only, perhaps, evil situations. In response, I first argued against situationism in general, echoing others who complain that situationists badly misunderstand the nature and constitution of moral character. Second, I argued that Zimbardo's own situationist-style skepticism about evil character is mistaken on a number of points, not least of which is its apparent inapplicability to most, if not all, of the paradigm instances of evil personhood discussed in Chaps. 2–4.

Of course, philosophers attempting to provide theories of evil personhood would do well to keep these three puzzles in mind as they proceed. However, there is no good reason for thinking that any of the puzzles addressed in this chapter could actually succeed in making such theories either impossible or uninteresting. Quite the contrary, as we will see in the next chapter, theories of evil personhood are both possible and very interesting.

Notes

1. Harman (1999: 316).
2. Harman (1999: 316).
3. Feinberg (2003: 142).
4. Feinberg (2003: 145).
5. de Wijze (2002: 213).
6. Morrow (2003: 3, 4, all italics mine).
7. Dawes (2013: 28).
8. From the Introduction to Part II of Caruth (1995: 153–154).
9. Kant (1793 [1996]: 58).
10. Sussman (2009: 613).
11. Cole (2006: 3).
12. Kant (1793 [1996]: 58).
13. Sussman (2009: 613, italics in original).
14. Cole (2006: 3).
15. The basic idea that intentional action requires that an agent sees the action, or some feature of the action, *sub specie boni*—that is, that he sees it as good—has a very long history in philosophy, going back to Plato and Aristotle. For more modern canonical discussions, see Anscombe (1957) and Davidson (1980) (especially the essays "Freedom to Act" and "Intending"). For a discussion of the possibility of desiring, or being motivated by, what is (thought to be) bad, see Stocker (1979).
16. Sussman (2009: 616). The example of people feeling an urge to throw themselves from high places or in front of trains comes from Kenny (1994: 95).
17. One might complain that none of Sussman's examples here involve an agent doing something morally wrong *because it is morally wrong*. This, it seems, would be closer to Kant's notion of a diabolical motive. But consider Augustine's famous example of stealing pears as a youth. In his *Confessions*, Augustine describes an episode in which he and some other "wretched youths" decided to steal pears from a nearby tree for no reason other than that it was wrong. The pears themselves were not especially good—he says they were "not particularly attractive either in color or taste". He did not steal them in order to satisfy his hunger—"this was not to feed ourselves; we may have tasted a few, but then we threw the rest to the pigs". Augustine concludes, "I became evil for nothing, with no reason for wrongdoing except the wrongdoing itself" (Augustine 1963: 45).
18. Haybron (2002: 261).
19. Feinberg (2003: 143–144).
20. Levi (1987: 395).
21. Levi (1987: 395).

22. As I mentioned before, Clendinnen's book *Reading the Holocaust* contains an essay called "Leaders" in which she tries to make some sense of the actions and motivations of the leaders of the Holocaust. As she puts it, the point of the essay is "to challenge that bafflement" that people typically experience in response to the Holocaust. In the essay, she responds directly to Levi's concerns, explaining how her job as a historian is precisely that of understanding the customs, habits, gestures, beliefs, attitudes, actions, and so forth, of other cultures, groups, or individual people, most of whom are very foreign to her. For instance, while researching Spanish bishop Deigo de Landa, who, she says, "inflict[ed] inventive, illegal, and hideous tortures on his new [Mayan] converts" (1999: 90), she came to "understand" de Landa to such a degree that she expected and could predict certain things before actually learning of them. "Although he always surprised me, I came to expect certain things of him, and I was, usually, right" (1999: 90.). But this surely does not mean that she in any way came to justify de Landa's actions, or to see his actions as justifiable.
23. Landesman (2002).
24. As I mentioned in Chap. 1, this book assumes without argument a basic sort of moral realism according to which there *are* objective moral truths or facts, some of which *can be known*. I also will not defend a particular theory of (moral) knowledge. I assume that it requires true beliefs, the contents of which are (moral) propositions, and *something else*—justification, warrant, reliable formation, or whatever. Readers are invited to apply their preferred theories of knowledge and justification as they see fit.
25. It is actually less clear than you might think what makes a belief count as delusional. For instance, almost all accounts of delusion stipulate that the belief must be false. But what about a case in which a person's mental disorder causes her to believe that her husband is having an affair, which, *by sheer coincidence*, happens to be true? The belief is surely still delusional, even if it is true. Presumably, then, delusion has more to do with *the process by which beliefs are formed* than with *the beliefs themselves*. As interesting as these issues are, though, I will not pursue them any further here.
26. Nomy Arpaly also contrasts schizophrenia with psychopathy when discussing the relationship between mental disorder and moral responsibility: "If a schizophrenic in an acute psychotic state kills a stranger because she believes her to be the devil from whom she must protect us […] she is obviously exempt from blame […] Of those disorders that do not serve as mitigating conditions, most famous, of course, is the condition of those who used to be called 'morally insane', then psychopaths or sociopaths, and now sufferers from Antisocial Personality Disorder" (2005: 291).
27. Arpaly (2005: 297–298).

28. Those who are familiar with the free will debate will likely recognize "the ability to do otherwise" as what is sometimes offered as a definition of free will. Though I generally find such accounts of free will plausible, I make no such commitments here, and focus instead on the general notion of agency.
29. As a reminder, there are nearly two million psychopaths in the United States, but only 25–50 serial murderers.
30. Arpaly (2005: 290–291).
31. Doris (2002: 30).
32. Isen and Levin (1972).
33. Isen and Levin (1972: 387).
34. Doris (2002: 30).
35. Darley and Latané (1968).
36. Darley and Latané (1968: 379).
37. Latané and Darley (1969: 255).
38. Latané and Darley (1969: 251).
39. Latané and Darley (1969: 252).
40. Valdesolo and DeSteno (2006). The humorous clip was from the comedy sketch program "Saturday Night Live," and the neutral clip was taken from a documentary about a small Spanish village.
41. Schnall et al. (2008). Similar effects have been observed with other negative emotions, like anger (Lerner et al. 1998) and sadness (Fogas and Bower 1987).
42. Zimbardo (2007: 56).
43. Zimbardo (2007: 158).
44. Zimbardo (2007: 195).
45. Zimbardo relates his work to both the Holocaust and the Rwandan genocide (see especially 2007: 10–16).
46. Zimbardo (2007: 211).
47. Kamtekar (2004: 477).
48. Adams (2006: 120, italics in original).
49. Kamtekar (2004).
50. Adams (2006: 115–130).
51. Miller (2010: 1).
52. Adams (2006: 115–139, see especially pp. 130–139).
53. Adams (2006: 121).
54. Haney, Banks, and Zimbardo (1973: 12).
55. Zimbardo (2007: 65). Zimbardo also admits to being (by his own description) "a radical, activist professor" who took particularly strong stances against military action and perceived injustices among law enforcement (2007: 91).
56. Zimbardo (2007: 68).

57. Prescott (2005).
58. In a recent retrospective interview with the *Los Angeles Times*, Guard Hellman (the especially cruel night shift guard) and Prisoner 8612 explain their behavior in the experimental prison by insisting that they were merely acting those roles in order to please Zimbardo. To his credit, Zimbardo acknowledges their recent testimony, but insists they are being disingenuous, that is, "acting new parts" in a movie "where everyone has a different view of what really happened" (2007: 218).
59. Zimbardo (2007: 195).
60. Zimbardo (2007: 208).
61. Zimbardo (2007: 182).
62. Zimbardo (2007: 206).

References

Adams, Robert. 2006. *A Theory of Virtue*. Oxford: Oxford University Press.
Anscombe, Elizabeth. 1957. *Intention*. Ithaca: Cornell University Press.
Arpaly, Nomy. 2005. How It Is Not 'Just Like Diabetes': Mental Disorders and the Moral Psychologist. *Philosophical Issues* 15: 282–298.
Augustine. 1963. *The Confessions of St. Augustine*. Translated by Rex Warner. New York: Mentor.
Caruth, Cathy, ed. 1995. *Trauma: Explorations in Memory*. Baltimore: Johns Hopkins University Press.
Clendinnen, Inga. 1999. *Reading the Holocaust*. Cambridge: Cambridge University Press.
Cole, Phillip. 2006. *The Myth of Evil: Demonizing the Enemy*. Westport: Praeger.
Darley, John M., and Bibb Latané. 1968. Bystander Intervention in Emergencies: Diffusion of Responsibility. *Journal of Personality and Social Psychology* 8: 377–383.
Davidson, Donald. 1980. *Essays on Actions and Events*. Oxford: Oxford University Press.
Dawes, James. 2013. *Evil Men*. Cambridge: Harvard University Press.
de Wijze, Stephen. 2002. Defining Evil: Insights from the Problem of 'Dirty Hands'. *The Monist* 85(2): 210–238.
Doris, John. 2002. *Lack of Character: Personality and Moral Behavior*. Cambridge: Cambridge University Press.
Feinberg, Joel. 2003. Evil. In *Problems at the Roots of Law: Essays in Legal and Political Theory*, 125–92. Oxford: Oxford University Press.
Fogas, J.P., and G.H. Bower. 1987. Mood Effects on Personal Perception Judgments. *Journal of Personality and Social Psychology* 51: 53–60.
Haney, Craig, Curtis Banks, and Philip Zimbardo. 1973. A Study of Prisoners and Guards in a Simulated Prison. *Naval Research Reviews* 30: 1–17.

Harman, Gilbert. 1999. Moral Philosophy Meets Social Psychology. *Proceedings of the Aristotelian Society* 99: 315–331.
Haybron, Daniel. 2002. Moral Monsters and Saints. *The Monist* 85(2): 260–284.
Isen, Alice, and Paula Levin. 1972. The Effect of Feeling Good on Helping: Cookies and Kindness. *Journal of Personality and Social Psychology* 21: 384–388.
Kamtekar, Rachana. 2004. Situationism and Virtue Ethics on the Content of Our Character. *Ethics* 114: 458–491.
Kant, Immanuel. 1793 [1996]. *Religion within the Boundaries of Mere Reason*. Translated by George di Giovanni. In *Religion and Rational Theology*, eds. Allen W. Wood and George di Giovanni, 39–216. Cambridge: Cambridge University Press.
Kenny, Anthony. 1994. *Action, Emotion, and Will*. Bristol: Thoemmes Press.
Landesman, Peter. 2002. A Woman's Work. *The New York Times*, September 15. Accessed March 1, 2016. http://www.nytimes.com/2002/09/15/magazine/a-woman-s-work.html?pagewanted=all.
Latané, Bibb, and John M. Darley. 1969. Bystander 'Apathy'. *American Scientist* 57: 244–268.
Lerner, J., J. Goldberg, and P.E. Tetlock. 1998. Sober Second Thought: The Effects of Accountability, Anger, and Authoritarianism on Attributions of Responsibility. *Personality and Social Psychology Bulletin* 24: 563–574.
Levi, Primo. 1987. *If This is a Man*, and *The Truce*. Translated by Stuart Wolf. London: Abacus.
Miller, Christian. 2010. Character Traits, Social Psychology, and Impediments to Helping Behavior. *Journal of Ethics and Social Philosophy* 5: 1–36.
Morrow, Lance. 2003. *Evil: An Investigation*. New York: Basic Books.
Prescott, Carlo. 2005. The Lie of the Stanford Prison Experiment. *The Stanford Daily*, April 28.
Schnall, S., J. Haidt, G.L. Clore, and A. Jordan. 2008. Disgust as Embodied Moral Judgment. *Personality and Social Psychology Bulletin* 34: 1096–1109.
Stocker, Michael. 1979. Desiring the Bad: An Essay in Moral Psychology. *Journal of Philosophy* 76(12): 738–753.
Sussman, David. 2009. For Badness' Sake. *Journal of Philosophy* 106(11): 613–628.
Valdesolo, P., and D. DeSteno. 2006. Manipulations of Emotional Context Shape Moral Judgment. *Psychological Science* 17: 476–477.
Zimbardo, Philip. 2007. *The Lucifer Effect: Understanding How Good People Turn Evil*. New York: Random House.

CHAPTER 6

Theories of Evil Personhood

In the next chapter, I answer the central question of the book—What makes someone an evil person?—by defending a theory of evil that will apply not only to persons, but also to actions, institutions, and anything else to which the label "evil" might apply. However, I am by no means the first to propose such a theory. Over the past couple of decades especially, the topic of evil has received a growing amount of attention from philosophers, and as a result of this, philosophical theories of evil have abounded. So before I get to my own theory, I want to survey the current landscape a bit, introduce readers to some of my competitors, and explain where and why these other theories are mistaken.

There is some debate among philosophers about whether the difference between evil and other moral categories like wrongness or badness is a difference of *quantity* or a difference of *quality*.[1] Suppose we can think of moral wrongness, or moral badness, as lying on a kind of continuum, with some actions or characters being more or less morally wrong, or bad, than others. For instance, presumably, stealing someone's car is *more morally wrong* than stealing someone's lunch, and *less morally wrong* than stealing a vital organ from someone's body. According to some philosophers, to say that an action or person is evil is just to say that the action or person lies near enough to the worst extreme end of this continuum—in other words, evil actions are just extremely morally wrong actions, and evil people are just extremely morally bad people. Call this the *extremity theory of evil*. According to extremity theories, the difference between evil and wrongness, or badness, is not qualitative, but merely quantitative—which is to say, it is not a difference in kind, but only in degree. As we will see below, Marcus Singer and Luke Russell both defend an extremity theory of evil action, but different types of theories of evil personhood.[2] Peter Brian Barry—whose survey about the most plausible candidates for evil personhood I mentioned earlier in the book—defends an extremity theory of evil personhood.[3]

What might motivate someone to adopt an extremity theory of evil? For one thing, extremity views pay respect to the fact that evil actions and persons typically have a profound (and profoundly negative) impact on our moral sensibilities. Whereas morally wrong actions might *offend*, or *disappoint*, or *hurt feelings*, evil actions seem to go beyond merely being offensive or disappointing. They *shock*; they *horrify*; they *repulse*; they *sicken*. These sorts of responses presumably underlie the apparent incomprehensibility of evil actions discussed in the previous chapter. Furthermore, and on a related note, some think that if we deny the extremity condition on evil actions—that is, if we deny that an action must be extremely morally wrong in order to count as evil—we thereby allow that there can be *trivial* evils, which is counterintuitive.[4] Finally, Barry defends his extremity theory of evil personhood partly on the grounds that it accommodates what is sometimes called the *mirror thesis*, which is the idea that evil persons are supposed to be a kind of perverse mirror image of moral saints.[5] If a moral saint is someone who is extremely morally good in virtue of possessing moral virtues to an extreme degree, then perhaps an evil person is someone who is extremely morally bad in virtue of possessing moral vices to an extreme degree.

For all that might be said in favor of an extremity theory of evil—whether of evil action, evil personhood, or both—I nonetheless think we should reject any such theory, for a few reasons. First, all of the above considerations that are supposed to count in favor of extremity views can be accommodated just as well by other sorts of theories. Suppose a theory of evil identifies some property E as the property in virtue of which an action or person counts as evil. As long as (a) E is something morally nontrivial, and (b) mature adult humans are psychologically disposed to be shocked, horrified, or repulsed by actions or persons with E, then this theory will be every bit as well suited to accommodate the first and second of the above considerations as any extremity view. Some of the theories analyzed later in this chapter, for instance, as well as my own theory in the next chapter, can explain why evil is nontrivial and why it often has such a profound effect on our moral sensibilities.

Second, Barry's point about an extremity view of evil personhood accommodating the mirror thesis only works if we first adopt an extremity view of moral sainthood according to which sainthood is a matter of being extremely morally virtuous. But this is controversial.[6] Here, too, we might alternatively define moral sainthood in terms of some separate property F, and then think of evil personhood as a kind of perverse mirror image of F. (Adams' religious conception of moral sainthood as participation in the interests of God, for example, might imply that an evil person is someone who actively opposes the interests of God—if we assume that something like the mirror thesis is correct. As I noted in Chap. 1, this may be plausible as a religious conception of evil.) In the next chapter, after defending my own theory of evil personhood, I explain what it might imply about moral sainthood if we accept the mirror thesis.

Third, and perhaps most significantly, extremity theories may actually give us reason to *abandon* the concept of evil. Rather than analyzing the concept of evil, extremity theories threaten to *analyze it away*. Take evil action, for example. If an evil action really is just an extremely morally wrong action, then apparently, to understand the nature of moral evil, we need look no further than our favorite theory in normative ethics—that is, any theory that offers an analysis of basic normative ethical concepts like moral rightness and wrongness. After all, presumably, an answer to the question "What makes an action *extremely* morally wrong?" will fall right out of an answer to the more basic question "What makes an action morally wrong?"[7] So, as long as our preferred normative ethical theory answers this latter question, it will thereby answer the former question as well. And if that is right, why even bother giving a theory of evil, if it is nothing over and above, or separate from, a theory of wrongness? For that matter, why even bother using the term "evil" at all?

In his own critique of extremity views, Calder explains, "If evil is just very wrong we can do without the term 'evil.' We can say everything we need to say using terms such as 'very wrong' or 'very very wrong.'"[8] But as I have been urging since Chap. 1, this just does not correspond with our intuitions about the relevant phenomena. Once again, here is Haybron, referring to people's ordinary intuitions with respect to things like serial murder and genocide: "Prefix your adjectives [like 'wrong' or 'bad'] with as many 'verys' as you like; you still fall short. Only 'evil', it seems, will do."[9] If someone were to say, "The Holocaust was bad," this would seem at best like a gross and irresponsible understatement, and perhaps worse, like a misuse of the term "bad" entirely. And adding that it was "*really* bad," or "*really, really* bad," or uttering the words in a particularly grave tone of voice, does not make the statement any better or more accurate. As I began Chaps. 2 and 3, by noting, serial murder and genocide stand out especially as paradigms of evil, but not because they are further down some sort of moral continuum from other murderous deeds with similar death tolls. Their status as evil seems to be less a matter of their simply having *a lot* of whatever property makes an action morally wrong, and more a matter of their possessing *some other property entirely*, in addition to whatever property makes an action morally wrong.

Of course, evil actions *are* typically very morally wrong and most evil people *are* typically morally bad, or morally vicious, in various respects. But this much can be acknowledged *without* accepting an extremity theory of evil. So in light of the above considerations, I will proceed on the assumption that evil is not simply a matter of extreme moral wrongness or badness. In other words, I assume that there is a qualitative, and not simply quantitative, difference between evil and other moral concepts.

I want to reiterate two other points from Chap. 1 before moving on. First, though there is some debate among philosophers about whether *evil action* or *evil person* is the more fundamental concept, my own approach is to assume that neither is more fundamental than the other, and instead that the concept of *evil* is fundamental to both. My focus throughout this chapter and the next will be on theories of evil personhood, but not because I take it to be more fundamental than the concept of evil action. Rather, it is only because I find the notion of evil personhood to be the more interesting of the two. As we will see in the next chapter, my own theory of evil applies equally well to both actions and persons, as well as to other things like events and institutions. Second, when we say of a person that he is evil, we make a judgment not simply about *what he has done*, but rather about *the sort of person he is*—that is, we say something about his *character*. As I put it in Chap. 1, not everyone who lies is a dishonest person. Even honest people tell lies from time to time, and when they do, we often explain the behavior by saying that they were acting "out-of-character." But this only makes sense as long as we recognize that character is not simply a matter of what you do; otherwise, presumably, anyone who acts dishonestly would therefore be a dishonest person. Likewise, not all *evildoers* are *evil people*. An evildoer, as I defined the term in Chap. 1, is just anyone who performs an evil action. But evil actions, like dishonest actions, can be performed out-of-character. A theory of evil personhood, then, has to tell us what it is about a person's *character* that makes him evil.

With these points in mind, and with extremity views set to the side, I think we can divide most contemporary theories of evil personhood into three types: *action-based* theories, *desire-based* theories, and *affect-based* theories. For each type of theory, I will explain its basic features, provide at least one example of a theory of that type, and then explain why theories of that type do not adequately account for evil personhood. This will then set the stage for my own theory, which I develop and defend in the next chapter.

ACTION-BASED THEORIES OF EVIL

An action-based theory of evil personhood, in simple terms, states that a person, S, is evil if and only if S performs, or is disposed to perform, actions of a given type. So obviously, proponents of action-based theories owe us an account of the type of action the performance of which makes a person evil. (If evil action really were more fundamental than evil personhood, then the account would presumably be as follows: S is evil if and only if S performs, or is disposed to perform, *evil* actions, whatever those are.) Action-based theories can be further divided into two subtypes: aggregative theories and dispositional theories. According to an aggregative theory, S is evil if and only if S has in fact performed the relevant type of action, and has done so in a way that meets or surpasses some threshold—by, for example, performing the action *enough* times, or with *enough* victims, or in a way that causes *enough* harm. As Russell puts it, according to aggregative theories, "[B]eing an evil person is equivalent to actually having done enough terribly wrong things."[10] On the other hand, according to dispositional theories of evil personhood, S need not have *actually performed* any actions of the relevant type. Rather, S is evil as long as S is *disposed* to perform them.

Marcus Singer defends an extremity theory of evil action, and then an aggregative action-based theory of evil personhood. Here he is putting the two theories together:

> [O]ne can imagine oneself jumping over the moon, or flying simply by flapping one's arms. But no ordinary decent human being, possessed of normal capacities for empathy and sympathy, can imagine himself treating someone else in a way that is evil. Hence the definition: *An evil action is one so bad, so awful, so horrendous that no ordinary decent reasonable human being can conceive of himself (or herself) doing such a thing. And an evil person or organization is one who knowingly performs, wills, or orders such actions, or*

> *remains indifferent to them when performed by another in a situation where one could do something to stop or prevent them.*[11]

So actions are evil in virtue of being extremely morally bad or wrong, where the relevant measure of extremity is to be understood in terms of incomprehensibility (recall my discussion of incomprehensibility from the last chapter). And persons are evil in virtue of the connection they bear to the performance of such actions, whether by performing the actions themselves, ordering others to perform them (think of Pauline Nyiramasuhuko ordering the mass rape of Tutsi women and girls), or sitting idly by while others perform them.

Now, in addition to owing us an account of the relevant type of action the performance of which makes a person count as evil, aggregative accounts owe us an account of the relevant aggregate: how much evil behavior is "enough" for a person to count as evil? Here is Singer's answer: "[O]ne who engages in a *pattern* of such behavior is evil."[12] One evil action cannot make you an evil person. Perhaps two are insufficient as well. But presumably, after three or four or five evil actions, performed closely enough in time and perhaps similar enough to each other to count as a "pattern," it is safe to say that the person performing the actions is evil.

Aggregative action-based theories of evil personhood are deeply problematic. First, as I just explained, to say that a person is evil is to make a judgment about that person's *character*, and judgments about character necessarily go beyond observations about the actions that a person has performed. Let's go back to the example of an honest person telling lies. Suppose this person cares very deeply about honesty and integrity, about respecting people's rights to know certain truths, and so forth, and, in fact, tells the truth far more often than not. But, suppose also that she compulsively lies whenever she feels nervous or insecure. The lies are rarely motivated by a concern for her own interest, and most times, she feels so guilty afterward that she begs the person to whom she lied for forgiveness. Here is someone who not only engages in dishonest behavior, but also does so often and consistently enough for it to be a pattern. But given all that we know about her, surely it would be a mistake to call her a dishonest person. As far as her character is concerned, she exhibits the virtue of honesty just as well as, if not more excellently than, most people—perhaps even people who tell fewer lies. Again, judgments of character are not judgments about what sorts of things a person has done; they are judgments about what sort of person she is. This basic point about character judgments does not change when the actions in question are evil rather than merely dishonest. Of course, most people who engage in a pattern of evil actions likely will have evil characters. But a pattern of evil actions can no more make a person evil than a pattern of dishonest actions can make a person dishonest. So aggregative theories, it seems, cannot adequately account for the difference between an evil person and an evildoer.

A related problem for aggregative theories is that they get the order of explanation between character and action backward. Presumably, when someone engages in a pattern of evil behavior, this reveals something about the person's character, which was not only *present all along*, but which also *explains* how they could do such evil deeds in the first place. But according to aggregative theories, the person only became evil *after*, and *because*, he performed the relevant number of evil deeds. So, whereas it seems natural to say something like, "He did those terrible things because he's evil," aggregative theories suggest counter-intuitively that the reverse is actually more accurate: "He's evil because he did those terrible things." As you recall, Ted Bundy's career as a serial killer began in 1974 with the brutal abduction, murder, and decapitation of Lynda Healy, and ended in 1978 with the rape and murder of 12-year-old Kimberly Leach. Intuitively, both murders are explained (at least partly) by the fact that Bundy was an evil person. But on Singer's aggregative theory, we cannot explain Bundy's first few murders by saying that he did them *because he was evil*, since he was not evil until he did them.[13]

Finally, aggregative theories fail to accommodate the possibility of character modification. We ordinarily think of a person's character as something that can change, whether for better or for worse. And yet, if (part of) a person's character is set or defined by *actions already performed*, then it is hard to see how a change in (that part of) the person's character could even be possible. If performing some number of evil actions is sufficient for being an evil person, and Tom has already met or exceeded that threshold, then he is an evil person. But now suppose that Tom spends the rest of his life not only abstaining from any such actions, but also making amends to former victims, influencing others to abstain from such behavior, and performing many other positive goods. Intuitively, we want to say that Tom is "a different person"—we want to say that he *was* evil, but is no longer. But for all of these changes to Tom and his life, it is still the case that he performed the requisite number of evil deeds. And so, according to aggregative theories of evil personhood, it is unfortunately, and counter-intuitively, still the case that Tom is evil.[14]

This is supposed to be one of the key advantages that dispositional action-based theories have over aggregative views. Since dispositional views define character not in terms of *actions already performed*, but rather in terms of *actions one is disposed to perform*, they leave adequate room for character modification. As long as Tom was once disposed to perform evil actions, but is no longer so disposed, we get the conclusion that seemed right: he *was* evil, but is no longer. Dispositional theories also seem to get the order of explanation right when it comes to the relationship between character and action. If evil character is a matter of being disposed to perform evil actions, then we can explain a person's evil action by saying that he did it because he was evil, even before any sort of pattern of behavior emerges. Bundy's first murder, just as well as his last murder, can be explained in terms of a disposition to do such things.

Russell offers the fullest and most sophisticated defense of a dispositional theory of evil personhood. Like Singer, Russell begins by defending an extremity theory of evil action, but Russell's is notably more complicated than Singer's. After considering a few different notions of extremity, and ironing out a few wrinkles associated with the notion of culpability, he arrives at the following definition of evil action:

> I propose that all evil actions are extreme culpable wrongs, where 'extreme' means appropriately connected to an actual or possible harm that is extreme for at least one victim, and 'appropriately connected' means that the action culpably produces or was intended to produce such a harm, or (more contentiously) that the action foreseeably would have produced such a harm if it was successful, or if it had its typical effects, or (even more contentiously) that the action is an appreciation of such harm.[15]

Whereas Singer couched extremity in terms of an action being incomprehensible to "ordinary decent reasonable human beings," Russell understands extremity in terms of the harm done to victims. Evil actions are extremely morally wrong actions, and they are extremely morally wrong in virtue of being extremely harmful. But like Singer, Russell wants his account of evil action to include actions that are not themselves extremely harmful, such as Nyiramasuhuko's ordering of the mass rape of Tutsi women and girls (as distinct from the subsequent acts of rape), or Eichmann's orchestration of the mass deportation of Jews to concentration and extermination camps. Even if these actions were not themselves extremely harmful, they were nonetheless "appropriately connected" to extreme harm, and are therefore evil.

Russell then adds an account of evil *feelings*, noting that emotions, like actions, are sometimes susceptible to moral evaluation. Just as there can be morally right and wrong actions, there can be morally right and wrong ways of responding emotionally to something; anger, for example, is often a right response, and indifference a wrong response, to injustice. But, can there be *evil* feelings?

> Which, if any, might warrant being called evil feelings? The most likely candidates come from within the class of antisympathetic feelings [here he cites McGinn; see below]: feelings of pleasure at another's pain, harm, or suffering, and feelings of pain at another's happiness or success. These are not merely pleasures that are caused by the suffering of others or pains that are caused by the pleasures of others. Rather, antisympathetic feelings are intentionally directed at the pleasure or suffering of others.[16]

One of the cases that Russell has in mind is that of the so-called harmless sadistic voyeur. This is supposed to be someone who is not himself disposed to perform (or even to order others to perform) actions that would cause anyone harm, but nonetheless greatly enjoys watching others perform extremely harmful actions, and does not renounce or repudiate these feelings in any way. If the harmless sadistic voyeur is evil—and Russell assumes that most people will agree he is—it apparently cannot be in virtue of any disposition to perform extremely harmful actions. It must then be a matter of his being disposed to evil feelings.

So with his accounts of evil action and evil feeling in place, Russell gives us the following theory of evil personhood:

> S is an evil person if and only if S is strongly and highly fixedly disposed to perform evil actions when in autonomy-favoring conditions, or S is strongly and highly fixedly disposed to have unrepudiated evil feelings when in autonomy-favoring conditions.[17]

Dispositions to act or feel a certain way are *strong* whenever the likelihood of their being realized is relatively great, and they are *highly fixed* as long as it would be difficult to change their strength over time. So, to borrow one of Russell's examples, I am currently strongly disposed to mispronounce French terms and expressions, since it is very likely that I will do so; but this disposition is not especially highly fixed, since it would be easy for me to learn how to pronounce them correctly. On the other hand, an incredibly racist person is strongly disposed to think racist thoughts, and this disposition is unfortunately likely to be very highly fixed, since incredibly racist people are not easily reformed.

Russell adds that the disposition has to be *strong* and *highly fixed* for a couple of reasons. First, as we have seen, there is some social psychological research that suggests that all or most of us are at least somewhat disposed to perform evil actions—think, for instance, of the Milgram experiment and dehumanization studies discussed in Chap. 3, or of some of the situationist research discussed in Chap. 5. The disappointing truth seems to be that, given the right combination of psychological and situational factors, most people will voluntarily inflict serious and undeserved harm on others. But surely, not all of us are evil. Evil people like Bundy and Eichmann stand out, in part, because of how uncommon they are. So, by adding that the disposition to perform evil actions must be both strong and highly fixed, Russell can apparently accommodate this intuition about the rarity of evil personhood, since most people are still relatively unlikely to engage in evil behavior (hence, not strongly disposed), and "the vast majority of us could be reformed or redeemed and lose our disposition to do evil" (hence, not highly fixedly disposed).[18] Second, intuitively, a disposition has to be relatively strong and highly fixed in order to count as a genuine character trait. On most accounts of character or virtue, infrequent, fickle, and especially short-lived dispositions are not sufficiently enduring to count as traits of character.[19] And finally, Russell adds that the disposition must be present in conditions that favor a person's *autonomy* in order to avoid it being the case that someone strongly and highly fixedly disposed to evil behavior, but only as a result of brainwashing, coercion, or some other uninvited outside force, counts as an evil person.

We have already seen a couple of the advantages that dispositional action-based theories of evil personhood have over their aggregative counterparts. Another point in favor of a dispositional theory like Russell's is that it apparently picks out the right sorts of people as evil. For instance, given all that we know about Bundy's psychology, it seems very likely that he was strongly and highly fixedly disposed not only to engage in extremely harmful behavior, but also to respond antisympathetically to his victims' pain. And again, unlike aggregative views, a dispositional theory makes no distinction between Bundy at the beginning of his killing career and Bundy at the end of his killing career: as long as he was strongly and highly fixedly disposed to evil actions and feelings at both points in time, then he was an evil person at both points in time, which seems right. Russell's dispositional view does, however, make a distinction between Nazi leaders, on the one hand, and Nazi commoners (like Melita Maschmann), on the other. And this, too, seems right. Maschmann may have engaged in evil behavior, but the sort of ambivalence that she exhibited at times during the Third Reich, and the sort of personal reform that she underwent soon after the war, suggest that her disposition to evil was nowhere near as strong and highly fixed as that of Eichmann. So Russell's view can apparently explain why Eichmann, but not Maschmann, was evil, even if both engaged in evil behavior.

For all that might be said in its favor, however, there are nonetheless some very serious problems for Russell's dispositional theory of evil personhood. As I explained above, in virtue of being an *action-based* view, the plausibility of Russell's theory of evil personhood depends first (and perhaps foremost) upon his account of evil action. And so, the first problem with Russell's theory of evil personhood is just that it depends upon a very problematic conception of evil action. There are controversies here on two fronts: Russell's account of evil action alleges that an action must be both (a) culpably morally wrong and (b) extremely harmful in order for it to count as evil, and there are good reasons for rejecting both of these conditions. As a way of illustrating the apparent non-necessity of culpable moral wrongness for evil action, Calder offers us the case of the so-called malicious hirer. It is a somewhat complicated case, so I will quote at length:

> In Malicious Hirer, A has the power to hire a candidate for a prestigious well-paying job: President of a charity organization called Good Deeds. Two people have applied: B and C. B has worked hard to acquire the education and experience for this specific job, and she is one of the two most qualified applicants for the job. A is aware of B's qualifications. A also knows that if B doesn't get the job she will be devastated and suffer a severe depression. A knows that C is equally well-qualified for the job but that C will not suffer a depression if she doesn't get the job. However, the situation is such that if C gets the job the lives of a lot of people will be greatly improved. C is a celebrity. If C gets the job, Good Deeds will receive a lot of publicity which will result in more donations. Let us say that it is obvious that hiring C rather than B will maximize the good and prevent some people from suffering more than B would suffer from the depression. A hires C reasonably expecting that she will bring about these good effects, but she does not really care about the overall good or about preventing suffering. She cares only about getting pleasure from the suffering of others. The reason A hires C rather than B is to take pleasure in the suffering this will cause B and not to maximize the overall good or to prevent suffering. This makes her act evil.[20]

Plausibly, it was not culpably morally wrong for A to hire C, especially if one accepts a broadly consequentialist theory of moral rightness and wrongness. But given what we know about A's sadistic motivation for doing so, it may seem as if A is behaving evilly. So perhaps Russell is mistaken to think that evil actions must involve culpable moral wrongdoing.

Russell's response to the case of the malicious hirer is interesting, since it appears to place him on the horns of a tricky dilemma. Basically, he thinks that the case conflates what are in fact two separate actions taken by A: first, there is the act of hiring C; second, there is the act of taking pleasure in B's suffering. It was not culpably morally wrong for A to hire C, he agrees, but it *was* culpably morally wrong for A to take pleasure in B's suffering. So the latter, but not the former, is an evil action.[21] The dilemma, however, arises from Russell's suggestion that *taking pleasure* in something is itself a kind of *action*. Russell certainly is not alone in thinking that affective responses can count as actions, but it does place him squarely in the minority among philosophers, the vast majority of whom, since Plato, have conceived of emotions and other affective phenomena (*pathe*) as markedly *passive* states. But the problem for Russell is not just that he conceives of affective responses in an unpopular way. Here is the dilemma: on the one hand, if Russell is right to think that taking pleasure in something could itself be an evil action, then it immediately becomes unclear why he felt the need to supplement his own theory of evil action with a separate account of evil feelings, if evil feelings (like the malicious hirer's sadistic pleasure) are just themselves evil actions; on the other hand, if Russell is wrong to think that taking pleasure in something can itself be an evil action, then it once again looks as if the case of the malicious hirer is a counter-example to his claim that evil actions must be culpably morally wrong.

Another problem with Russell's theory of evil action is that its emphasis on *degree* of harm, as opposed to *type* of harm, leaves him unable to explain why only certain actions tend to stand out as paradigm instances of evil. As I began Chaps. 2 and 3 by noting, there is something peculiar about both serial murder and genocide that makes these actions seem so evil to so many people. While it may initially seem as if this is due to the *extremity* of the harm caused by these actions, on further reflection and closer examination, it seems it must be something else. After all, in some cases, serial murderers may actually cause less overall harm than other murderers—by, for example, having fewer victims or killing their victims relatively quickly and painlessly (before then dismembering, or engaging in sex acts with the corpses). As I explained at the beginning of Chap. 3, not only might some acts of genocide actually involve less overall harm than other instances of mass killing, such as that involved in war, but also, the category of actions that most would consider instances of genocide might even include actions that involve no killing at all, and relatively little harm—for example, imagine one ethnic group forcing all of the women of another ethnic group to be sterilized, effectively "killing off" the targeted ethnicity, but doing so in a relatively humane way (i.e., by medical standards of humaneness). This is why I felt it necessary to dig so deeply throughout Chaps. 2–4 into the psychological mechanisms underlying purportedly evil actions and the people most notorious for performing them—that is, because only by doing so can we recognize that, even though people like Bundy and Eichmann were indeed responsible for causing extreme harm to others, this is not what made their behavior evil. Rather, it apparently has more to do with the *type* of harm inflicted on victims, for example, the way serial murderers objectify their victims, the way genocidal leaders dehumanize their victims, and the way human traffickers commodify their victims.

So Russell's dispositional theory of evil personhood is problematic in virtue of relying on a problematic conception of evil action. But even aside from worries about his account of evil action, we should reject any account of evil personhood that defines it ultimately in terms of a *disposition* to this or that type of action (or feeling). Russell understandably focuses on the different *ways in which* a person might be disposed to some behavior—strongly or not, highly fixedly or not, and so on. As I explained above, these features of behavioral dispositions are indeed relevant to their counting as traits of character. But what Russell neglects to consider is that there are also different *reasons or motives for which* a person might be disposed to the behavior in question. Here, again, is Adams:

> It is very doubtful that a direct behavioral disposition is sufficient to constitute a virtue. At a minimum, we may think, one must have a good motive for the behavior in question if the disposition is to count as a virtue. It seems possible to have a direct disposition to behave honestly out of fear of social consequences of dishonest behavior without caring much at all about honesty and other people's rights for their own sake. Such a disposition, badly motivated though it be, will still be socially *useful*, [...] but few will think it is *excellent* enough to be a virtue.[22]

It seems as if we can imagine two people, both strongly and highly fixedly disposed to behaving honestly in autonomy-favoring conditions, but for markedly different reasons or motives. Maybe one behaves honestly out of fear of social consequences, or perhaps, like Kant's famous shopkeeper example, he behaves honestly solely to secure whatever benefits come with having an honest reputation (e.g., increased business due to increased customer trust). The other person, though, behaves honestly because he cares about honesty, and respects others' rights to know certain truths. Presumably, only the latter person, and not the former, counts as a genuinely *honest person*, even though both are strongly and highly fixedly disposed to honest behavior in autonomy-favoring conditions. Adams' point in the above quotation is that we are not yet talking about virtue until and unless we say something about the reason or motive behind the virtuous behavior. And the point applies just as well to moral character more generally: if you want to say something about a person's character, you have to go beyond merely noting the *ways in which* he or she is disposed to behave and say something about the *reasons or motives for which* he or she is disposed to behave, that is, the reasons or motives that *explain why* he or she is disposed to behave in those ways.

The mistake that Russell makes here is akin to that of confusing a symptom, or set of symptoms, for the disease that underlies them. Though we may casually speak as if the common cold *consists in* such things as a runny nose and sore throat, as we also well know, these are not the disease, but only symptoms of the disease. The disease itself is a viral infection of the upper respiratory system. And the viral infection is what underlies and explains the runny nose, sore throat, and other symptoms. Likewise, honesty does not *consist in* being strongly and highly fixedly disposed to honest behavior, even though honest people *will* be disposed in these ways. Rather, honesty consists in the trait or traits that underlie and explain the strong and highly fixed disposition to honest behavior—for example, caring about honesty and respecting others' rights. In the same way, evil personhood does not *consist in* being strongly and highly fixedly disposed to evil actions or feelings, even though evil people *will* be disposed in these ways. Rather, evil personhood, or evil character, consists in whatever trait or traits underlies and explains the strong and highly fixed disposition to evil actions or feelings.

So, in one sense, Russell's dispositional theory of evil personhood is correct: evil persons *will* be disposed to evil actions and evil feelings. But the correctness here is merely superficial. It tells us something interesting about evil persons, but very little about the actual nature of evil personhood. For that, we would need to know more about what it is about these people that underlies and explains why they are disposed in these ways.

Desire-Based Theories of Evil

According to desire-based theories of evil personhood, S is an evil person if and only if S regularly has desires of a certain sort. But desires *for what*, exactly? Much like the action-based theories discussed in the previous section, desire-based theories of evil typically associate evil with harm. So, for example, in Chap. 2, I briefly mentioned the desire-based view of Manuel Vargas, according to which someone is evil as long as he "desire[s] to see other people harmed for no reason beyond the desire itself."[23] Claudia Card defines evil in terms of reasonably foreseeable and intolerable harm, and explains, "Someone may be rightly judged an evil person on the basis of persistent and effective evil motives or intentions (or both) or on the basis of persistent gross negligence or recklessness."[24] Calder then clarifies,

> [A]n evil motive is a desire for someone else's intolerable harm for its own sake, that is, a desire for intolerable harm as an end in itself or as part of a whole that is desired. An evil intention "is an [inexcusable] intention to do someone intolerable harm, or to do something with that foreseeable result."[25]

Already, we can see some of the advantages that desire-based theories have over their action-based counterparts. For one thing, unlike aggregative action-based views, desire-based theories can accommodate the possibility of character modification, since, presumably, an evil person's desire for another's intolerable harm can weaken over time, and perhaps be lost entirely. Also unlike aggregative action-based views, desire-based theories seem to get the order of explanation between evil personhood or character and evil action right, since, presumably, desires often figure into explanations of actions. So desire-based theories can make good sense of claims to the effect that "he did it *because he was evil*." Finally, desire-based theories avoid the problem just raised for Russell's dispositional view, since they purport to tell us what it is about a person's character that underlies and explains his strong and highly fixed disposition to cause others extreme or intolerable harm, namely, the fact that he regularly desires to do so.

Calder begins his own defense of a desire-based theory of evil personhood by adapting W. D. Ross's account of the relationship between vicious action and vicious character.

> According to Ross, vicious characters are those characters from which vicious actions spring and vicious actions are those actions that spring from certain sorts of desires. For instance, three types of desires that lead to vicious actions are the desire to do what is wrong, the desire to bring into being some bad state of affairs, and the desire to inflict pain on another.[26]

Presumably, having an evil character is one way of having a vicious character. But, Calder goes on to note that of the three types of desires noted by Ross, only one could have anything to do with evil. Desiring to do what is wrong cannot be evil, he thinks, since a person can persistently desire to do very trivial wrongs, and this would not make him evil. Nor is it evil to desire to bring about "the admiring contemplation of ugly pieces of art, which some, such as G. E. Moore, believe are objectively bad states of affairs."[27] So if evil character is to be understood in terms of any of these three types of vicious desires, it is apparently a matter of desiring to inflict pain on another. But since Calder thinks a desire to inflict some very minor or trivial pain on another should not be sufficient to make a person evil, he arrives, for now, at the conclusion that evil character or personhood has something to do with a desire to inflict some *significant* harm on another.

Going a bit further, Calder suggests that S cannot be an evil person if his desire to cause significant harm to another is consistently overcome by a *stronger* desire to *refrain* from causing harm. For this reason, he claims that evil personhood is a matter of being regularly or consistently motivated by what he calls an "e-desire set":

> I call combinations of desires for other people's significant harm or for objects or states of affairs inconsistent with other people's being spared serious harm, together with the lack of a [stronger] desire that they not be significantly harmed, e-desire sets. I contend that e-desire sets are constitutive of the motivation necessary for evil.[28]

But what if S desires another's significant harm and this desire is not overcome or outweighed by any stronger desire that the other be spared significant harm, but the desire itself is had for good reason? For instance, perhaps he only desires another's significant harm because this is unfortunately necessary in order to spare others from an even more serious harm. Surely, then, he is not an evil person, and it would not be evil for him to act on this desire. In light of this possibility, Calder adds that it only counts as an e-desire set if the desire for another's harm is itself morally unjustified. As he puts it elsewhere, it is only an e-desire set if the desire for another's harm is had "for an unworthy goal."[29] His preferred way of conceiving of the *worthiness* of a goal is in terms of hedonistic consequentialism. As he explains, "A goal is worthy of a harm when it makes for a state of affairs that is on balance more valuable than if the harm had not occurred," and the value of a state of affairs is presumably to be understood in terms of its overall balance of pleasure or happiness to pain or suffering.[30]

We are now in a position to see clearly Calder's accounts of both evil action and evil character. For Calder, an action is evil if and only if two conditions are met. First, the action must cause some significant harm to at least one victim, where the harm counts as "significant" as long as "a normal rational human being would take considerable pains to avoid [it]."[31] Second, the action has to be motivated by an e-desire set. Both of these conditions are necessary, and together they are sufficient, for an action to count as evil. And a person is evil as long as he is regularly or persistently motivated by e-desire sets.

> I contend that e-desire sets are the defining characteristic of evil character. Those who have these desire sets will also be inclined to carry out their despicable plans and take pleasure in the fruition of these plans. However, they may not do so. Their evil plans may be spoiled by their own cowardice or incompetence or by other inhibiting factors, and they may not derive pleasure from accomplishing their despicable deeds. Thus, it seems that all that is required for evilness of character is a consistent propensity for e-desire sets.[32]

So, like Russell's dispositional view, Calder's theory of evil personhood does not require that a person actually perform evil actions in order to count as an evil person. If S is regularly motivated by e-desire sets, but S's desire for another's significant harm is always frustrated either by ignorance, incompetence, or unforeseen circumstances—so S never actually performs any harmful acts—S will still count as an evil person.

Despite its advantages over action-based theories, Calder's desire-based theory of evil faces a number of serious problems. For one thing, by stipulating that the desire for another's harm must be had for an unworthy goal, and then conceiving worthiness in hedonistic consequentialist terms, Calder may open himself up to a kind of objection that often arises in general discussions of hedonistic consequentialism. Recall Calder's own case of the malicious hirer. This is someone who desires another's significant harm for a goal that is *apparently* unworthy of the harm caused, namely, his own sadistic pleasure. But again, as Calder understands the worthiness of a goal, it is ultimately a matter of the value of the resulting state of affairs; and according to hedonism, the value of a state of affairs is supposed to be a matter of its overall balance of pleasure to pain. So, what if the malicious hirer's sadistic pleasure is sufficiently great in magnitude that it far outweighs even the significant harm caused to B? And, what if the malicious hirer knows this will be the case ahead of time? Could it not, then, be the case that his malicious desire actually *does* "[make] for a state of affairs that is on balance more valuable than if the harm had not occurred"? It seems so. But if that is right, then he is actually *not* being motivated by an e-desire set, since it would not be the case that his malicious desire is had for an unworthy goal. And if he is not motivated by an e-desire set, then he is not engaged in evil.

Another problem for Calder's view—and this one may apply more widely to other desire-based views as well—is that it is supposed to be a theory of evil *character*, but it fails to acknowledge and accommodate the fact that even persistent desires can be so disconnected from one's moral identity that they are not actually a part of one's character. In his now famous account of what it means to be a person, Harry Frankfurt distinguishes between two types of desires: first-order desires and second-order desires.[33] First-order desires can be directed at a wide variety of objects, including actions, circumstances, food, drink, material possessions, experiences, conditions (e.g., physical fitness, wealth), accomplishments (e.g., graduating, getting a job), and so on. Second-order desires, however, are only directed at other desires. The desire to exercise is a desire of the first-order. But suppose I do not actually want to exercise, but instead, I *want to want* to exercise. In this case, I have a second-order desire for the first-order desire to exercise. This may sound strange, but we actually say things like this all the time—for example, when someone says, "I wish I were more of a reader," or, "I wish I didn't crave chocolate so much." These are expressions of second-order desires: in the first case, a positive second-order desire for the first-order desire to read; and in the second case, a negative second-order desire to lack the first-order desire for chocolate.

As a way of illustrating the significance of second-order desires to our moral identities, Frankfurt introduces readers to the so-called unwilling addict. This is someone with two competing first-order desires—a very strong desire for drugs and a considerably weaker desire to refrain from using drugs—and a second-order desire that the first-order desire to refrain be effective. Unfortunately, though, this second-order desire often goes unsatisfied, since his first-order desire for drugs is so powerful. Here is how Frankfurt characterizes the unwilling addict:

> The unwilling addict identifies himself [...] through the formation of a second-order volition, with one rather than with the other of his conflicting first-order desires. He makes one of them more truly his own and, in so doing, he withdraws himself from the other. It is in virtue of this identification and withdrawal, accomplished through the formation of a second-order volition, that the unwilling addict may meaningfully make the analytically puzzling statements that the force moving him to take the drug is a force other than his own, and that it is not of his own free will but rather against his will that this force moves him to take it.[34]

In other words, despite being persistently motivated by the first-order desire for drugs, the unwilling addict nonetheless *identifies himself* with the weaker of the two first-order desires, to such a degree that the desire for drugs is not really *his own*. He has so withdrawn himself from the first-order desire for drugs that it might as well have been put there, artificially, by some outside source—via brainwashing, a chip on his brain, manipulation by an evil demon, or whatever. Either way, that desire is not constitutive of *the sort of person he is*, even if it happens to be a desire on which he acts fairly regularly. It seems the unwilling addict can point to his first-order desire for drugs and say, sincerely and truthfully, "That's not who I am."

If this is right, then Calder's desire-based theory of evil personhood, not to mention any other theory according to which evil personhood is a matter of regularly having and being motivated by a (first-order) desire to engage in evil behavior, is at best incomplete. After all, it is apparently possible for someone to be motivated by something like an e-desire set, and yet to identify himself so strongly with the weaker of the two first-order desires (i.e., the desire that others not be significantly harmed) that the stronger desire for harm is not constitutive of the sort of person he is. He may, then, engage in legitimately evil behavior, but it hardly seems right to say that he is an evil *person*—that he has an evil *character*—especially when we contrast him with another person who also has an e-desire set, but identifies himself very much with the stronger desire for another's harm, and perhaps even wishes that he lacked entirely the weaker desire that others be spared significant harm. In short, it seems as if claims about a person's desires are not yet claims about the person's character, until something is added about how the desires are had, what relationship they bear to the desirer's identity, and so forth.

Finally, recall my brief discussion of genocide at the beginning of Chap. 3, where I made the point that, while it can be easy to assume that the relevant feature of genocide that makes it an instance of evil is the fact that it involves *so many deaths*, further reflection forces us to look a bit deeper than this for the relevant evil-making property. The extreme death tolls may be sufficient for making genocide count as an atrocity, but there are other atrocities with similar death tolls that many would not count as evil—in the same sense of "evil," at least—such as wars. (Furthermore, as I have noted before, we can imagine genocidal policies that would not involve such enormous death tolls—perhaps no deaths at all—but would nonetheless count as evil.) Our intuitions suggest that there is something unique about genocide in particular that sets it apart from other atrocities as an instance of evil—just as there is something unique about serial murder that sets it apart from other homicidal acts as an instance of evil. To assume, then, that acts of genocide are evil because of their enormous death tolls is to settle too quickly for the appearances of things, and to miss the deeper truth about what is in fact its evil-making property, which, as I have hinted already, and will argue in the next chapter, has more to do with the way in which the victims are seen, or regarded, by the perpetrators.

I repeat this point about the evil of genocide because I think Calder makes a similar mistake when he claims that the relevant evil-making property of persons has something to do with their either desiring another's significant harm or desiring something inconsistent with others being spared significant harm. Of course, many evil people do desire such things. But this is like admitting that most cases of genocide do involve enormous death tolls. Even if the observation is correct, we should not assume from this that what we are observing is in fact what makes a person evil.

Even if Ted Bundy arguably was not motivated by a desire for his victims' harm, but rather a desire to possess another person as one might possess a potted plant—as you recall, his closest biographers called this "the key to understanding Ted"—Calder could just say that Bundy was evil in virtue of desiring something inconsistent with others being spared significant harm. So he was still motivated by an e-desire set, apparently. But what about some of the other people discussed in Chaps. 2–4? Take Adolf Eichmann, for instance. Throughout his entire career as a Nazi officer, Eichmann was motivated first and foremost by a desire for "a Jew-free Germany." And of course, he eventually acted to satisfy this desire by orchestrating the extermination of several million innocent people, most of them Jews. But as I mentioned in passing in Chap. 3, genocide was not his first plan for satisfying his desire. At one point, for instance, he met with a number of Zionist leaders, and even toured Palestine, all in the hope of coordinating a mass Zionist emigration of Jews out of Germany.

In fact, according to some historians, it was not until after the Nazis invaded Russia in 1941 that extermination was even seriously considered by the Nazi leaders.[35] Until that time, their efforts were focused on a policy of resettlement, moving Jews—voluntarily or not—out of Germany and into eastern Poland. Once they moved into Russia, it became clear that resettlement was no longer practical: cities were already clogged, ghettos over-flowing, and the Nazis had just "inherited" a population of Russian Jews. Let us assume—falsely, of course, but for the sake of argument—that resettlement could have been pulled off without causing significant harm to any Jews—perhaps the Nazis could have persuaded Jews to resettle "for their own good." There still would be something grossly evil about the Nazis' treatment of the Jews, since it would still be the case that they regarded the Jews as something *less than persons*—that is, as *things* to be packed up and shipped elsewhere, even if no significant harm is involved. But if this is right, then neither desiring another's significant harm nor desiring something inconsistent with another's significant harm is necessary for being evil.

If you find this bit of revisionist history unpersuasive, consider instead some of the characters discussed in Chap. 4. Madoff, it seems, was motivated by a pair of desires: first, a desire for money; and second, a desire for a kind of social status that, earlier in life, he felt others enjoyed to his exclusion. Now, as a matter of fact, the way he went about satisfying these two desires did involve causing significant harm to thousands of victims. But, strictly speaking, neither wealth nor social status is *inconsistent* with others being spared significant harm. There are morally legitimate ways of acquiring both. Likewise, human traffickers are typically motivated simply by a desire for money, and this, again, is a desire the satisfaction of which is strictly speaking consistent with others being spared significant harm.

But unfortunately, like Madoff, their preferred means of satisfying their desire for wealth did in fact involve causing massive amounts of undeserved suffering. If this is right, then neither Madoff nor human traffickers (nor their actions) are evil, since neither is motivated by an e-desire set. After all, it is not their desires that are inconsistent with others being spared significant harm, but rather the means by which they acted to satisfy their desires. But surely it is evil to knowingly and willfully participate in a business in which the "products" are human children, and "success" typically involves these children being brutally raped upward of tens of thousands of times.

Calder has a response to this sort of objection, but in my view, it will only raise a further and more interesting problem for him. His response is to allow that there may actually be two different kinds of evil persons or characters: *positive* and *privative*.[36] To be positively evil is just to be regularly motivated by something like an e-desire set. But after conceding to Haybron that someone can qualify as evil "even if he never has evil motives or intentions," Calder writes, "We might say this sort of person has a privative evil character because it is their lack of empathy and concern that makes them evil rather than anything they want or try to do."[37] So perhaps he could say that Madoff, human traffickers, and our reimagined Nazis may not be *positively* evil, since their desires were neither for another's harm nor for anything inconsistent with others being spared significant harm. But these people were *privatively* evil in virtue of how uncaring they were toward their victims.

There are two problems with this response, though. One immediate problem is that it will apparently force Calder to accept a similarly bifurcated account of evil action as well, since it is apparently possible to act evilly even in the absence of an e-desire set. But a potentially more serious problem with Calder's now-bifurcated theory of evil personhood is this: what is it about positively and privatively evil characters that makes them both count as evil? To say that two different things are both *round*, for instance, is either (a) to say that, despite their differences, they share some relevant feature in common (e.g., resemblance to a circle), or else (b) to use the term "round" in two difference senses—as, for example, when we say both that an opera singer's face is round (in the sense of resembling a circle) and also that his voice is round (in the sense of being rich or mellow). Assuming, then, that Calder is using "evil" in the same sense when he applies it to both positively and privatively evil characters, what is the relevant feature or property that both characters have in common, such that they both count as instances of evil? And whatever *that* property is, why not unify the theory by identifying evil personhood with possession of *it*? So, what may have initially seemed like a quick and easy solution to the problem that e-desire sets are not necessary for evil ends up compelling us to look elsewhere entirely for a satisfactory theory of evil personhood.

Affect-Based Theories of Evil

A final category of theories of evil personhood includes those that identify evil with a certain sort of affective response. Colin McGinn, for instance, has us imagine two hypothetical species: G-beings and E-beings.

> The G-beings are such that when another member of the species experiences pleasure they too experience pleasure, while when another experiences pain they feel pain. [...] The E-beings, on the other hand, exemplify the opposite laws of social psychology: pleasure in one causes pain in another, and pain causes pleasure. [...] If an E-being sees another stub his tow and yelp, she experiences a rush of pleasurable sensation, while if she sees someone enjoying a fresh melon, she feels a nasty sensation.[38]

He goes on to suppose that, given their affective dispositions, "the E-beings will promote and seek out painful sensations in others [They] will be apt to become torturers, sadists, thieves, rapists, child abusers—whatever causes distress in others."[39] After noting that the affective dispositions of the two hypothetical species are similar to those of many humans, he explains,

> My point in introducing them [the G-beings and E-beings] is to provide a model for two types of moral psychology: that of the virtuous person, and that of the evil person. Focusing on the evil person, then, and simplifying for the moment, the basic idea is that an evil character is one that derives pleasure from pain and pain from pleasure.[40]

So, according to an affect-based theory of evil personhood of the sort defended by McGinn, S is an evil person if and only if S is regularly pleased by others' pain or pained by others' pleasure.

Hillel Steiner defends a different sort of affect-based view. Steiner begins by noting that some features of actions *intensify* their moral wrongness without simply *increasing* it along a kind of spectrum or continuum, as mentioned above in conjunction with extremity theories. His model for this is the difference between assault and *aggravated* assault.[41] Aggravated assault is worse than assault, but it is not clear that the worseness here is merely a matter of its possessing *more* of whatever wrong-making property is already possessed by simple assault. Two assailants might incite in their victims equal amounts of fear, or cause equal amounts of harm, or whatever, but the fact that one of the assailants used a deadly weapon "aggravates" the wrongness of the act. Along these lines, Steiner argues that evil actions are worse than morally wrong actions, but not because they are on the extreme end of a continuum of wrongness or badness. Rather, they are worse in virtue of possessing some feature that "aggravates" their wrongness. The relevant aggravating feature is that the wrongdoer takes pleasure in doing wrong.[42] While Steiner only intends for this to be a theory of evil action, it is not hard to imagine what a Steiner-like theory of evil personhood would look like: S is an evil person if and only if S regularly takes pleasure in wrongdoing (and perhaps also despises doing what is right).

For both of these affect-based theories, evil is a matter of *having* a particular sort of morally *inappropriate* affective response—the sort that Russell dubbed "evil feelings." But, as Calder rightly pointed out in connection with so-called privative evil, there are also cases in which people seem evil in virtue of *lacking* a particular sort of morally *appropriate* affective response. For instance, Haybron asks, "What would we say of a sane man who allows, without compunction, a six-year-old to drink from a bottle of Drano, and impassively watches the child suffer an agonizing death?"[43] The man takes no pleasure in the child's suffering. Nor does he take any pleasure in the fact that his negligence is seriously morally wrong. Rather, he feels nothing at all. And it is precisely because he feels nothing at all that he (or at least, his behavior) seems so evil.

We need not imagine hypothetical cases in which evil people are utterly indifferent to another's pain. There is no evidence that Madoff took any sort of sadistic or perverse pleasure in the suffering of his victims, or in the wrongfulness of his deeds. The same is apparently true of most human traffickers. Rather, part of what makes these people seem so evil to us is how frighteningly business-like they are able to be while knowingly and willfully destroying the lives of so many innocent victims. Likewise, while some perpetrators of genocide clearly do take pleasure in the suffering of their victims, not all of them do. After the war, many Nazi leaders and henchmen claimed only to be disinterestedly (or even reluctantly) "doing their jobs," as if actively participating in the extermination of millions of innocent people is, like plumbing or selling insurance, just another way to make a living. Suppose some of them were being sincere. Does it really make them seem any less evil, their actions any less horrific, that they were able to remain so indifferent while leading innocent men, women, and children into gas chambers to be killed (or ordering others to do so)? Doctors and scientists of Japan's notorious Unit 731 were apparently completely unaffected while performing gruesome experiments on their Chinese prisoners, and this unimaginable *absence* of an affective or emotional response, given the circumstances, can seem every bit as evil as the *presence* of pleasure in McGinn's E-beings.

So perhaps a more plausible affect-based theory would say that S is an evil person if and only if S responds affectively to others' suffering in morally terrible and inappropriate ways, allowing that there are two ways of doing this—either sadistic pleasure or callous indifference. But, even if this theory would have an obvious advantage over affect-based theories that identify evil with only one sort of affective response, there are still serious problems for such a view. For one thing, the affect-based theorist still needs to say more about the amount or type of suffering that is relevant here. After all, most people take some pleasure in the very minor suffering of others—think, for instance, of the popularity of television programs like *America's Funniest Home Videos*, which regularly feature videos of people slipping, tripping, falling, crashing, and running into things—but surely we are not evil for doing so. Steiner's view faces a similar sort of problem, since it counter-intuitively implies that even a very minor wrong—a white lie, for example—could be an evil action as long as the wrongdoer takes pleasure in the act.[44]

Ultimately, though, the most significant problem for affect-based theories of evil personhood is similar to the one I raised above for dispositional action-based views. What makes a person evil is not *that* he responds affectively in morally terrible and inappropriate ways, but *why* he responds affectively in morally terrible and inappropriate ways. This, again, is the nature and depth of moral character. Character does not consist in certain affective responses or even in dispositions to certain affective responses, just like it does not consist in dispositions to certain actions. Rather, our character is what underlies and explains why we (are disposed to) act *and react* in the ways that we do. Two people might be regularly indifferent to others' suffering, but for importantly different reasons—perhaps one is cripplingly depressed, and as a result, struggles to engage emotionally with others, despite still recognizing the moral significance of others' suffering; while the other, Pauline Nyiramasuhuko perhaps, is indifferent to others' suffering because she sees them as *inyenzi*, mere cockroaches in need of extermination. I suspect most will have the intuition that only the latter of these two people ought to count as evil, even if they are both regularly indifferent to others' suffering. And this highlights the fact that, whatever it is that makes a *character* evil, it has to be something psychologically deeper than (dispositions to) affective responses.

Concluding Thoughts

In this chapter, I introduced you to four theories—or categories of theories—of evil personhood: extremity theories, action-based theories, desire-based theories, and affect-based theories. There are theories which I have not discussed to this point, but for the most part, these other views just combine elements of the types of theories already mentioned.

For instance, Haybron divides theories of evil personhood into three very similar categories: harm-based accounts, motive-based accounts, and affect-based accounts. After dismissing harm-based views—because they pay too little attention to considerations of motive and affect—Haybron then argues that motive-based and affect-based accounts are right insofar as they go, but both are incomplete. Since character is a matter of both motive *and* affect, he thinks, a more plausible theory of evil character or personhood would be a kind of hybrid of motive-based and affect-based views. So, he defends what he calls an "affective-motivational account," according to which S is an evil person if and only if S is "consistently vicious" in the sense of being "either wholly unaligned with the good, or moved and motivated by it so little that it makes no significant difference to the moral quality" of S's character.[45] And "alignment with the good," according to Haybron, is a matter of being moved (affectively) or motivated in ways that are responsive to moral reasons. So, for Haybron, evil personhood is a matter of not having any kind of "good side"—that is, being morally bad or vicious through-and-through.

At some points, Haybron sounds like he is defending an extremity view like Barry's above, according to which evil is a matter of being extremely morally vicious. If this is right, then Haybron's view should be rejected for the same reasons that Barry's view should be rejected. But at other points, Haybron's view sounds more like a straightforward combination of Calder's desire-based theory and the "more plausible" affect-based theory that I suggested in the previous section. If this is right, then his view will apparently just inherit the problems of both.

In the next and final chapter, I defend a theory of evil that not only avoids the problems raised in this chapter for other views, but also better accommodates the psychological data gathered in Part I of the book. In my view, evil is not a matter of the actions that one performs, or is disposed to perform. Nor is it a matter of one's desires or affective responses. Rather, evil personhood is a matter of the way in which one *sees*, or *regards*, fellow persons or members of the moral community.

Notes

1. See Russell (2007) and Calder (2013).
2. See Russell (2007, 2010, and 2014). Most of the discussion below will draw from Russell (2014).
3. See Barry (2009, 2011, and 2013).
4. See, e.g., Russell (2014: 46ff). As Russell explains, "Almost all contemporary accounts of evil action build in an extremity condition" (2014: 46). He then goes on to cite several theorists who appear to do just that, including Card (2002: 8), Morton (2004: 13), Singer (2004: 193), Kekes (2005: 1), and Formosa (2008: 228).
5. See Barry (2009 and 2011). Steiner urges a similar thesis with respect to evil actions, which he calls the Negative Counterpart Thesis: "[E]vil acts are simply the negative counterparts of supererogatory ones" (Steiner 2002: 185).
6. See, for example, the well-known exchange between Susan Wolf (1982), who defends something like Barry's conception of a moral saint, and Robert Adams (1984), who argues that sainthood is a religious concept, and defines moral sainthood in terms of participation in the interests of God.
7. Calder (2013: 182–187) shows how this works with respect to a few of the more prominent normative ethical theories.
8. Calder (2013: 178).
9. Haybron (2002: 260).
10. Russell (2014: 133).
11. Singer (2004: 196, italics in original).
12. Singer (2004: 197, italics added).
13. For more on the issue of evil character or personhood being an explanatory concept, see Garrard (2002) and Russell (2009).
14. For a more detailed statement of this objection to aggregative views, see Russell (2014: 144–147). Russell suggests that aggregative views might avoid the objection by supposing a person's life to be divisible into "life segments"—for example, we might say that Tom was evil in a previous life segment, but since he has not performed the requisite number of evil deeds in the present life segment, he is presently not an evil person. But, just as soon as Russell proposes this option for aggregative views, he goes on to argue that it will eventually generate contradictions (see especially 2014: 145).
15. Russell (2014: 62).
16. Russell (2014: 177).

17. Russell (2014: 192).
18. Russell (2014: 170).
19. See, e.g., Adams (2006: 18).
20. Calder (2013: 183–184).
21. Russell (2014: 41–42).
22. Adams (2006: 121).
23. Vargas (2010: 75).
24. Card (2002: 21).
25. Calder (2009: 23), quoting from Card (2002: 20).
26. Calder (2003: 364).
27. Calder (2003: 365). See Moore (1903 [1993]).
28. Calder (2003: 366). Initially, Calder identifies e-desire sets as combinations of (a) a desire for another's significant harm together with (b) the *total lack* of a desire that others be spared significant harm. But he then goes on to recognize that it is probably unnecessary that the agent totally lack a contrary desire. Rather, all that is required is that the agent's malicious desire be *stronger* than any contrary desires, that is, that the malicious desire be strong enough to be *effective*.
29. Calder (2007: 378). See also Calder (2013: 188).
30. Calder (2007: 379). In the same context, Calder endorses hedonism as the "best known non-privation theory of nonmoral evil" (2007: 378).
31. Calder (2013: 188).
32. Calder (2003: 369).
33. Frankfurt (1971).
34. Frankfurt (1971: 13).
35. Clendinnen (1999: 95–100). Clendinnen also references Browning (1992) in this context.
36. Calder (2009: 22–27).
37. Calder (2009: 25). Calder essentially just identifies privative evil with psychopathy, writing, "Privative evil characters are genuine psychopaths, not just habitual criminals. Some psychologists estimate that about 1 percent of the general population are psychopaths" (2009: 26). But this is almost certainly too strong a claim, since, as we saw in Chap. 2, there is much more to being a psychopath than merely lacking empathy.
38. McGinn (1997: 61).
39. McGinn (1997: 61, 62).
40. McGinn (1997: 62).
41. Steiner (2002: 184).
42. Steiner (2002: 189).
43. Haybron (2002: 271).
44. Russell (2007: 669–670). See also Calder (2013).
45. Haybron (2002: 269–271).

REFERENCES

Adams, Robert. 1984. Saints. *The Journal of Philosophy* 81(7): 392–401.
———. 2006. *A Theory of Virtue*. Oxford: Oxford University Press.
Barry, Peter B. 2009. Moral Saints, Moral Monsters, and the Mirror Thesis. *American Philosophical Quarterly* 46(2): 163–176.
Barry, Peter B. 2011. In Defense of the Mirror Thesis. *Philosophical Studies* 155(2): 199–205.
——— 2013. *Evil and Moral Psychology*. New York: Routledge.
Browning, Christopher. 1992. *The Path to Genocide: Essays in the Launching of the Final Solution*. Cambridge: Cambridge University Press.
Calder, Todd. 2003. The Apparent Banality of Evil. *Journal of Social Philosophy* 34(3): 364–376.
———. 2007. Is the Privation Theory of Evil Dead? *American Philosophical Quarterly* 44(4): 371–381.
———. 2009. The Prevalence of Evil. In *Evil, Political Violence, and Forgiveness: Essays in Honor of Claudia Card*, eds. Andrea Veltman and Kathryn J. Norlock, 13–34. Lanham: Lexington Books.
———. 2013. Is Evil Just Very Wrong? *Philosophical Studies* 163(1): 177–196.
Card, Claudia. 2002. *The Atrocity Paradigm: A Theory of Evil*. Oxford: Oxford University Press.
Clendinnen, Inga. 1999. *Reading the Holocaust*. Cambridge: Cambridge University Press.
Formosa, Paul. 2008. A Conception of Evil. *Journal of Value Inquiry* 42(2): 217–239.
Frankfurt, Harry G. 1971. Freedom of the Will and the Concept of a Person. *The Journal of Philosophy* 68(1): 5–20.
Garrard, Eve. 2002. Evil as an Explanatory Concept. *The Monist* 85(2): 320–336.
Haybron, Daniel. 2002. Moral Monsters and Saints. *The Monist* 85(2): 260–284.
Kekes, John. 2005. *The Roots of Evil*. Ithaca: Cornell University Press.
McGinn, Colin. 1997. *Ethics, Evil, and Fiction*. Oxford: Clarendon Press.
Moore, G. E. 1903 [1993]. *Principia Ethica*. Revised edition with 'Preface to the second edition' and other papers, edited by Thomas Baldwin. Cambridge: Cambridge University Press.
Morton, Adam. 2004. *On Evil*. New York: Routledge.
Russell, Luke. 2007. Is Evil Action Qualitatively Distinct from Ordinary Wrongdoing? *Australasian Journal of Philosophy* 85(4): 659–677.
———. 2009. He Did It Because He Was Evil. *American Philosophical Quarterly* 46(3): 267–282.

———. 2010. Dispositional Accounts of Evil Personhood. *Philosophical Studies* 149(2): 231–250.
———. 2014. *Evil: A Philosophical Investigation*. Oxford: Oxford University Press.
Singer, Marcus. 2004. The Concept of Evil. *Philosophy* 79: 185–214.
Steiner, Hillel. 2002. Calibrating Evil. *The Monist* 85(2): 183–193.
Vargas, Manuel. 2010. Are Psychopathic Serial Killers Evil? *Are They Blameworthy for What They Do?* In *Serial Killers: Philosophy for Everyone*, ed. S. Waller, 66–77. Malden: Blackwell.
Wolf, Susan. 1982. Moral Saints. *The Journal of Philosophy* 79(8): 419–439.

CHAPTER 7

A New Theory of Evil

In this chapter, I defend a theory of evil according to which evil is not a matter of the actions one performs, or is disposed to perform. Nor is it a matter of any of one's desires or affective responses. Rather, in my view, evil is a way of seeing, regarding, or caring about others. In terms that I shall define below, evil is a matter of having a kind of moral disregard for others. As I have been saying since the introductory chapter, my view is very much inspired by some of the work of political philosopher Hannah Arendt. So, before I can state my theory, I first want to review some of Arendt's most noteworthy contributions to the philosophical literature on evil. After that, I will attempt to locate my notion of moral disregard among other familiar terms and concepts in contemporary ethical theory. Then, after laying out my theory of evil, and explaining how it applies not only to persons, but also to actions, institutions, policies, events, and other things, I defend the theory against a number of potential objections.

HANNAH ARENDT ON EVIL

Arendt was born into a family of assimilated German Jews in 1906, and grew up with what can only be described as a complicated relationship with her own Jewishness, having internalized at a young age some of the anti-Semitism of the surrounding German culture. After a brief stint at the University of Berlin, during which she studied classics and Christian theology, she enrolled at Marburg University in 1924 to study philosophy with Martin Heidegger. A couple of years later, she moved to Heidelberg, where she wrote her dissertation on the concept of love in Augustine's thought, under the direction of Karl Jaspers. Arendt and Jaspers would remain lifelong friends, corresponding through letters, which have since been collected and published.[1]

Fearing Nazi persecution, Arendt fled Germany in 1933—the year Hitler became German Chancellor—eventually settling in Paris, where she worked to help other Jewish refugees. In 1937, she was stripped of her German citizenship. In 1940, after the Nazis invaded and began their occupation of northern France, Arendt was interned at Camp Gurs, a refugee camp in southwestern France. After only a few weeks of internment, Arendt left France for the United States, eventually becoming a naturalized American citizen in 1950. She spent much of the rest of her life doing freelance writing for various publications, writing a handful of books—mostly on political topics—and serving as a visiting scholar and lecturer at a number of American universities.

As I mentioned in Chap. 1, it was during the twentieth century, and especially since the Holocaust, that philosophers began giving special attention to a narrower and more explicitly moral conception of evil. And according to some, Arendt was the first to do so.[2] But she never actually defended her own theory of evil. Instead, her contribution to the philosophical literature on evil consists primarily in a number of interesting and puzzling claims that she made about its nature. My aims in the remainder of this section are twofold. First, since my own theory of evil is to some degree inspired by some of Arendt's claims about evil, I want to discuss three of these claims in particular, offering my own interpretations of their meanings. Second, I want to address what some—even Arendt herself, apparently—perceive as an important change in her thinking about evil, which took place around the time of the Eichmann trial in 1961. Like Bernstein,[3] I think her pre-Eichmann and post-Eichmann claims about evil are actually more consistent than they may seem.

The most famous of Arendt's claims about evil is her claim that evil is somehow banal. It appears in the subtitle of her report on Eichmann's trial, *Eichmann in Jerusalem: A Report on the Banality of Evil*. But the claim actually appears only once in the original text of the book. After recounting Eichmann's final moments before execution and "the grotesque silliness of his last words," she writes,

> It was as though in those last minutes he was summing up the lesson that this long course in human wickedness had taught us—the lesson of the fearsome, word-and-thought-defying *banality of evil*.[4]

Eichmann in Jerusalem was, and remains, an intensely controversial book. For one thing, as I explained in Chap. 3, many thought that Arendt painted Eichmann in far too sympathetic a light. But much of the controversy has surrounded that one phrase in particular—"the banality of evil." What could it mean to say that evil is banal? In other contexts, to call something banal is to say that it is so ordinary, so utterly "ho-hum," as to be boring and uninteresting. But, how could anyone suggest such a thing about the evil of Eichmann's participation in the Holocaust? And of all people, how could Arendt suggest such a thing, when just a dozen years earlier in *The Origins of Totalitarianism* (1951), she had written, "There are no parallels to the life in the concentration camps. Its horror can never be fully embraced by the imagination"?[5] Surely, if something is ever horrific enough to defy all powers of imagination, it must therefore be the furthest thing from banal.

Nowadays, philosophers working on evil have more or less converged on an interpretation of Arendt's claim according to which "the banality of evil" has to do specifically with the motives of evildoers. The idea is that evil is banal in the sense that it does not require any special or peculiar sort of motivation on the part of the evildoer. Indeed, this is how Arendt herself clarified things several years after publishing the Eichmann book, writing,

> I spoke of 'the banality of evil' and meant with this no theory or doctrine but something quite factual, the phenomenon of evil deeds, committed on a gigantic scale, which could not be traced to any particularity of wickedness, pathology, or ideological conviction in the doer, whose only personal distinction was a perhaps extraordinary shallowness.[6]

What Arendt came to believe, after observing Eichmann during his trial, is that evil actions can apparently arise out of some rather banal psychological sources—not necessarily a monstrous desire to make others suffer, but perhaps even a perfectly ordinary, "ho-hum" motive, such as a desire to advance in one's career. Russell explains,

> In claiming that the Eichmann trial revealed the banality of evil, Arendt appears to be committed to the view that the concept of evil action is psychologically thin. Arendt seems to believe that all evil actions are extreme culpable wrongs, but that these actions could flow from a very broad range of motives that need not include malice, sadistic pleasure, or defiance of morality. Nor does Arendt posit any other psychological hallmark of evil action.[7]

Now, as I explained in Chap. 3, Arendt probably just badly underestimated the extent to which Eichmann was motivated by hatred of the Jews and other ideological considerations. But, the basic point about the banality of evil, as here interpreted by Russell, may, nonetheless, be right: perhaps, evil is banal in the sense that it bears no peculiar psychological hallmark; in other words, perhaps there is no psychological feature or trait whatsoever that a person must possess in order for his or her actions to count as evil. Sometimes evil arises out of malice, sadistic pleasure, or defiance of morality; but other times, it might arise out of something as mundane as professional ambition.

For my own part, I think Russell and others go too far in their interpretation of Arendt's remark about the banality of evil. It is one thing to say that evil is compatible with a variety of *motives* or *desires*. It is another thing, however, to suggest that evil bears *no psychological hallmark at all*. Even if no two evildoers are motivated in the same way, there may nonetheless be some *other* feature of their psychologies that they not only share in common, but also explains why their behavior is evil. Indeed, later in this chapter, I defend a theory according to which evil does have a peculiar psychological hallmark, just not anything to do with a particular motive or desire.

Will this put me at odds with Arendt? Perhaps, if she really did mean by "the banality of evil" that evil bears no psychological hallmark at all. But, there are good reasons for denying that that is what she meant. After all, in *Eichmann in Jerusalem*, and throughout much of her later writing about evil, she does ascribe to him and other evildoers a peculiar psychological feature—something she refers to as "thoughtlessness." Here, again, is an example from one of her later works:

> [W]hat I was confronted with was [...] a manifest shallowness in [Eichmann] that made it impossible to trace the uncontestable evil of his deeds to any deeper level of roots or motives. The deeds were monstrous, but the doer—at least the very effective one now on trial—was quite ordinary, commonplace, and neither demonic nor monstrous. There was no sign in him of firm ideological convictions or of specific evil motives, and the only notable characteristic one could detect [...] was something entirely negative: it was not stupidity but thoughtlessness.[8]

(Notice the connection of thoughtlessness to *shallowness*, a term she also used above in her explanation of the meaning of "the banality of evil.") As we saw in Chap. 3, some interpret her claim that Eichmann was thoughtless as implying that he lacked the capacity to think deeply about moral matters—that he was a kind of moral imbecile. But as you can see in this quotation, Arendt is quite explicit in denying that Eichmann's thoughtlessness was a matter of any kind of stupidity. And Russell apparently interprets the claim that Eichmann was thoughtless as implying only that Eichmann lacked the sort of malicious or sadistic motivating thoughts or desires that many assume he had.[9] But again, if that is what Arendt had in mind when calling Eichmann thoughtless, then she was apparently just wrong about that, as he almost certainly was motivated in malicious and sadistic ways.

As I pointed out in my earlier discussion, there is a way of interpreting Arendt's suggestion that Eichmann was thoughtless that both (a) preserves her claim that his thoughtlessness was not a matter of moral stupidity, and (b) spares her from being committed to the historically inaccurate claim that Eichmann lacked any malicious or sadistic desires or motivations. On this interpretation, Eichmann's thoughtlessness consisted not so much in an *inability to think*, but rather in the conspicuous *absence* of a particularly important thought, namely, that of his victims' humanity. Like other perpetrators of genocide, Eichmann saw his victims in a way that dehumanized them. He was thoughtless, then, in the sense that he did not see his victims as things to which he should have *given a thought*.

At one point, abstracting away from Eichmann in particular, Arendt refers to what she perceived as a kind of "strange interdependence of thoughtlessness and evil."[10] This remark is significant for a couple of reasons. First, it implies that she meant something else by "thoughtlessness" than just the absence of malicious or sadistic motives and desires. After all, it would be very strange indeed for her to suggest that evil actually *depends upon* the absence of such motivational states. Second, it implies that she actually did think that evil has a peculiar psychological hallmark—namely, thoughtlessness—contrary to what has become the standard interpretation of her claim about the banality of evil. So, while I will not go so far as to say that my take on the meaning of "thoughtlessness" is exactly what Arendt had in mind, it is apparently more faithful to her actual words than the interpretations offered by others.

Unfortunately, that one phrase, "the banality of evil" has come to more or less define Arendt's contribution to the philosophical study of evil. This is unfortunate because it is actually in her earlier, pre-Eichmann work that I believe she comes closest to identifying the real nature of evil. Not long before *The Origins of Totalitarianism* appeared in bookstores, Arendt sent a copy of the book to Jaspers. He apparently thought quite highly of it, but still wondered, in a letter back to her, "Hasn't Jahwe faded too far out of sight?" In her response, Arendt notes how she struggled to come up with an answer to his question, and then adds,

> Evil has proved to be more radical than expected. In objective terms, modern crimes are not provided for in the Ten Commandments. Or: the Western tradition is suffering from the preconception that the most evil things human beings can do arise from the vice of selfishness. Yet we know that the greatest evils or radical evil has nothing to do anymore with such humanly understandable, sinful motives. *What radical evil really is I don't know, but it seems to me it somehow has to do with the following phenomenon: making human beings as human beings superfluous* (not using them as a means to an end, which leaves their essence as humans untouched and impinges only on their human dignity; rather, making them superfluous as human beings). This happens as soon as all unpredictability—which, in human beings, is the equivalent of spontaneity—is eliminated.[11]

This idea of a kind of moral "superfluity" is an important theme in her earlier work on evil, but its meaning is never exactly defined, only gestured at—as, for example, when she speaks here of the elimination of spontaneity. What could it mean to make human beings superfluous as human beings?

In *The Origins of Totalitarianism*, Arendt argues that totalitarian regimes aim at nothing less than "the transformation of human nature itself."[12] They do this by making humanity superfluous through a process of "total domination," which has three essential steps. The first step is "to kill the juridical person in man," by systematically stripping people of their protection under the law.[13] The Nazis did this, for instance, "by placing the concentration camp outside the normal penal system, and by selecting its inmates outside the normal judicial procedure in which a definite crime entails a predictable penalty."[14] The second step is "the murder of the moral person in man by making martyrdom, for the first time in history, impossible."[15] A martyr's death is significant, but a concentration camp inmate's death *could not be less significant*, since, as we have already seen, these inmates are treated "as if they no longer existed, as if what happened to them were no longer of any interest to anybody, *as if they were already dead.*"[16] The third step is "the destruction of the individuality of man To destroy individuality is to destroy spontaneity."[17] In other words, the camps were designed to destroy the inmates' statuses, both as *individuals* and as *agents*, and to effectively transform them into mere "bundles of reactions."[18]

These three steps result in total domination, but not the total domination *of humans*, for by this point, as far as the Nazis were concerned, their victims' humanity had been all but completely extinguished. Of course, the concentration camp inmates were still human in a strictly *biological* sense. But in ethical contexts, the term "humanity" is often used to refer to whatever it is about human beings that is supposed to make them matter morally, whatever it is that gives us our moral significance—for example, our individuality, agency, or autonomy (see my discussion of Kant in the next section). This is humanity in the *ethical* sense, and it is precisely what, according to Arendt, totalitarian regimes seek to destroy. She writes, "Precisely because man's resources are so great, he can be fully dominated only when he becomes a specimen of the animal-species man."[19]

Now, of course, in a certain objective sense, human beings *cannot* be made superfluous, since we cannot actually lose our moral significance. Even after being "totally dominated" in the ways described above—even as they were being forced from their homes, packed into train cars, and eventually led into gas chambers—every single one of the Nazis' victims remained as morally significant as he or she ever was before. They may not have had the same *legal* rights as they did before the Nazis assumed power, but surely all of their *moral* rights were intact. So, when Arendt suggests that evil is somehow a matter of making others superfluous, this should not be interpreted as implying that totalitarian regimes could ever be successful in actually transforming their victims into things that no longer matter morally. Rather, they "make" their victims morally superfluous only in the sense that they "make (them) *out to be*" superfluous in this way, that is, by *treating* or *regarding* their victims as if they no longer mattered as humans. To make human beings superfluous as human beings, then, is to take dehumanization as far as that concept will allow. It is not simply to think of others as *inferior* or *subhuman*. It is to regard them as if they have been removed from the category of humanity entirely.

So that you might get a better grip on the sort of superfluity that I have in mind, consider a very rudimentary example. Suppose there is a stack of receipts from recent purchases sitting on my kitchen counter. Now contrast two scenarios: in the first scenario, I am considering returning one of the recently purchased items, and so, I need to find that particular receipt; in the second scenario, I am finished chewing a piece of gum, and just want a scrap of paper in which to place the gum before throwing it away. Depending on the scenario, my attitude toward the receipts will be very different; I will think of them—perhaps even look at them—in very different ways. In the first scenario, the receipts themselves matter to me *as receipts*, and I will attend to each one individually as if its particular identity were of some practical significance. But in the second scenario, the receipts do not matter to me *as receipts*, rather, they matter to me only as *potential pieces of trash*, and their individual identities are of no significance at all.

The attitude had by the Nazis toward their victims was, in an important sense, similar to my attitude toward the receipts in this second scenario. Their victims no longer mattered to them *as humans* or *as persons*, which is why their individual identities were of no significance to the Nazis whatsoever. This is the sense in which, as Arendt put it, *making superfluous* is a matter of destroying individuality; it is to regard others in such a way that their individuality, their identity, is no longer of any significance. Instead, the Nazis regarded their Jewish victims as something akin to human refuse. If they mattered at all, they mattered only as things to be discarded or eliminated.

I mentioned above that Arendt's thinking about evil apparently underwent some sort of change around the time of the Eichmann trial. In her earlier work, she used the term "radical evil," which she borrowed and adapted from Kant, to signify the utter separateness of this moral category. But soon after publishing *Eichmann in Jerusalem*, she wrote in a letter to Gershom Scholem, "I changed my mind and do no longer speak of 'radical evil.' It is indeed my opinion now that evil is never 'radical,' that it is only extreme, and that it possesses neither depth nor any demonic dimension."[20] Whatever she meant by this, there is nonetheless an interesting and illuminating continuity between her earlier and later thoughts about the nature of evil. A central theme of her earlier work is the apparent relationship between evil and making others morally superfluous. A central theme of her later work is the "strange interdependence of thoughtlessness and evil." As I have interpreted them here, both of these ideas actually come together in the person of Adolf Eichmann, and this is what made him evil—that is, not any of his actions, desires, or affective responses, but the way that he *regarded* (or, rather, *disregarded*) his victims as morally superfluous.

In this section, I have offered interpretations of a few of Arendt's more noteworthy claims about evil, which not only give us some insight into her thinking about the nature of evil, but also unite some of her earlier and later thoughts on the topic. The basic idea is that people are due a kind of moral recognition that is denied them when they are the victims of evil. As individuals, agents, or autonomous persons, we matter in ways that others are obligated to recognize. To exhibit "thoughtlessness" toward others, then—that is, to "make others out to be morally superfluous"—is to fail to show them the sort of basic moral regard they are owed as members of the moral community. It is instead, as I will explain in the next section, to show them a form of moral *disregard*. But first, I want to survey some relatively familiar territory in ethical theory, so that we might locate my own somewhat unfamiliar notion of moral disregard among other normative ethical concepts.

Moral Recognition, Regard, and Disregard

Perhaps the most noteworthy feature of modern ethical thought—something that many think distinguishes it from premodern ways of thinking about morality—is its emphasis on things like equality, freedom, and universal human rights, all rooted in something like human dignity. Of course, premodern moral philosophers discussed things like freedom and equality, but it was not until modernity that philosophers began thinking it a basic—maybe *the* basic—requirement of participation in the moral community that members of the community *recognize* each other as free and equal persons.

This notion of moral recognition is significant in a couple of ways. For one thing, it seems to bear a kind of normative significance: if I recognize you as an autonomous person, a free and equal individual, that recognition alone implies that I have certain obligations to you—such as an obligation to refrain from unjustly compromising your autonomy in any way. Furthermore, some think that *being recognized* as an autonomous person is a necessary step in the development and maintenance of one's own moral or practical identity, or the way in which one sees oneself as a member of the moral community. If this is right, then failures of recognition are not just wrongful omissions, but harmful omissions as well, and the particular harm involved is a matter of ruining (even if only temporarily) another's conception of himself or herself as fully deserving of others' respect. As Taylor notes,

> [S]ome feminists have argued that women in patriarchal societies have been induced to adopt a depreciatory image of themselves. They have internalized a picture of their own inferiority, so that even when some of the objective obstacles to their advancement fall away, they may be incapable of taking advantage of the new opportunities. [...] An analogous point has been made in relation to blacks: that white society has for generations projected a

demeaning image of them, which some of them have been unable to resist adopting. Their own self-depreciation, on this view, becomes one of the most potent instruments of their own oppression.[21]

We saw a particularly disturbing example of this in the discussion of human trafficking in Chap. 4, in which a woman named Silpa—a victim of human trafficking who was eventually "promoted" to a madam-like status at an Indian brothel—had apparently become so confused about her own moral status, as well as that of the younger girls now under her "care," that she no longer considered rape in brothels to be a harmful act. In light of such examples, Taylor concludes, "Due recognition is not just a courtesy we owe people. It is a vital human need."[22]

As I mentioned before, many who now work in ethics take it to be a fundamental requirement of membership and participation in the moral community that one recognize others in some normatively significant way. Korsgaard, for instance, argues that recognizing our obligations to others is a matter of first recognizing their fellow humanity.[23] Scanlon argues that there is a particular sort of "relation with others the value and appeal of which underlies our reasons to do what morality requires. This relation, much less personal than friendship, might be called a relation of mutual recognition."[24] According to Darwall, members of the moral community typically occupy what he calls the second-person standpoint, which is "the perspective you and I take up when we make and acknowledge claims on one another's conduct and will."[25] As he later explains, the legitimacy of these claims is grounded in a kind of mutual or shared recognition of each other as possessing whatever dignity or normative authority is required to make claims on another's will.[26] What all of these philosophers have in common is that their ideas about recognition and its normative significance are inherited more or less directly from Kant.[27] (Readers who are already familiar with the basics of Kantian ethics are welcome to skip the next few paragraphs.)

A central element of Kant's moral philosophy is his notion of autonomy, which, as far as he is concerned, is the feature of persons that gives them their moral significance. Whereas many (especially nonphilosophers) now use the term "autonomy" to mean something like *the freedom to do what one wants*, Kant had something more specific and interesting in mind. In its most literal sense, the word actually means something like *self- (auto-) law (nomos)*. For Kant, autonomy is not merely a freedom to do what one wants, but rather the capacity to make something a law unto oneself, that is, the capacity to rationally reflect on one's potential reasons for action, and to endorse one or another consideration as *the* reason for which one will act. For the sake of illustration, recall Frankfurt's example of the unwilling addict, discussed in the previous chapter. This, again, is someone with a very strong first-order desire for drugs, a weaker first-order desire to refrain from using drugs, and a second-order desire that the first-order desire for drugs not be effective (or that the first-order desire to refrain be effective). The unwilling addict is still *autonomous*, since he can engage in this second-order reflection on his own desires, and then rationally endorse one of them as the desire on which to act, thereby making it a law unto himself. However, when he unfortunately succumbs to the stronger first-order desire for drugs, he is not *acting autonomously*, even if he is in some sense doing what he wants. The unwilling addict does not act autonomously because he does not obey his own law, but another.

For Kant, being a morally good person is a matter of having what he calls a "good will," and having a good will is a matter of exercising one's autonomy in a particular sort of way. The person with a good will rationally reflects on her potential reasons for action, and endorses *moral duty* as the reason for which she will act, thereby making the moral law a law unto herself. In other words, the person with a good will does her moral duty *because it is her moral duty*. She does whatever is the right thing to do, but not because it is convenient or advantageous for her to do so. Nor does she do the right thing because it feels good to do what is right. Rather, she does the right thing for the simple reason that it is the right thing to do. (For the record, according to Kant, the evil person—the person with the "diabolical will," as discussed in Chap. 5—is supposed to be the opposite of someone with a good will. The evil person, then, is someone who critically reflects on her potential reasons for acting, and then endorses *violating* her moral duty as the reason for which she will act. She therefore does the wrong thing, not because it is convenient, or advantageous, or feels good, but rather because it is wrong.)

What remains for Kant to explain, then, is: what *is* our moral duty? What *is* the right thing to do? Of course, Kant recognizes that the answer to this question is going to depend very much on the relevant circumstances. But, in *all* circumstances, he thinks, the right thing to do is whatever is prescribed by the Categorical Imperative. Kant sets out to establish "the supreme principle of morality," and later identifies this principle as the Categorical Imperative. But to the confusion of philosophy students ever since, he actually articulates the Categorical Imperative in a few different ways. These are supposed to be different formulations or expressions of the same basic principle. Here I want to focus on only one of these formulations, the so-called Principle of Humanity: "Act in such a way that you treat humanity, whether in your own person or in the person of another, always at the same time as an end and never simply as a means."[28] Two things are especially worth noting about this principle. First, as I noted in the previous section, the term "humanity" is used here to refer not to a particular biological species, but rather to whatever feature or features of humans give them their moral significance (e.g., autonomy). Second, the term "simply" (other translations use "merely") is especially significant. What the Principle of Humanity forbids is *not* treating another as a means, but rather, treating another *simply* as a means, or as a *mere* means. When I ask you for the time, I thereby treat you as a means to learning the time. But I do not thereby reduce your moral status to *nothing but* that of a time-giver.

So on a fairly standard interpretation of Kant, as well as a number of contemporary moral philosophers, participation in the moral community is a matter of having and exercising one's autonomy, that is, rationally reflecting on and endorsing reasons for action. And the most fundamental obligation had by those in the moral community is to recognize both themselves and others as autonomous, and therefore deserving of moral recognition or regard. To regard others as anything less than this is therefore to violate the most fundamental of one's moral obligations to others.

My aim in drawing this simple sketch of Kantian ethics is not to convince anyone that Kant was right about all of this. Rather, I do so for the following two reasons. First, as the discussion so far implies, the basic idea that our first and most fundamental obligation to others is a matter of *seeing* them, *recognizing* them, or *regarding* them, as possessing a certain moral status is nowadays quite common among moral philosophers, and not peculiar to just Kant. But fully understanding and appreciating this idea requires that we acknowledge its Kantian origins. Second, this notion of a kind of moral recognition, or moral regard, which is at the same time both a fundamental moral obligation and a "vital human need," as Taylor put it, is important for my overall aims in this chapter, since the theory of evil that I defend will actually depend and build on it. Let me now explain how.

In the previous section, I claimed that Eichmann's evil consisted not in anything that he did, or was disposed to do. Nor did it consist in any of his desires or affective responses, as other theories of evil might have it.

Rather, his evil consisted in the kind of regard that he apparently had for his victims. Clearly, Eichmann failed to regard his victims as free and equal persons, as autonomous individuals or agents, and in so doing, he failed to fulfill this most basic of moral obligations. But importantly, not all failures of regard, or failures of recognition, are *evil*. Recall Taylor's examples of sexism and racism perpetrated against women and blacks. Sexist and racist acts always involve some kind of failure to give to victims their due recognition. But not all sexist and racist acts are morally evil, though it might be fair to say that they are *reminiscent* of evil. (I will say more about this later.) What, then, is the difference between a recognition failure that *does* amount to evil and one that does *not*?

Philosophers working on the nature and significance of moral recognition generally use the term "recognition" as interchangeable with other terms like "regard," as I have done to this point. For my purposes here, however, I actually prefer the term "regard" for the following reason. Unlike recognition, we commonly speak of regard as something that can be both *had for* and *shown to* others, whether in speech or in action. To have a certain regard for someone or something is just to think of that person or thing in a certain evaluative manner, that is, to "see them in a certain light," as it were. But one can have a kind of regard for someone without ever showing it in or through any of his actions. Just as well, someone can show a kind of positive or negative regard for someone by acting toward that person in a certain way, despite thinking of the person very differently—for example, acting respectfully toward one's boss despite thinking very poorly of him. This feature of regard—that it can be both *had* in one's mind and *shown* in one's behavior—will be important in the next section when I distinguish between evil personhood and evil action.

Now, to answer the question I just raised, I want to distinguish between two kinds of failures of moral regard, namely, moral *misregard* and moral *disregard*, the latter being a subspecies of the former. To have or to show proper moral regard for someone or something is to give the person or thing its due recognition. To fail to give someone or something its due recognition, that is, to fail to have or show proper moral regard, is to engage in a form of moral misregard. In Kantian terms, we are guilty of moral misregard whenever we violate the Principle of Humanity—which is to say, whenever we fail to regard others as ends in themselves. Or, in terms perhaps more familiar to readers, we are guilty of moral misregard whenever we fail to acknowledge and appreciate a thing's moral status *as it is*, that is, whenever we treat another as "less than," or as inferior, or as a second-class citizen, or as subhuman, when a higher form of regard than this is in fact owed or deserved. (It is important to add this last point about the regard or recognition being owed or deserved, since not all cases of treating another as "less than," or as second-class, count as failures of moral regard. When two parents are trying to make a difficult decision about some family matter—for example, deciding whether or not one should accept a job offer that would require them all to move to another part of the country—they might ignore the opinions of their young children without thereby being guilty of a form of moral misregard. This is because, in this case, the children are not *owed* an equal say in the matter.)

There is an important and generally unremarked-upon difference, however, between regarding a thing as having a lesser moral status and regarding a thing as having no moral status at all. It would be one thing for me to regard some group of persons—another gender, perhaps, or members of another race—as *less than fully human*, or as *subhuman*. It would be another thing, however, for me to regard these people as *removed from the moral community entirely*. The former would be an instance of what I am calling moral misregard. The latter, however, is what I call moral *disregard*.

Moral misregard is, unfortunately, very common. Indeed, most (if not all) forms of moral wrongdoing—including, but certainly not limited to, lying, cheating, stealing, manipulating, insulting, abusing, betraying, and even raping, torturing, and murdering—involve some failure to give to another the moral regard that he or she is due. And as I noted before, most instances of sexism, racism, ageism, ableism, and other forms of wrongful discrimination also involve some degree of moral misregard. But thankfully, moral disregard is relatively rare. We commonly regard others as if their interests matter less than ours, or less than they actually matter, but we rarely regard others as if they do not even have interests that could or should matter at all.

Arendt gestures at this distinction between moral misregard and moral disregard in some of her descriptions of Nazi concentration camps. For instance, recall (from Chap. 3) her description of the difference between the treatment of concentration camp inmates and that of slaves or forced laborers:

> Forced labor as a punishment is limited as to time and intensity. The convict retains his rights over his body; he is not absolutely tortured and he is not

> absolutely dominated. [...] Throughout history slavery has been an institution within a social order; slaves were not, like concentration-camp inmates, withdrawn from the sight and hence the protection of their fellow-men; as instruments of labor they had a definite price and as property a definite value. The concentration-camp inmate has no price, because he can always be replaced; nobody knows to whom he belongs, because he is never seen. From the point of view of society he is absolutely superfluous.[29]

Arendt likely has a couple of Kantian distinctions in mind here (she wrote these words when she still preferred the term "radical evil," which, again, she borrowed and adapted from Kant). The first is the distinction noted above between treating another as an end and treating another simply as a means, or as a mere means. The second is another of Kant's famous distinctions, between things with dignity and things with a price. To get a sense of the distinction, imagine me offering you some amount of money for one of your possessions. You may not agree to sell the item, but strictly speaking there would be nothing wrong with me offering in the first place. And perhaps, given a large enough offer, you might even begin to reconsider your attachment to the item. This is because even our most sentimentally valued possessions are things that—in theory, at least—have a price. Now imagine me offering you some amount of money for your child, or your spouse, or another person in your life. In this case, it seems I am guilty of a kind of moral misstep simply by offering in the first place. You would be right to be offended, and not because the offer was to your mind unreasonably low. Rather, you take offense at the suggestion that a child, spouse, or other person could—even in theory—have a price. In Kantian terms, persons do not belong to the category of things with a price; rather, persons—or rational, autonomous individuals—are things with *dignity*. To regard a person as if he or she had a price would be, again, to engage in a form of moral misregard.

Arendt's point, then, is this: the slave or forced laborer may be treated as a mere means, or as something with a price—and that is of course seriously morally wrong—*but at least he has a price*. The concentration camp inmate, by contrast, is not even regarded as *highly* as a mere means, but rather as something lower even than that. He is regarded as priceless, but not in the same way that someone with dignity is priceless. Rather, he is regarded as priceless in the same way that a piece of trash, or a disease, or a cockroach beneath one's foot has no price.

Evil as Disregard: Seeing Others as Morally Superfluous

Before I can state my theory of evil outright, I need to preemptively address two potential points of concern. Unfortunately, the kind of regard that we have for and show to others is not always under our control. For example, suppose that Tom was raised in an extremely racist household, and as a consequence of this, he espoused a number of racist beliefs and attitudes throughout his childhood and teenage years. Now an adult, however, he has since disavowed the racist beliefs and attitudes that he once held in his youth, and sincerely believes that members of the other race are in fact his moral equals. Nonetheless, Tom finds that he still occasionally responds negatively to people of the targeted race. When his daughter began dating someone of the race in question, for instance, he initially responded to the boy with suspicion and hostility. Soon after, though, it occurred to him why he responded in this way, and he felt deeply ashamed, apologized to the boy and his daughter, and resolved once again to put his earlier racism behind him. On some level, it seems, Tom still harbored a kind of moral misregard for members of the targeted race. But importantly—especially as far as Tom's blameworthiness is concerned—he no longer *owns*, or *identifies with*, this misregard. Just as the unwilling addict might point to his first-order desire for drugs and truthfully say, "That's not who I am," Tom can point to this latent misregard of members of another race and say, "That's not who I am."

Evil, in my view, is a matter of seeing others as morally superfluous, and to see or think of others in this way is to morally disregard them. But just as Tom's misregard of members of the targeted race might plausibly be thought of as separate from *who he is*—separate, perhaps, from his moral character—someone could in theory likewise disown or withdraw himself from his own disregard of others. Toward the end of Chap. 3, I described the confusing psychological basis of Pauline Nyiramasuhuko's participation in the Rwandan genocide. She is most notorious for ordering the mass rape and murder of many thousands of Tutsi women, but in addition to being a woman herself, she was also a Tutsi by her own country's patrilineal standards (and she likely knew this at the time). Now in prison, suppose that, over a period of years, Nyiramasuhuko eventually comes to terms with her own genetic heritage, the significance of her crimes, and so forth, and is overcome with intensely sorrowful regret. Suppose, like Tom, she disavows her hateful beliefs about and attitudes toward Tutsi people, and resolves to do whatever she can with the rest of her life to make amends to former victims and their families. However, suppose also that, despite her sincere change of heart, she still catches herself from time to time slipping back into old ways of thinking—maybe some of her fellow inmates are Tutsis, and occasionally, as if it were instinct, she finds herself regarding them not as fellow humans, nor even as subhuman, but as cockroaches, much like she once saw her victims. But when she notices herself thinking this way, she immediately feels regret, both at the thoughts themselves and also at her own inability to avoid them.

My own view is that there is an important difference between Nyiramasuhuko in 1994 and the Nyiramasuhuko we are now imagining many years later, even if both are guilty of morally disregarding others. In the case of the older, wiser Nyiramasuhuko, moral disregard may still be *a thing she does*, but it is no longer a part of *who she is*. She *was* evil, but is no longer. So evil is primarily a matter of seeing others as morally superfluous, or morally disregarding them. But in order for a person to be evil, her moral disregard for others must plausibly still be a part of her moral character. It cannot, therefore, be something that she has disowned or withdrawn herself from, but rather must be something she still owns or identifies with. (Importantly, S need not consciously endorse a mental state, like a belief or attitude, in order for S to own the state in the relevant sense. S counts as owning, or identifying with, a mental state as long as it is the case that S would not consciously reject or disavow the belief or attitude, under present conditions.)

Now imagine a different sort of case. Suppose there is a species of organisms, call them Xs, and according to our best and most current sciences, Xs do not have the capacities required to have interests in the relevant sense, whatever those capacities might be. And so, humans go about using Xs as means to various human ends, or even just destroying Xs en masse, all without having or showing any kind of moral regard for Xs. Eventually, though, we discover that scientists have been wrong about Xs all along, and in fact, Xs do have morally significant interests just like us. Immediately, we revise our thoughts about, and attitudes toward, Xs, and adapt our behavior accordingly. Before the discovery, it would perhaps be fair to say that we both (a) saw Xs as morally superfluous, and also (b) owned or identified with this way of seeing them. But it would not be right to say that we were therefore evil. This does count as an instance of moral disregard, since, presumably, the Xs were *owed* some degree of moral regard all along, but were instead shown none. However, in this case, the disregard itself is plausibly morally innocent, since it seems reasonable to think that we could not have known any better.

One of the issues lying at the intersection of ethics and epistemology is the idea of *epistemic responsibility*. Epistemology is the philosophical study of knowledge, and epistemologists often concern themselves with the matter of what is required for a belief to be justified, or for a believer to be justified in holding the belief. But as some epistemologists recognize, justification may not be the only dimension along which beliefs and believers might be evaluated.[30] Sometimes, for instance, when we say, "You ought not believe that," or, "How could you think such a thing?" we imply not (or not *merely*) that the believer is or would be unjustified in holding a particular belief, but (also) that the believer is or would be blameworthy for holding the belief. This is often the case when people form beliefs about others on the basis of stereotypes that are not only false, but also demeaning. Such beliefs are unjustified, of course. But to say only that the people who hold them are not justified in doing so would be to fall short of fully capturing the extent to which they have failed in their responsibilities as believers. Epistemic responsibility is not simply a matter of being justified, or being able to justify one's belief to others. To be epistemically responsible is—perhaps among other things—to be appropriately responsive to the right kinds of reasons for believing, and also to be genuinely concerned for the truth.

In the example above, even if we were guilty of morally disregarding the Xs before discovering that they have morally significant interests, the fact that we were, nonetheless, epistemically responsible in doing so ought to absolve us from counting as evil. This effectively distinguishes us, then, from Nazi and Hutu leaders who, regardless of whatever justification they might have tried to offer for their beliefs about and attitudes toward their victims, are nonetheless rightly blamed for *having* such moral disregard for the victims, much less *showing* such moral disregard in their actions. For ease of reference, I shall henceforth refer to the combination of moral disregard and these other two conditions—(a) owning, or identifying with, the moral disregard, and (b) being epistemically irresponsible in one's disregard of others—as *problematic moral disregard*.

We are now finally in a position to answer the central question of the book: what makes someone an evil person? Here is the view in a nutshell: S is an evil person if and only if S has problematic moral disregard for others—that is, if S sees or thinks of others as morally superfluous, owns or identifies with this way of seeing or thinking, and is epistemically irresponsible in doing so. In Chap. 5, I briefly discussed the constitution of moral character—noting, in that context, that while situationists tend to conceive of moral character as mostly or entirely composed of direct dispositions to various stereotypical behaviors, many others who work on moral character take a wider view according to which a person's character is also constituted by things like values, concerns, motives, ways of caring about things, and ways of seeing things. In my own view, our habits of moral regard—that is, the ways and degree to which we have and show moral regard, misregard, and disregard for and to members of the moral community—are among the most important "ways of caring about things" and "ways of seeing things" that make up our moral characters. Habitual moral disregard for others, then, is itself a trait of character, the possession of which is both necessary and sufficient for counting as an evil person, unless one either disowns the disregard (as Tom disowns his misregard for members of the targeted race) or is epistemically responsible in one's disregard for others (as in the case of the Xs above).

Evil character or personhood is not a matter of the actions one performs, or is disposed to perform. Nor is it a matter of the desires or affective responses that one regularly has. Rather, evil character or personhood is fundamentally a matter of the way in which one sees or thinks of others. Now suppose, for the moment, that S sees members of another race as morally superfluous, and owns or identifies with this way of seeing them. Presumably—especially in light of some of the social psychological studies discussed in previous chapters—S will therefore be far more disposed than the rest of us to harm members of the targeted race, and also to respond with either indifference or sadistic pleasure to their being harmed. In this way, my theory of evil can perhaps explain some of the intuitive appeal had by some of its peers, discussed in the previous chapter.

An evil action, in my view, is any action in which the agent or agents *show* moral disregard to or for others—in other words, any action in which members of the moral community are treated as if they were morally superfluous. I assume a relatively permissive sense of "show" here, so that it is possible for you to show a kind of moral regard for someone even if you neither *have* that kind of regard for the other nor *intend* to show it in your behavior. Note that I do not include the conditions of ownership and epistemic irresponsibility in this account of evil action. This is as it should be. When Tom initially responds to his daughter's boyfriend with suspicion and hostility, his *behavior* is still racist (since it shows a form of moral misregard) even if *he*, perhaps, is not (since he disowns the misregard shown).

Likewise, while we were destroying Xs en masse, our *actions* were still evil (since fellow members of the moral community were being treated as if they were morally superfluous) even if *we* were not (since we were being epistemically responsible in believing that they lacked morally significant interests). This explains how it could be the case that not only (a) not all evil persons are evildoers, but also (b) not all evildoers are evil persons. According to some, like Russell, any plausible theory of evil ought to be able to accommodate both of these intuitions at once.[31]

Finally, my account works just as well for other things to which the label "evil" might apply, such as institutions, policies, and events. These are all evil in virtue of whatever connection they might bear to moral disregard. For instance, if, by "institution," we mean something like an organization or association with some sort of membership—like a government, society, or corporation—then it will count as evil if either (a) its members or leaders are evil persons, or (b) its members or leaders perform evil actions in the name of, or for the sake of, the organization. On the other hand, if, by "institution," we mean something like a social practice—like slavery, marriage, or war—then it will count as evil as long as its normal operation typically involves some form of moral disregard. A policy is evil if its successful enactment would cause, involve, or otherwise contribute to some form of moral disregard (recall Arendt's description of the way certain Nazi policies contributed to the total domination of Jewish victims). An event is evil if it includes some form of moral disregard.

Now that I have stated the theory, let us briefly examine how it applies to some of the cases examined in Part I of the book. As I noted in the introductory chapter, and then elaborated on in the chapters that followed, psychopathic serial murderers and genocidal leaders consistently rank highest among those people most commonly thought to be evil. Ultimately, the aim of Chaps. 2 and 3, was to investigate why this is the case. What is it about psychopathic serial murderers, as opposed to other murderers—even other murderers with similar victim counts—that sets them apart as evil? One response that is understandably common is that most psychopathic serial murderers are sexual sadists, and that they are evil in virtue of deriving such pleasure from the suffering they inflict on their victims. But as I argued in Chap. 2, this would be to settle for a superficial understanding of the motivations of most serial killers—many of whom, it is important to note, are apparently not sexual sadists.

What was revealed in Chap. 2, among other things, is that psychopathic serial murderers are motivated first and foremost not by a desire to receive sexual or otherwise sadistic pleasure from another's pain, but rather by a deeper need to feel as though they have total possession of, and total control over, another person. But in a darkly ironic sort of way, in their efforts to satisfy this need for control, they typically end up regarding their victims as if they were not actually *persons*, but rather objects, human dolls, mere playthings. Most of the harm done by Bundy to his victims was reserved for after he had already knocked them unconscious, so it was apparently not their conscious suffering that he was after. Rather, in his own words, he was after the sensation of "possessing them physically, as one would possess a potted plant, a painting or a Porsche."[32] But in order to achieve this end, he often had to go out of his way to manipulate his encounter with a potential victim so that she would not—again, in his words—"emerge as a person and thereby lose her symbolic value."[33] She mattered to him, then, but not *as a person*. Rather, she mattered to him merely *as a symbol*—in particular, a symbol of that which he sought to possess and control. Since she was only a symbol, her individual identity was therefore utterly irrelevant and unnecessary, since *any* woman, in theory, could have held precisely the same symbolic value to him. To Bundy, then, women were morally superfluous.

In order to feel like they have total possession and control over another person, psychopathic serial murderers typically exploit their victims in ways that most other murderers do not. Bundy, you will recall, often dressed his victims up in different outfits and applied makeup to their faces, sometimes after he had already killed them. He also kept the severed heads of several victims in his apartment as keepsakes. Kemper occasionally removed parts of his victims' bodies to then use as sex objects. Berdella tortured his victims in so many different ways—from electrocuting them to applying bleach, drain cleaner, and other chemicals to their eyes, vocal chords, and other body parts—that he felt the need to keep a notebook of all of his methods and their effects, complete with photos of the victims. Others, perhaps most notoriously Jeffrey Dahmer, cannibalize their victims. Many engage in acts of necrophilia. In all of these ways and others, psychopathic serial murderers quite literally *objectify* their victims; to them, their victims are not persons with identities and interests that matter morally, but rather life-sized human dolls over which to exercise complete control, and then, eventually, to discard. Habitually objectifying others in this way is one way of problematically morally disregarding them.

In Chap. 3, we examined the various levels at which the Nazi "machine" operated, from the lower-level Nazi "commoners," like Melita

Maschmann, up to the Nazi leaders, like Adolf Eichmann. As I explained along the way, this was necessary in order to appreciate some of the social and psychological differences between functionaries at the different levels. What motivated and explains Maschmann's actions is something different from what motivated and explains the actions of Nazi "henchmen," such as the Nazi doctors and officers of the SS. Likewise, there are important psychological differences between the leaders of genocides and those working under them, such that the leaders are more deserving of their ranking among history's most evil people.

What emerged as a common theme *throughout* our discussion of genocide, however—something that seemed to be present at *all* levels of the Holocaust, not to mention every other genocide in history—was the element of dehumanization. Indeed, as I argued there, this is ultimately what makes genocide itself evil, and not anything to do with the amount of lives lost or the amount of harm caused. Maschmann admits that her own participation in the mistreatment of Jews and other victims depended on her having come to see them as subhuman. The actions of SS officers and Nazi doctors—as well as other "henchmen"-type perpetrators of genocide, such as members of Rwanda's violent Hutu militia (the *Interahamwe*) or scientists in Japan's notorious Unit 731—are evidence of what psychologists like Bandura, Zimbardo, and others have since confirmed, which is that, when it comes to group violence, there is no more powerful disinhibitor than dehumanization.

However, to be clear, I do not believe that all instances of dehumanization are evil. Nor do I think that all who dehumanize are evil persons. For one thing, as I explained above, the concept of dehumanization apparently spans my notions of moral misregard and moral disregard. One might dehumanize another by thinking of him as subhuman, as someone whose interests matter less than one's own, and in so doing, exhibit a form of moral misregard. But, in my view, this would not be evil, though it would of course be seriously morally wrong. On the other hand, one might dehumanize another by thinking of him as removed from the category of humanity entirely, as something without interests that matter morally. This would be a form of moral disregard. For another thing, not all who dehumanize would own or identify with their dehumanization of others. As I put it at the end of Chap. 3, this is what separates genocidal leaders like Eichmann from commoners like Maschmann: dehumanization is not merely a *thing that they do*, but rather a *way that they are*. Eichmann and Nyiramasuhuko were not in any way psychologically conflicted while performing their evil actions, because their own utter moral disregard for their victims had become a part of their moral characters, a part of who they were. So Eichmann was an evil person, but Maschmann was not, even if some of her actions were.

Finally, to be honest, I am not sure whether any of the people discussed in Chap. 4 should count as evil persons. As you may recall, my primary aim in that chapter was just to investigate what kind of relationship there might be between money and evil, in the hope of gaining a better, more complete understanding of the real nature of moral evil. What the investigation revealed was that money often has the effect of altering our perception of others, so that we go from seeing them as persons, as fellow members of the moral community, to instead seeing them either as means to, or as obstacles in the way of, the pursuit of our own interests. In other words, money has the effect of provoking in us a kind of business-like frame of mind from which others come to be regarded as objects, or commodities, to be used (or even used up) for our own benefit.

Certainly some of the actions described in Chap. 4 are evil actions—such as Madoff's fraud and the various evils involved in human trafficking—in virtue of the sort of moral disregard shown to and for the victims. And if intensive animal farming ought also to count as an evil, then this, too, will be because of the utter moral disregard shown to, and for, the animal victims. But, whether or not any of the perpetrators of these actions is an evil person will, on my view, depend on whether or not problematic moral disregard is plausibly thought to be a part of their moral characters. I think this is perhaps most plausible in the case of Madoff, and so, I am inclined to consider him an evil person. But, I am admittedly less sure about this than I am that Bundy and Eichmann ought to count as evil persons. For the record, though, I do not consider it a weakness of my view that it is not especially clear whether and how the view applies to certain people, like Madoff, human traffickers, and intensive animal farmers. Indeed, as I have acknowledged since Chap. 1, their conspicuous absence from lists like Barry's suggests that it is just *generally* unclear whether these people belong among the ranks of Bundy, Eichmann, and other paradigm cases.

Moral disregard can take a number of different forms, and some of those forms are highlighted by the discussions in Chaps. 2–4. Objectifying, dehumanizing, and commodifying others are all potentially ways of showing them moral disregard, depending on how they are done. What makes these actions evil, when they are evil, is that the victims are treated not simply as if their interests matter less, but rather as if they do not even have interests that matter at all—that is, as if they are morally superfluous. And what makes the people who perform these actions evil, when they are evil, is that they see their victims as morally superfluous, own or identify with this way of seeing others, and are epistemically irresponsible in doing so. They are evil, that is, in virtue of having problematic moral disregard for others.

The title of the book, *The Meaning of Evil*, is meant to be ambiguous. On the one hand, we sometimes use the term "meaning" to refer to a thing's content—specifically, to the semantic content of a word, phrase, sentence, gesture, and the like. In this sense, you might think of the book as an investigation into the semantic contents of claims about evil, when they are true. But on the other hand, we also sometimes use the term "meaning" to refer to the *importance or significance* of a thing, oftentimes things without semantic contents. So, for instance, we can ask about what a particular possession, experience, or relationship means to a person. In this sense, we might wonder what, if anything, the book has revealed about the importance or significance of evil.

The significance of evil, as I have defined it here, seems to me twofold. First, in identifying evil as a particular way of seeing, we have learned a valuable lesson about the nature and depth of moral character. At its deepest, character is not a matter of *what we do, what we want*, or *how we feel*. Rather, it is a matter of *how we see the moral world and its inhabitants*. And it is at this deep level of moral character that evil resides. And second, a point related to the first, thinking of evil in this way serves as a kind of reminder that our responsibilities to others (and ourselves) cannot be reduced to rules of behavior, duties to act one way or to refrain from acting another way. Even before we could break one of those rules, or violate one of those duties, we owe it to others to see them as they are, morally—that is, to see them not only as fellow persons, but further, as individuals whose particular identities afford them just the same moral significance as our own identities afford to us.

Before moving on in the next section to defend the view against potential objections, I want to briefly show how it avoids some of the objections that I raised for other theories in the previous chapter. Against Russell's dispositional action-based theory, my main complaint was just that dispositional theories of evil *cannot* be theories of evil *character*, since we do not yet know the state of a person's character until we have some idea *why* he is disposed to act in the relevant ways. As I explained there, even dishonest people can be strongly and highly fixedly disposed to honest behavior, in autonomy-favoring conditions. Being an honest person, then, must be a matter of something psychologically deeper than one's disposition to honest behavior, such as the way in which one cares about honesty and the respect that one has for others' rights to know certain truths. At the conclusion of my critique of Russell's view, I said that evil personhood, or evil character, must consist in whatever trait or traits *underlie* and *explain* the strong and highly fixed disposition to evil actions or feelings. My view identifies that trait as problematic moral disregard. The reason that evil people tend to be strongly and highly fixedly disposed to evil actions and feelings is that they see others as morally superfluous, and own or identify with this way of seeing.

My main complaint against affect-based theories of evil personhood was similar. In a sense, these theories are certainly right: evil people do tend to respond either unsympathetically or antisympathetically to others, whether by taking sadistic pleasure in others' pain or merely by being indifferent to their suffering. But as I explained before, this fact alone does not give us enough insight into the state of their character, since there are a number of reasons for which one might fail to respond sympathetically to others' suffering, only some of which appear to have anything to do with evil. In other words, what makes a person evil is not *that* they respond affectively in these deeply inappropriate ways, but rather *why* they do. Someone who regularly fails to sympathize with others' pain or suffering only because he is severely depressed, or afflicted with some other mental illness, disorder, or handicap, surely should not count as an evil person. On the other hand, someone who regularly fails to respond sympathetically to others' suffering because he sees them as morally superfluous, and owns or identifies with this way of seeing them, does seem to be an evil person. But now it seems clear that the evil-making property is not the pattern of inappropriate affective responses itself, but rather this deeper feature of his character that both *underlies* and *explains* the pattern of inappropriate affective responses—that is, the problematic moral disregard that he has for others.

And finally, against Calder's desire-based theory of evil personhood, I argued that e-desires as he conceives them are not necessary for evil personhood. His response to this sort of objection, it seems, is to concede the point, and then to allow that there might be two types of evil persons or characters: *positively* evil characters, for which e-desires *are* necessary, and *privatively* evil characters, so named for the absence of appropriate affective responses to others' suffering. But then my objection was this:

assuming "evil" has the same meaning when it is applied to both positive and privative evil, what is the relevant feature or property that both types of character have in common, such that they both count as subcategories of the more general category *evil*? And whatever that deeper feature is that both characters have in common, why not unify the theory by identifying evil personhood with possession of *it*? My theory allows us to do just that: what unites positively evil characters (like, perhaps, Bundy and Eichmann) with privatively evil characters (like, perhaps, Madoff) is the problematic moral disregard that both have for others.

So, in addition to accommodating all of the psychological data gathered from Part I, as well as some of our other intuitions about evil, my Arendt-inspired theory of evil as a matter of moral disregard avoids some of the most significant problems faced by its competitors. In the next section, I consider a few potential objections to my own view, and offer my replies.

Objections and Replies

Some might argue that my theory of evil action is less intuitive than it may at first seem. In some cases, the account will seem too permissive, allowing even some very minor or trivial wrongs to count as evil actions. In other cases, the account will seem too restrictive, since it will apparently exclude some actions that most would consider evil. So, let me briefly address the kinds of cases that I have in mind, before returning to my theory of evil personhood.

In the previous chapter, I briefly discussed Steiner's theory of evil action, according to which an action counts as evil as long as it is morally wrong, and the wrongdoer takes pleasure in his or her wrongdoing. As I explained there, one common objection to Steiner's view is that it is too permissive, allowing even very minor wrongs to count as evil, as long as the wrongdoer is sufficiently pleased by the act. For instance, someone who tells a little white lie, but also derives pleasure from knowing that the action is morally wrong, would apparently be guilty of evil. But surely that cannot be right. After all, one of the intuitions that people commonly have about evil is that it always involves a kind of moral gravity, such that there can be no such thing as a trivial evil. This, you may recall, is one of the primary motivations behind extremity theories.

Perhaps my own theory of evil action faces a similar problem. Imagine Eichmann stopping at a German restaurant for lunch, knowing in advance that, at this particular establishment, it is customary for diners to bus their own tables when they are finished with their meals. But, suppose he also knows that the entire restaurant staff is Jewish, and, evil man that he is, he regards these people as utterly morally superfluous. So rather than cleaning up after himself, he leaves his mess behind, crumbs and all, for one of the restaurant staff members to deal with. Eichmann's action here is surely *rude*, but would my theory go so far as to say that it is *evil*? If so, my view commits the same sort of mistake as Steiner's, since it apparently allows for the possibility of trivial evils, which our intuitions forbid.

According to my theory of evil action, Eichmann's rude behavior in this example counts as evil only if it is actually the case that his action *shows* moral disregard to or for others. Of course, since it is Eichmann that we are talking about, we can plausibly assume that he *has* problematic moral disregard for the members of the restaurant staff. But as I explained above, we do not always *show* the kind of regard or disregard that we, in fact, *have* for others, and vice versa. So, it need not be the case that *all* of Eichmann's actions toward Jewish people are, or were, evil, even if he never once had the slightest moral regard for any of them. Whether or not an action shows a particular sort of regard or disregard for others depends more upon the nature of the action itself than anything to do with the psychology of the person performing it. By offering to shake a person's hand, for instance, I show respect for the other person *regardless* of whether I actually have any respect for this person. In the hypothetical example above, Eichmann's act of leaving a mess at his table surely shows a degree of disrespect or misregard for the restaurant staff, but it just is not plausible that such an act could ever show the kind of utter moral disregard that I described earlier. Indeed, very few actions are of the sort that could plausibly be thought to show moral disregard to or for others, and it seems likely that no such action would ever be trivial. So while Steiner's view may indeed be too permissive, mine is not, since it does have a way of disallowing trivial evils.

Indeed, as I have defined the notion of moral disregard, it should be relatively clear why trivial evils are actually impossible in my view. This is one of the reasons that I earlier thought it worthwhile to discuss the nature and significance of moral recognition or regard. It is nowadays quite common in normative ethics for philosophers to suppose that the first and most fundamental obligation had by members of the moral community is to give to others whatever kind of basic recognition or regard they are due. A failure to do so, according to Taylor, is not merely a *wrongful* omission, but a potentially *harmful* omission as well, since recognition is itself a "vital human need." For an action to show any kind of misrecognition or misregard, then, is for it to violate this primary moral obligation. So, if an action shows moral *disregard*, it does not merely violate our first and most fundamental obligation to others; rather, it violates this obligation to the greatest possible degree. Whereas other philosophers tend to conceive of the "extremity" or nontriviality of evil in terms of the degree of pain or suffering caused to victims, I prefer to think of it in terms of the degree of disrespect or disregard shown to victims.

What about the charge that my theory of evil action may be too restrictive, in virtue of excluding some actions that are intuitively evil? My earlier discussion of recognition and regard explicitly allows that misregard can be shown in varying degrees—depending, in part, on the nature of the action. Some actions, like rape, apparently show a much greater degree of misregard than others, like white lies. But if this is right, then it seems as if we can at least imagine actions showing a very great degree of misregard, but still something short of utter moral disregard. And in my view, these actions will not count as evil. For example, imagine a sadistic torturer who makes a point of not inflicting pain on his victims beyond a certain threshold; maybe, for instance, there are some torture devices that even he refuses to use, thinking them too vicious or barbaric. In this case, it does seem as if the torturer is giving *some* consideration to his victims' interests, though obviously not nearly enough. So, while this is surely a terrible failure of moral regard, it is apparently not quite an instance of moral disregard. And if his actions do not show moral disregard to his victims, then in my view, they are not evil. But this is a problem for the view, if indeed most people will have the intuition that the sadistic torturer's actions *are* evil.

There are two things to say in response to this worry. First, as I explained in response to the last objection, whether or not an action shows moral disregard depends more on the nature of the action itself than on anything to do with the psychology of the person performing it. Plausibly, torturing another person for pleasure is among the types of actions that show moral disregard to or for others regardless of whatever regard the torturer himself or herself may in fact have for his or her victims. So my theory does not actually exclude cases like this one as examples of evil action. Second, the broader point about it not always being clear whether an action shows moral disregard or just a very great degree of moral misregard is well taken. This is why, in the brief mention of racism and sexism above, I allowed that there can be actions that are *reminiscent* of evil, or that exhibit *shades* of evil. Even if some extremely wrongful acts are not evil in my view, it may nonetheless be accurate to say that there is something evil *about* them. For instance, some have the intuition that there may be a sense in which acts of rape or torture are actually *worse* than murder, contrary to the common assumption that murder is the worst thing that you can do to a person. If there is any truth to this, my theory of evil may provide the resources for an explanation: acts of rape or torture are perhaps worse in virtue of their showing a greater degree of misregard for victims, perhaps even something approaching utter disregard. In this way, acts of rape or torture bear a greater *resemblance* to evil than an act of murder.

Similar objections might be raised to my theory of evil personhood—that is, that it is either too permissive, in virtue of allowing too many people to count as evil, or else too restrictive, since it may exclude some people who seem to many of us to be evil. According to my view, a person is evil as long as he or she has problematic moral disregard for others (even if such disregard is never actually shown to others). But, someone might ask, how many "others" must a person problematically morally disregard in order to count as evil? Ted Bundy apparently thought of *all women* as morally superfluous; indeed, as a psychopath, it might be the case that he thought of *all people* as morally superfluous. Adolf Eichmann apparently thought of *all Jews* as morally superfluous, while Pauline Nyiramasuhuko thought of *all Tutsis* as morally superfluous. All of these paradigm instances of evil people apparently had problematic moral disregard for huge numbers of people. But what about someone who only problematically disregards *one* person, having and showing proper moral regard for everyone else? Would even this person count as evil, deserving of being counted among the Bundys and Eichmanns of the world? If that is what my theory implies, then it may seem as if the view is implausibly permissive.

My answer is that such a person absolutely would count as evil, and I do not think that makes the view too permissive. Let us briefly consider a real-life case of someone apparently having such moral disregard for only one person.[34] Barbara "Barbie" Atkinson had a total of six children. Immediately after giving birth to her second child—a girl named Lauren—Atkinson gave the girl up for adoption, only to then fight for and regain custody a couple years later. Starting around this time, and lasting for a period of six years, Lauren endured some of the worst abuse ever suffered by a child. She spent almost the entirety of the six years living on the floor of her mother's bedroom closet, having to sit, stand, and sleep in her own blood, vomit, urine, and feces. Lauren was sometimes allowed to sit at the dinner table with her family, but Atkinson would use this as an opportunity to torture and humiliate the girl in front of her siblings, allowing Lauren to put food in her mouth, but refusing to let the girl swallow a single bite. Most times, if Lauren was let out of the closet, it was so that either Kenneth Atkinson, Barbie's husband, or any other interested pedophile from whom the Atkinsons regularly accepted payments, could rape the girl. After Kenneth, for whatever reason, revealed "Barbie's little secret" to one of their neighbors, police were called and they found and rescued Lauren, eventually returning the girl to her original adoptive parents. At the time of her rescue, she was eight years old, and weighed only 25 pounds—the weight of an average two-year-old.

Suppose that, in all of her other relationships with people, Barbie Atkinson was able to have and show proper moral regard for others. There was just this one person for whom she apparently had no moral regard at all. In my view, Atkinson is no less evil than Bundy or Eichmann because her disregard was aimed at only one person. Indeed, it seems absurd to think that one's status as evil could depend on the number of others for whom he or she has problematic moral disregard. Was Eichmann *less* evil at the end of the war than he was at its start, since there were *fewer* Jews around for him to disregard? Of course not. What matters is not the number of others for whom a person has moral disregard. Rather, what matters is that the disregard itself is plausibly thought to be a part of the person's character, and that the person is rightly blamed or blameworthy for having such disregard for others. So yes, on my theory of evil personhood, a person can count as evil even if he or she has problematic moral disregard for a single person; but no, I do not think this makes the view too permissive.

Finally, one might complain that my theory of evil personhood is too restrictive, in virtue of excluding some people who, intuitively, are evil. A good example might be the sadistic torturer described above, who apparently does not completely disregard his victims, but rather shows some very small consideration for their interests. Surely this man is evil, some will think, even if he has *some* moral regard for his victims. I have two things to say about cases like this. First, there is a well-known (even if sometimes difficult to detect) difference between acting *in* the interest of another and acting *for* the interest of another. As a matter of fact, it often happens in the actual world that people who hold others captive for sadistic or otherwise self-interested reasons cater to some degree to the interests of their victims, for example, by providing them with food, clean clothes, activities to pass the time, and a bed to sleep on. But in most of these cases, it seems clear enough that the captor is not actually considering the interests of his or her victims, that is, the captor is not actually moved by a sense of obligation to the victim as a fellow member of the moral community. Rather, the captor does these things for his or her own sake, thinking that the more comfortable the victim is, the more compliant the victim will be. In this way, one can act *in* (but not *for*) the interest of another person while still having utter moral disregard for the other person. So it is not clear that my theory of evil personhood really would exclude the sadistic torturer.

Second, if the sadistic torturer really does see his victims to some degree as autonomous persons whose interests matter not just prudentially, but *morally*, then he is not an evil person. So either our intuitions are mistaken in this case, or else the case itself is poorly described. There may be a bunch of other moral labels that could readily apply to this person—he may be corrupt, vicious, depraved, malicious, despicable, and vile. But in my view, he is not quite an evil person. In the same way that some actions may be reminiscent of evil, as I allowed above, he too may bear a striking resemblance to evil people. But he is not an evil person, as long as he does not actually have problematic moral disregard for others.

Concluding Thoughts

As if the book has not been controversial enough to this point, I want to conclude with a few more provocative thoughts, which I will leave mostly undefended, and intend only for further reflection. I began Chap. 1 by recounting an event that took place during the 2008 US presidential race between Barack Obama and John McCain. Each candidate was asked a series of question by Saddleback Church pastor Rick Warren, while the other candidate sat backstage unaware of his opponent's answers. One of the questions that Warren asked them was: "Does evil exist?" Both agreed that it does. Then, as a kind of follow-up, Warren asked them what, if anything, we should do about evil—ignore it, negotiate with it, contain it, defeat it? Now, given the context, it seems reasonable to assume that these questions were meant to prompt each candidate to talk about his plans for responding to terrorism, an issue that did not come up in this book, and will not be addressed here. But readers may nonetheless have a similar question in mind at this point: assuming that evil is a matter of seeing others as morally superfluous, and this kind of moral disregard for others often precipitates grossly immoral and extremely harmful behavior, is there anything that we can do about it? Are there ways of confronting evil, correcting evil, or perhaps even preventing evil, as I have defined it in this chapter? I have a few things to say in response, some of them pessimistic, others optimistic.

Let me get the pessimism out of the way first. As we have seen, serial murderers are among the people most commonly thought to be evil, and many—though perhaps not all—of these people are psychopaths. Indeed, for many, the term "psychopath" is practically synonymous with "evil." But I think, we need to be very careful here: not all psychopaths are evil, and not all evil people are psychopaths. Even so, there *does* seem to be some kind of relationship between psychopathy and evil, such that psychopaths, due primarily to emotional and other cognitive deficits and abnormalities rooted in prior amygdala malfunction, are significantly more likely than nonpsychopaths to see or regard others as morally superfluous. If there is any truth to this, then I am afraid the prospects of confronting and correcting evil in *these* people are very dim. And this is because there is apparently very little, if anything, that can be done to treat—much less *cure*—psychopathy. Robert Hare, one of the world's leading experts on psychopathy, once remarked, "[T]he shortest chapter in any book on psychopathy should be the one on treatment. A one-sentence conclusion such as, 'No effective treatment has been found,' or, 'Nothing works,' is the common wrap-up to scholarly reviews of the literature."[35] Of course, there may be methods for preventing psychopaths from engaging in violent or otherwise harmful behavior—from early detection and close monitoring in schools to various methods and technologies for criminal investigation and law enforcement. But as far as getting a psychopath to see and appreciate others as autonomous individuals, free and equal persons, never to be treated as a mere means, and so forth, I share Hare's pessimism and doubt that anything really can be done.

On a more optimistic note, however, not all evil is related in this way to some apparently untreatable or incurable personality disorder. Rather, some of it, as we have seen, is instead the effect of racist hatred and dehumanizing ideology. And in other cases, it seems to have more to do with greed and the (morally) blind pursuit of wealth. Might there be ways of confronting, correcting, and perhaps preventing evil in these cases? Here I am more optimistic. For one thing, since evil is ultimately a matter of the way we see people, or the kind of regard that we have for them, it seems plausible that one way to correct and prevent evil ways of seeing others is simply for people to spend more time with each other. After all, there is perhaps no more effective way to correct your misperception of another than to spend time actually getting to know that person.

This may seem like an overly sentimental and insufficiently philosophically rigorous point for me to make, but the facts speak for themselves. Recall Maschmann's firsthand account of what she dubbed the "fatal schizophrenia" of many Germans at the time of the Holocaust—that is, the ability of many non-Jewish Germans to see some Jews as persons, but to see others as "*the* Jews, an evil power, something with the attributes of a spook."[36] What made the difference? It was simple, really: social proximity. For the most part, the Jews who were their friends, classmates, co-workers, and neighbors were seen as people. But the Jews who were strangers, with whom they were not nearly as close socially, were seen as the cells of an infection from which their beloved country suffered. And what was it that eventually changed Maschmann's own mind toward those she had previously hated and dehumanized? Toward the end of her book *Account Rendered*, Maschmann recounts how, while a student at Frankfurt University, she "belonged to a group in which Americans, French (both white and coloured) and Germans met Asians of very varied nationalities"—some of the same people she was once taught were racially inferior. What kind of effect was had by her spending time with people of other races, ethnicities, and nationalities?

> The conclusion to which my observations compelled me (I later spent almost a year in France and had a chance to look about amongst this 'racially tainted and degenerate nation') was as follows. The National Socialist racial theory was erroneous, based on fiction and not on fact. For reasons which cannot be gone into here, we as a nation worked ourselves up to a state of self deification, the obverse of which could only be contempt and hatred for the other 'inferior' nations. In so doing we sank into the narrowmindedness of a primitive tribe that believes its own tribal gods to be the most powerful in the world.[37]

If racist and dehumanizing ideology is a powerful force for evil, then social proximity and engagement with diverse peoples are similarly powerful forces against it. What changed Huck Finn's mind about the moral status of slaves like Jim? Time together.

Another apparently powerful force against evil—though one significantly harder to actually recommend, for reasons I hope are obvious—is that of *forgiveness*. Here again, rather than waxing on about the power of forgiveness, I am happy to let the facts speak for themselves. In Rwanda, a nonprofit peace-building organization known as *Association Modeste et Innocent* (AMI) offers a month-long program for small groups of Hutu perpetrators and Tutsi victims, consisting primarily of group counseling sessions, and finally culminating in the perpetrators' formal request to survivors for forgiveness. If forgiveness is granted by the victim or victims, "the perpetrator and his family and friends typically bring a basket of offerings, usually food and sorghum or banana beer. The accord is sealed with song and dance."[38] Scenes like this continue to take place in Rwanda even today, more than two decades since the genocide. And by many Rwandans' own lights, this has been essential to the country's ability to heal, recover, and move on. In a recent op-ed for the *Huffington Post*, Ange Kagame, daughter of Paul Kagame, the current President of Rwanda, writes,

> Hate, like many other vices, is a learned behavior—it is a choice, a bad choice, but a choice nonetheless. And yet, I believe—I know—that forgiveness works the same way. I have experienced the power of forgiveness in my life—and I have seen it work its healing power in Rwanda today.

> Confronted with the horror of our history, we have a choice. We can choose forgiveness, or we can surrender to a natural reaction and choose revenge. On an individual level, choosing forgiveness is making a conscious decision to live above unimaginable circumstances.[39]

Against the natural human impulse to respond in kind, Rwanda has found that the most effective way of putting evil behind them and preventing its future reoccurrence is forgiveness.

Maschmann had her own run-in with forgiveness, and it may have had an even greater effect on her than her time at a cosmopolitan university. For as long as possible after the war, Maschmann went out of her way to avoid contact with any Jews, perhaps as a means of avoiding having to confront her own guilt and remorse. But on one occasion, she encountered a Jewish woman who had recently returned to Germany after losing both of her parents in an extermination camp and going into exile. Amazingly, this woman and her husband not only returned to the country from which they had recently been driven, but even adopted a couple of non-Jewish German teenagers who had both been active members of the Nazi Party. Here is how Maschmann describes the encounter:

> When I met the woman she knew about my political past, which made me all the more uneasy. I will never forget the glow of spontaneous kindness in this person's eyes when she first held out her hand to me. It bridged all the gulfs, without denying them.

> At that moment I jumped free from the devil's wheel. I was no longer in danger of converting feelings of guilt into fresh hatred. The forgiving love which I had encountered gave me the strength to accept our guilt and my own. Only now did I cease to be a National Socialist.[40]

Of course, it would be a mistake to think that victims of evil are ever *obligated* to forgive those who wronged them. But the theory of evil defended in this chapter suggests that forgiveness may nonetheless have an interesting and important role to play in confronting and correcting evil, a role that is evident across Rwanda as well as in this account from Maschmann. Evil, in my view, is a matter of seeing or treating others as if they were morally superfluous, as if their individuality and autonomy were no longer of any concern to anyone, as if they were not merely subhuman, but removed from the moral community entirely. But notice, since forgiveness is something that can only ever be *given*, and never *taken*, the act of forgiveness itself both assumes and asserts a certain degree of moral authority over the person receiving the forgiveness. And since forgiveness can only be given *by the victim*, and no one else, the act of forgiveness also both assumes and asserts the moral significance of the forgiver's individuality and autonomy. In this way, forgiveness is itself a way of confronting and correcting the particular sort of moral misperception that lies at the heart of evil—and, hopefully, preventing future occurrences.

Finally, I want to say something about an issue that I mentioned at the beginning of Chap. 6. As I explained there, some are led to adopt extremity theories of evil because they think this is the best way of accommodating another thesis often held by philosophers with respect to the nature of evil, namely, the *mirror thesis*. The mirror thesis, again, is the claim that evil is in some sense a kind of perverse mirror image of moral sainthood or saintliness. But, of course, the "reflected" image will depend upon one's theory of either evil or moral sainthood. For instance, if one starts with a religious conception of moral sainthood according to which moral sainthood is a matter of participation in the interests or purposes of God, and then one adopts the mirror thesis, evil will look something like an opposition to the interests or purposes of God. On the other hand, if one starts with a conception of moral sainthood according to which the moral saint has some or all of the moral virtues to an extreme degree, then the mirror thesis will imply that evil is a matter of being maximally morally vicious. As I mentioned in passing in the previous chapter, my theory of evil apparently has its own implications regarding moral sainthood, that is, as long as we adopt something like the mirror thesis. I want to close the book by spelling out what those implications might be.

In my view, the evil person is someone who has problematic moral disregard for others—that is, someone who sees or thinks of others as morally superfluous, as if they do not have interests that matter morally at all. If a moral saint is in some sense the opposite of an evil person, then my view implies that the moral saint is not someone who sees or thinks of others as his or her *equals*, but rather someone who sees or thinks of others as *superior* to himself or herself in some moral sense. In other words, if the evil person is someone who has disregard for others, then the moral saint is someone who has what might be called a kind of *super*-regard for others, that is, someone who, whether in thought or deed, elevates others to a status *above* himself or herself.

Philosophers working on the nature and significance of moral recognition, respect, or regard, often distinguish these notions from other, related concepts. One such concept is that of *esteem*. Whereas basic moral recognition or regard is supposed to be owed to fellow members of the moral community strictly in virtue of their being fellow members of the moral community, esteem is something owed or given to others in virtue of particular good-making properties they possess in addition to their basic moral status. So for instance, while my neighbor is due proper recognition or regard in virtue of his basic moral status, I might in addition to this *esteem* him for being an excellent musician, or for his expertise with lawn care, or for some accomplishment of his, such as climbing a mountain or winning a prestigious award. Esteem might be thought of as a kind of super-regard, since it does seem to involve thinking *especially highly* of another person. But this is not the kind of super-regard that would be the signature of the moral saint, since there is nothing particularly saintly about regarding another highly when the other rightly *deserves* or *merits* the high regard.

On the other hand, on one very common conception of love—in particular, the Greek notion of *agape*—love is at least partly a matter of thinking, especially highly of others *regardless* of whatever good-making properties they might possess. In other words, rather than serving as a kind of fitting response to certain valuable or respectable traits in another, this love in effect *creates* value *in* its object.[41] The kind of love I have in mind here is typically distinguished from both *eros* love—which is a matter of passionate, romantic desire for another—and *philia* love—which is a matter of friendly feelings toward one's family and friends, and perhaps other close relationships, such as co-workers and neighbors. In contrast with these, *agape* love does not assume any kind of relationship between lover and beloved, but rather depends only on the will of the lover toward the beloved, without any consideration at all for whether the love is earned or deserved. Interestingly, especially in light of the discussion of evil and incomprehensibility in Chap. 5, Soble notes how it is essential to *agape* love that it is had for, and shown to, others without any consideration of whether they are worthy of such love, and concludes that such love is, therefore, rationally "incomprehensible."[42]

I will not defend this claim here, but suggest it only for further reflection: suppose moral sainthood is not a matter of moral perfection, but rather a matter of having this kind of love, this kind of unmerited high regard, for others. On such a conception of moral sainthood, the moral saint would indeed be a kind of mirror image of the evil person, as I have defined evil personhood here. But perhaps more interestingly, this discussion suggests that a reorganizing of our familiar moral concepts may be in order. We often speak of the contrast between "good and evil," as if the opposite of evil were goodness. Indeed, as I explained in Chap. 1, this is how many philosophers have used the term "evil." But, if what I have suggested here about moral sainthood is on point, then perhaps the familiar contrast between good and evil is mistaken. The opposite of goodness may not be evil, but badness. Maybe the opposite of evil is love.

Notes

1. Arendt and Jaspers (1992).
2. Calder (2014).
3. See Chaps. 7 and 8 of Bernstein (1996).
4. Arendt (1963 [1977]: 252, italics in original). For the record, after announcing his own disbelief in the afterlife, Eichmann's last words were these: "After a short while, gentlemen, *we shall all meet again*. Such is the fate of all men. Long live Germany, long live Argentina, long live Austria. *I shall not forget them*" (Arendt 1963 [1977]: 252, italics in original).

5. Arendt (1951 [1973]: 444).
6. Arendt (1971: 417).
7. Russell (2014: 76).
8. Arendt (1978b: 3–4).
9. Russell (2014: 71ff).
10. Arendt (1963 [1977]: 288).
11. Arendt and Jaspers (1992: 165–166, italics added).
12. Arendt (1951 [1973]: 458).
13. Arendt (1951 [1973]: 447).
14. Arendt (1951 [1973]: 447).
15. Arendt (1951 [1973]: 451).
16. Arendt (1951 [1973]: 445, italics added).
17. Arendt (1951 [1973]: 455).
18. Arendt (1951 [1973]: 456). Keeping in mind that much of Arendt's early thinking about evil was apparently inspired by Kant, it seems likely that she has in mind here Kant's notion of "spontaneity." Just what Kant had in mind by this term, however, is a matter of some dispute. But the basic idea seems to be this: something is spontaneous to whatever degree it is undetermined, and therefore unpredictable (or at least, not predictable to anything like the degree to which determined events in the physical universe are predictable). When Arendt speaks of the destruction of spontaneity, then, she apparently has in mind something like the capacity that free and autonomous agents have to set *their own* course in life, determine *for themselves* what decisions to make, actions to perform, and so forth. The characters in a story are not spontaneous, since their decisions, actions, and fates are determined for them by the story's author. Spontaneity, then, is something like *self-authorship*.
19. Arendt (1951 [1973]: 457).
20. Arendt (1978a: 250). Despite what she says here, it is unclear just how significantly her general view of evil really did change, since, as some argue, her pre-Eichmann and post-Eichmann thoughts appear to be more or less consistent (see Chaps. 7 and 8 of Bernstein 1996).

    Also, for the record, some may read "radical" and "extreme" as synonymous, and so wonder what Arendt could possibly be saying here. But since she quite explicitly borrowed the term "radical evil" from Kant, we can safely bet that she was not using it to refer to evil to an extreme degree. As Bernstein nicely explains, Kant used the term "radical" in the etymologically original sense of the term *radikal*, which has to do with *the root or fundamental aspects of thing* (2002: 19–35).
21. Taylor (1992: 25–26).
22. Taylor (1992: 26).
23. Korsgaard (1996: 142–143).

24. Scanlon (1998: 162).
25. Darwall (2006: 3).
26. Darwall (2006: 20–22).
27. Korsgaard, of course, is quite explicit in characterizing her own moral philosophy as a direct descendant of Kant's. Scanlon acknowledges up-front that his own account of right and wrong "is likely to strike many as a Kantian theory," admitting that it "does have an obvious similarity to Kant's Categorical Imperative" (1998: 5). Darwall also acknowledges the obvious Kantian overtones in his own views (2006: 26–35), even going so far as to offer a second-personal interpretation of the Categorical Imperative (2006: 35, 115–118).
28. Kant (1785 [1993]: 36).
29. Arendt (1951 [1973]: 444).
30. See especially Alston (2005).
31. See Russell (2014: 135ff).
32. Michaud and Aynesworth (1999: 113).
33. Michaud and Aynesworth (1999: 125).
34. Farwell (2013).
35. Hare (1993: 194).
36. Maschmann (1964: 40).
37. Maschmann (1964: 210–211).
38. Hugo and Dominus (2014).
39. Kagame (2015).
40. Maschmann (1964: 213).
41. Nygren (1989: 87–88).
42. Soble (1990: 5).

References

Alston, William. 2005. *Beyond "Justification": Dimensions of Epistemic Evaluation.* Ithaca: Cornell University Press.
Arendt, Hannah. 1951 [1973]. *The Origins of Totalitarianism.* San Diego: Harcourt, Inc.
———. 1963 [1977]. *Eichmann in Jerusalem: A Report on the Banality of Evil.* New York: Penguin Books.
———. 1971. Thinking and Moral Considerations: A Lecture. *Social Research* 38(3): 417–446.
———. 1978a. In *The Jew as Pariah*, ed. Ron H. Feldman. New York: The Grove Press.
———. 1978b. *The Life of the Mind.* New York: Harcourt Brace Jovanovich.
Arendt, Hannah, and Karl Jaspers. 1992. In *Hannah Arendt/Karl Jaspers Correspondence, 1926–1969*, eds. Lotte Kohler and Hans Saner. New York: Harcourt Brace Jovanovich.

Bernstein, Richard. 1996. *Hannah Arendt and the Jewish Question*. Cambridge: Polity.
Calder, Todd. 2014. The Concept of Evil. *The Stanford Encyclopedia of Philosophy*, Ed. Edward N. Zalta. http://plato.stanford.edu/archives/win2014/entries/concept-evil/.
———. 2002. *Radical Evil: A Philosophical Interrogation*. Cambridge: Polity.
Darwall, Stephen. 2006. *The Second-Person Standpoint: Morality, Respect, and Accountability*. Cambridge: Harvard University Press.
Farwell, Scott. 2013. The Girl in the Closet. *The Dallas Morning News*. Accessed February 22, 2016. http://res.dallasnews.com/interactives/2013_October/lauren/#.VsvGCMd-Hww.
Hare, Robert. 1993. *Without Conscience: The Disturbing World of the Psychopaths among Us*. New York: Guilford Press.
Hugo, Pieter and Susan Dominus. 2014. Portraits of Reconciliation. *The New York Times Magazine*, April 4. Accessed February 24, 2016. http://www.nytimes.com/interactive/2014/04/06/magazine/06-pieter-hugo-rwanda-portraits.html?_r=1.
Kagame, Ange. 2015. From Victim to Victor: The Healing Power of Forgiveness. *The Huffington Post*, September 21. Accessed February 24, 2016. http://www.huffingtonpost.com/ange-kagame/from-victim-to-victor-the-healing-power-of-forgiveness-in-rwanda_b_8168036.html.
Kant, Immanuel. 1785 [1993]. *Grounding for the Metaphysics of Morals*. Third edition. Translated by James W. Ellington. Indianapolis: Hackett.
Korsgaard, Christine. 1996. *The Sources of Normativity*. Cambridge: Cambridge University Press.
Maschmann, Melita. 1964. *Account Rendered: A Dossier on my Former Self*. Translated by Geoffrey Strachen. London: Abelard-Schuman.
Michaud, Stephen, and Hugh Aynesworth. 1999. *The Only Living Witness: The True Story of Serial Sex Killer Ted Bundy*. Irving: Authorlink Press.
Nygren, Anders. 1989. Agape and Eros. In *Eros, Agape, and Philia: Readings in the Philosophy of Love*, ed. Alan Soble, 85–95. New York: Paragon House.
Russell, Luke. 2014. *Evil: A Philosophical Investigation*. Oxford: Oxford University Press.
Scanlon, T.M. 1998. *What We Owe to Each Other*. Cambridge: Harvard University Press.
Soble, Alan. 1990. *The Structure of Love*. New Haven: Yale University Press.
Taylor, Paul. 1992. The Politics of Recognition. In *Multiculturalism: Examining the Politics of Recognition*, ed. Amy Gutmann, 25–73. Princeton: Princeton University Press.

INDEX

A

Abu Ghraib, 17
action-based theories of evil personhood, 18, 161–71, 182, 210, 211
Adams, Robert, 147, 169, 170, 183n6, 184n19
affect-based theories of evil personhood, 18, 161, 179–82, 211
aggregative theories of evil personhood, 161–4
amygdala, 34, 35, 48n22, 136, 218
Arendt, Hannah, 9, 18, 70, 71, 73–5, 78, 82n39, 117, 187–95, 200, 201, 206, 212, 224n18, 224n19
Aristotle, 118, 152n15
Arpaly, Nomy, 133, 136, 153n26
Augustine, 152n17, 188
autonomy, 101, 165, 166, 170, 193, 195–8, 211, 221
Aynesworth, Hugh, 25, 43

B

banality of evil, 73, 82n39, 188–91
Bandura dehumanization experiment, 66–8
Barry, Peter Brian, 15, 53, 158, 159, 182, 183n3, 183n5, 183n6
Berdella, Robert, 46, 47, 50n46, 207
Bernstein, Richard, 188, 223n3, 224n20
Breivik, Anders, 48n21
Bundy, Ted, 10, 15, 24–8, 41, 54, 85, 90, 124, 126, 131, 150, 163, 176, 215
Bush, George, 3, 5, 15
business decision frame, 96–8, 103
bystander effect, 139–41

C

C. K., Louis, 3
Calder, Todd, 159, 167, 171–6, 178–80, 182, 183n1, 183n7, 184n28, 184n29, 184n30, 184n37, 184n44, 211

Card, Claudia, 71, 82n33, 171, 183n4, 184n25
character, moral, 78, 119, 130, 138–51, 170, 181, 202, 203, 205, 209, 210
Chase, Richard Trenton, 24, 131, 132
Cleckley, Hervey, 33, 37
Clendinnen, Inga, 74, 80n3, 82n39, 184n35
Cole, Phillip, 6, 19n1, 121, 122
Collector, The, 31
commodification, 85–111, 209
concentration camps, 70, 73, 189, 200
conscience, 24, 32, 36–45, 47n16, 74, 91
consequentialism, hedonistic, 173, 174

D

Dahmer, Jeffrey, 15, 28, 87, 207
Dawes, James, 69, 78, 82n43, 120
dehumanization, 53–83, 86, 166, 193, 209
Des Forges, Alison, 79, 127, 146
desire-based theories of evil personhood, 171–9, 182, 211
determinism, 134, 135
de Wijze, Stephen, 119
diffusion of responsibility, 66, 67
dime experiment, 138, 139
dispositional theories of evil personhood, 161, 164–71, 210, 211
dispositionism, 142, 149
dispositions, behavioral, 146–8, 169
disregard, moral, 18, 72, 78, 187, 189, 195, 199, 200, 203–6, 208–17, 222
Doris, John, 138, 139

E

Eichmann, Adolf, 15, 53, 72–5, 124, 133, 150, 177, 194, 208, 216
emotional impairment, 34, 35

emotions/feelings, 29, 33, 34, 58, 61, 67, 68, 71, 75, 81n14, 89, 90, 93–5, 110n20, 138, 139, 141, 154n41, 158, 165, 166, 168, 170, 180, 210, 221, 223
empathy, 33, 34, 37, 48n19, 161, 178, 184n37
epistemic responsibility, 204
esteem, 222
evil, pure *vs.* impure, 5–7, 9
extremity theories of evil, 157–61, 221

F

factory farming, 104–7
Fish, Albert, 24
forgiveness, 162, 219–21
Formosa, Paul, 183n4
Frankfurt, Harry, 174, 175, 197

G

Gacy, John Wayne, 15, 28
Garrard, Eve, 183n13
God, 7–9, 159, 183n6, 221, 222

H

Hare, Robert, 33, 48n19, 49n26, 218
harm, 29, 30, 39, 49n36, 64–7, 71, 72, 85, 86, 103, 107, 119, 161, 164–6, 168, 169, 171–8, 180, 182, 184n28, 195, 205, 207, 208
Harman, Gilbert, 119, 143
Haybron, Daniel, 10, 13, 108, 159, 178, 180, 182
Hick, John, 19n3
Himmler, Heinrich, 15, 53, 126
Hitler, Adolf, 3, 10, 15, 53, 54, 56, 59, 60, 126, 188

Holocaust, 9, 10, 53, 55–7, 63, 65, 72, 73, 75, 80, 82n43, 126, 150, 153n22, 154n45, 159, 188, 189, 208
human trafficking, 86, 98–104, 107, 124, 126, 196, 209

I
Imperial Japanese Army, 68, 150
incomprehensibility, 57, 70, 119–27, 158, 162, 223

K
Kant, Immanuel, 196–8
 diabolical being, 121, 122
 dignity vs. price, 201
 Principle of Humanity, 111n59, 198, 199
Kekes, John, 183n4
Kemper, Edmund, 10, 31, 43–5, 49n36, 49n37, 62, 90–2, 137, 207

L
Levi, Primo, 126, 152n20, 152n21
Lewis, C.S., 19n3
love, 16, 31, 37, 46, 85, 86, 94, 103, 107, 126, 188, 219, 221, 222

M
Madoff, Bernie, 16, 86–92, 95, 97, 98, 103, 108, 109n4, 129, 134, 138, 150, 177, 178, 180, 209, 212
malice, 123, 189, 190
Mao Zedong, 15
Maschmann, Melita, 60–2, 72, 75, 81n14, 167, 208, 209, 219, 220

mass murder, 9, 29, 68, 71, 75, 77
McGinn, Colin, 165, 179, 181
Mengele, Josef, 15, 53
mental illness/disorder, 47n16, 49n35, 118, 130–7, 151, 211
Michaud, Stephen, 25, 28, 43, 49n41
Milgram obedience experiment, 63–6
Milton, John, 7, 121, 124
mirror thesis, 158, 159, 221–3
moral agent vs. moral patient, 128
moral judgment, 141, 142
moral knowledge, 130–4, 153n24
moral luck, 55, 56, 62, 79
moral sainthood, 18, 158, 159, 183n6, 221–3
Morrow, Lance, 120
Morton, Adam, 183n4
motivational internalism, 41, 42
Mussolini, Benito, 15

N
Nagel, Thomas, 55, 56, 79
Nanking Massacre, 68
Nazism/Nazi ideology, 59, 60, 74
Nietzsche, Friedrich, 7
Nyiramasuhuko, Pauline, 72, 76–8, 83n44, 85, 133, 162, 164, 181, 202, 203, 208, 215

O
Obama, Barack, 1, 2, 4, 5, 15, 217
objectification, 23–50, 86, 207, 209

P
perverse motivation, 120–4
Plantinga, Alvin, 19n3
Pol Pot, 15
Ponzi scheme, 86, 87, 89, 91
positive vs. privative evil, 178, 211, 212
Prescott, Carlo, 143, 145, 148

problem of evil/suffering, 8–10, 19n3
psychopathy, 32–45
  causes of, 23, 34–6
  performance on moral-conventional task, 39–41
  treatment of, 32, 218
  vs. sociopathy, 48n21

Q
qualitative *vs.* quantitative difference, 157–160

R
racism, 39, 56, 61, 62, 199, 200, 202, 214
Rwandan genocide, 16, 53, 58, 59, 79, 81n21, 82n43, 154n45

S
sadism/sadistic pleasure, 29, 30, 45, 168, 174, 179–81, 189, 190, 205, 207, 211
Satan, 7, 121, 124
schizophrenia, 61, 75, 127, 129, 131, 132, 138, 153n26, 219
secular *vs.* religious theories of evil, 7, 124
serial murder, definition of, 28, 29
sexism, 199, 200, 214
Singer, Marcus, 158, 161–4, 183n4
situationism, 142, 143, 146–151
slavery, 70, 82n33, 98–104, 201, 206
spree killing, 29
Stalin, Joseph, 15
Stanford Prison Experiment, 17, 143–6, 148, 149
Staub, Ervin, 57–9, 62, 81n30

Steiner, Hillel, 179, 180, 183n5, 184n41, 184n42, 184n44
Stone, Michael, 23
superfluity, moral, 192–5

T
Taylor, Richard, 195, 196, 198, 199, 213
terrorism, 217
thoughtlessness, 73–5, 82n39, 190, 191, 194, 195
Tourette syndrome, 135, 138
trivial evils, 158, 212, 213

U
understanding, 10, 13, 16, 23, 30, 34, 37, 38, 56, 57, 59, 60, 62, 65–7, 81n3, 91, 98, 103, 105, 117, 120, 122, 124–7, 129, 153n22, 176, 198, 206, 209
Unit 731, 69–71, 78, 181, 208

V
Vargas, Manuel, 39, 40, 42, 45, 171
violence, reactive *vs.* instrumental, 34, 136

W
West, Fred and Rosemary, 28, 46
Wolf, Susan, 183n6

Z
Zimbardo, Philip, 16–18, 19n10, 119, 143–6, 148–51, 154n45, 154n55, 155n58, 208